THE
MEN
WHO
ROBBED
BRINK'S

THE
MEN
WHO
ROBBED
BRINK'S

━━━━━━

THE INSIDE STORY OF ONE OF THE MOST
FAMOUS HOLDUPS IN THE HISTORY OF CRIME

AS TOLD BY **Specs O'Keefe**
ONE OF THE RINGLEADERS

TO **BOB CONSIDINE**

IN CO-OPERATION WITH THE
FBI

━━━━━━

RANDOM HOUSE NEW YORK

Thanks are due the following for permission to reprint material:

Associated Press: Copyright, 1950, by Associated Press.

Boston American: Copyright, 1953, 1956, by the Hearst Corporation.

Boston Globe: Copyright, 1953, 1960, by the Boston Globe Corporation.

Boston Record: Copyright, 1956, 1960, by the Hearst Corporation.

Boston Traveler: Copyright, 1956, 1958, by the Herald Traveler Corporation.

PREFACE

THIS IS THE STORY OF A TITANIC STICK-UP, THE MOST FAMOUS and best-planned cash robbery in the history of the nation and, perhaps, in the annals of crime. It is told largely by the only man at liberty to reveal its bizarre details. He is an articulate, self-educated man christened Joseph James O'Keefe, called Joe, called Specky, called Specs.

It is the story, too, of the men of the Federal Bureau of Investigation, of the Boston police department, and of other champions of law and order who brought O'Keefe and his co-conspirators to book.

It is something beyond a simple morality play, we think, more than the inevitable conquest of Good Guys over Bad Guys. It is a study of greed. If honor existed among thieves, Specs and the others who committed the Brink's robbery would never have been caught. They would never have been apprehended despite the utmost efforts of the Commonwealth of Massachusetts and the ingenuity, courage, research and patience of the finest detective force in the world, the FBI.

The lust for a fast buck, as old as man's first fumbling attempts at larceny, intervened in this case and ruptured the superbly organized and trained band of robbers. One of the eleven who robbed the great Boston counting house was, in turn, robbed of his share of the fabled loot.*

* $1,218,211.29 in cash; $1,557,183.83 in checks, money orders, etc.

v

That would be O'Keefe. His revenge, after years of soul-searching, was so terrible and so sweeping that it dispatched eight surviving associates to prison for life, plus sentences "beyond life" totaling about eighty years. One man, McGinnis, who was not even present at the robbery, was given *nine* life sentences, and more.

As this first authentic and approved account of the Brink's Robbery is presented, Specs O'Keefe is unanimously regarded by foe and friend as the worst insurance risk among 180,-000,000 of his fellow Americans. Three known efforts have been made to murder him. His reaction to this savagery and the loss of his money was absolute. He turned state's evidence and cracked a case that had thwarted a great state and the Federal Government for six expensive years.

Two blazing efforts to do Specs in were made at close range by one of the most accomplished and cold-blooded assassins of the crime-laden twentieth century, Elmer "Trigger" Burke, later removed from society in the electric chair at Sing Sing for murdering a man whose hapless fate in life was that he was Trigger's friend. O'Keefe's survival in the face of this point-blank fire must be classed as providential.

But Trigger Burkes grow on trees in the world Specs O'Keefe knew and now is attempting to put away. The men his testimony jailed for the rest of their natural lives, and more, have by now spent on lawyers and appeals—up to and including the Supreme Court—probably almost as much money as they were convicted of stealing from Brink's. Their friends, sympathizers or plain ordinary crackpots will hardly begrudge the additional expense and danger of permanently perforating O'Keefe, the reluctant informer.

"It figures that some day I'll get hit," Specs, a philosopher, says with the barest suggestion of a sigh. And then he adds:

"All I hope is that when they try again I'll be ready. I'd feel so . . . well . . . so *foolish,* if I didn't have something in my hand to whack back with."

It was so perfectly planned, so intensely researched, so painstakingly rehearsed. The night before it happened, two of the men—O'Keefe and Pino—went over the plot for the thousandth time, checking each of the myriad details.

It couldn't miss.

The two finished their dinner and strolled contentedly from the restaurant. They paused briefly in front of the place, picking their teeth and quietly luxuriating in the knowledge that they had concocted the perfect crime.

Just then, by astonishing coincidence, a Brink's armored truck hammered past. On its steel side flapped a banner. It read:

BRINK'S CELEBRATES ITS 90th BIRTHDAY
NEXT MONTH

The men stared at it reflectively. It was Pino who spoke. He took the toothpick out of his mouth and said:

"They'll never make it."

"Anthony could be an amusing bastard, at times," O'Keefe was to say years later of a man who is now a lifer.

THE ROBBERS

JOSEPH JAMES O'KEEFE
JOSEPH F. MCGINNIS
ANTHONY PINO
ADOLPH MAFFIE
VINCENT JAMES COSTA
STANLEY ALBERT GUSCIORA
MICHAEL VINCENT GEAGAN
HENRY BAKER
JOSEPH SYLVESTER BANFIELD
JAMES IGNATIUS FAHERTY
THOMAS FRANCIS RICHARDSON

1

IN THE CLAMMY MURK OF EARLY NIGHT—BOSTON, JANUARY
17, 1950—seven men tumbled out of a canvas-covered Ford
truck parked near Brink's, Incorporated, and strolled casually
toward the front door of that internationally famous money-
handling organization's prime office in New England.

They were in no hurry. They had been there before. Each
knew every inch of the remainder of the way to what they
sought.

They were dressed alike: Navy pea coats, such as were
worn by Brink's truck drivers and guards, chauffeur hats and,
as seemed proper for the bad night, rubbers. There was one
exception—one man who was to remain a nonconformist
until the end of the incredible story which at that moment
was nearing one of its many climaxes. Specs O'Keefe, who
led the seven on the scene, characteristically chose to be
different. He wore a pair of good crepe-soled shoes he had
purchased—a somewhat eccentric way for him to acquire
property at that time—at Filene's, a fine Boston department
store.

The group, carrying under their arms the familiar Brink's
type of canvas moneybags, empty now, strolled through the
concrete and terraced playground that runs along one side
of the ugly garage building that houses the Brink's offices
and counting rooms. Then it turned into Prince Street and
advanced on the securely locked front door.

3

O'Keefe did not fumble for an instant with the five keys he held in his gloved hand. He inserted an immediately chosen one into the lock, swung open the door and stepped inside, followed by the other men. He possessed the poise and stillness of a family cat returning home.

When the last of the men was inside and the door closed, they did a remarkable thing for the ostensible company employees they appeared to be. They reached their gloved hands into the pockets of their short coats and pulled out limpid, pliable masks. They took off their chauffeur hats, pulled the cover-all masks down over their heads, put the caps back on when they had adjusted the mask-slits to their eyes, and followed Specs up a flight of steps to the door at its summit.

Specs had a key for that one, too; he shoved it home and noiselessly turned it in its lock. He opened this door more carefully than the first. The men padded in behind him. One of them propped the door open with a special door-stop he took from his pocket. Like other interior doors, it was considered best to have it ajar in case of an enforcedly fast exit.

And so they were led through Brink's darkened offices and corridors by Specs and his unerring keys until finally they stood outside a particularly formidable door. Specs dropped soundlessly to all fours, pressed an ear against the razor edge of light that cut across the bottom of the barrier and listened for a tense moment. Whatever he heard, or did not hear, plainly reassured him. He jumped up, chose the last of his keys, slipped it in the lock and opened the door.

Like ghosts, the seven men stepped into the vault room of Brink's. They had been in there many times before, but never when it was so brightly lighted. Or populated by Brink's employees.

"We took out our guns and spread out, fast, in front of the wire screen that separated us from them," Specs remembers—as do the others, for this was the biggest score of their lives.

"There they were, the five of them . . . counting the money, checking papers, sorting checks, working around the main vault. The vault was wide open. It was kind of shocking. They hadn't noticed we were with them.

"For a little bit they all kept working. Then they looked up, looked through the wire at us. It was terrible, in a way. To say they froze isn't enough. They suffered from a great case of shock. You could see it on their faces. They seemed to be saying, 'This can't be happening to us! This can't be happening to *Brink's!*'

"But it sure was."

Thomas B. Lloyd, the cashier of the little Brink's group, told the Associated Press later that momentous night:

"I had just come out of the vault when I looked toward the wire mesh cage with the locked gate.

"Seven men—all wearing Navy-type pea jackets and Hallowe'en plastic rubber masks over their faces—stood behind the wire with drawn guns.

"I exclaimed, 'Oh, my God!' None of us had heard them approaching because all of them—except one who had shoes with crepe soles—wore rubbers.

"Grell was standing at my right. I guess we both saw the gunmen at the same time.

" 'Open up this door,' one of them shouted. 'This is a stickup. Don't give us any trouble.' I told Grell to open the gate. Grell was armed, but it would have been sure death for him to reach for his gun.

"Likewise, it would have been sure death for perhaps all of us if I had reached into a nearby rack containing several sawed-off shotguns.

"When the cage door was opened the gunmen filed into where we were going over the money. Just as they entered, Allen came out of the dispatcher's office. The shotgun rack was not far from him but he, too, decided not to grab for a weapon.

5

"We noticed that all wore gloves and each carried a length of heavy corded rope, knotted on each end. They ordered us to lie face-down on the floor, as though they had planned it for a long time . . ."

Specs won't forget the scene:

"Gus—that's Gusciora, who's dead now—was tying them up, as planned. We went into the vault and started putting the stuff in the sacks we had brought along, and into containers we found there. We worked fast. As Gus got each of the Brink's people tied up, hand and foot, he rolled them over and planted a strip of adhesive tape over their mouths.

"There wasn't a sound from them. The only sound in the place was the little commotion we made as we stuffed the money, the checks, and what have you, into our bags and theirs.

"We were busier than any of us had ever been in our lives when, suddenly, a buzzer sounded. Somebody was at the back door, which was right next to the vault room. The 'kitchen door' we called it.

"We stood there like statues. Then we looked at each other. I realized that I didn't recognize anybody on account of the masks, and that was quite a feeling. Then, by the way he moved, I recognized Gus. Gus went over to Lloyd, who was on the floor, ripped the tape off his mouth and asked him, quiet-like, 'What does that mean?' Meaning the buzzer.

" 'It means someone wants to come in,' Lloyd said.

"Gus thought that over. Then he said, 'If he don't get in, what effect will that have?'

"Lloyd said, 'Well, then perhaps he'll realize there's trouble here.'

"I pulled the coat of the guy nearest me—it turned out to be Geagan—and I motioned to him to follow me outside. We'd go to grab the guy who was ringing that buzzer, not through the 'kitchen door' but around the other way—out

6

the Prince Street front door and around through the garage. I thought that would reduce the guy's chances of getting away and sounding an alarm, if we closed in on him that way.

"But by the time we got into the garage we saw that he was a watchman of some kind and he had left the 'kitchen door' and was headed across to the other side of the garage where there was a little office. Obviously, he had gotten tired of pushing the button of the buzzer and given up. We decided it wasn't worth it, grabbing him. He went into his little office and started eating his dinner.

"Geagan and I went back into Brink's to help load the stuff and carry it out. There was so much of it! And nobody to squawk. The Brink's people just lay there on the floor, bound and gagged. We kept stuffing the bags with the dough.

"I noticed a big heavy metal box, a hamper kind of box, marked 'General Electric.' Gus worked on it for a bit but we didn't have the tools to open it, I'm sorry to say. So we left it there. We learned later that there was $800,000 in untraceable payroll cash in that box.

"Anyway, we carried and dragged the sacks back through the offices and threw or pulled them down the steps to the Prince Street entrance. The truck had pulled around there by now, and the street looked empty. I went back to the vault room for a bit, to look for my cap. I had lost it in the confusion. The Brink's people were still on the floor. I never did find the cap. I came back where the rest of the guys were and helped them load the stuff into the truck. There was a mountain of it. We climbed in on top of it and pulled the canvas top closed.

"We got away from there. It wasn't just a good getaway, either.

"It was perfect."

Without realizing what he was saying to the AP, Lloyd expressed a great truth when he said, "They ordered us to

7

lie face-down on the floor, *as though they had planned it for a long time . . ."*

They had planned it for a very long time, each in his own way.

Specs, for example . . .

2

SPECS WAS THE SIXTH OF FIFTEEN CHILDREN BORN IN BOSTON to God-fearing, law-observing Edward C. and Catherine Herne O'Keefe. Nine of the fifteen lived. Eight of them grew in the image of their hard-working, second-generation Irish-American parents. Specs was different. Specs grew like a crooked twig.

He was a wiry, feisty little boy, fast on his feet and quick of mind. In 1914 he started his criminal career. It was to become a fabled life of crime, but its origin could be classed as unique, too.

Specs was six years old.

As perhaps America's youngest hoodlum he joined the older boys of the C Street Gang shortly after the family moved from Boston's Old Cove district to a seventeen-dollar-a-month house in South Boston's Rogers Street near Andrews Square. The father, who worked in various penal institutions, at least one of which eventually cooped his son, did not earn enough to pay the meager sum charged by the nuns of St. Monica's parochial school. Specs was placed in the John A. Andrew public school. It was a rough-hewn school, even in its tenderest grades. But Specs was up to every challenge, even to the challenge of playing hooky a great deal yet keeping up with his studies. He was never kept back, he recalls today with quiet pride. With remarkable calm he concealed from his family the activity that most interested him. He concealed from it also the fact that his best friend was a roly-poly Italian immigrant boy named Anthony Pino, who was a year older and a grade ahead of Specs during their limited stay in school. It was an association destined to be climaxed on the evening of January 17, 1950, when Specs led the others into Brink's to carry out an epochal robbery whose chief architect was Pino. But as children they were content with lesser loot.

"We fell in with a group that liked to do the same things we liked to do," Specs recalls. "You know, like running around, going downtown, and doing crazy little things like sneaking in shows and sporting events and into stores— stealing and so forth.

"We'd steal aything we could. It wasn't because of the value of the things we stole; it was just to be doing that type of thing. It was more or less a contest among the kids, to see who could get away with the most. The idea of bravado, I guess.

"We never did anything constructive, like work. Some of the other boys in our classes would work to help their families. We wouldn't. It's just a division between groups, between fellows. It was that way all my life. People I grew up with, went to school with, they became successful people in all walks of life—you know the old clichés: policemen, firemen, priests, whatever. It was that way all through my adolescence.

"I don't really remember when this life of mine started. It seems to me now like the old saying that men and water meet their own level; that the good stays in its element and the bad finds its own."

Specs was sent away the first time when he was twelve. He was caught robbing a hockshop of a handful of cheap jewelry. He was sentenced to Lyman Reform School at Westborough, Massachusetts. He remained there six months, was released and returned to John A. Andrew School.

"Subconsciously, I felt separated from the other kids," he told us. "Perhaps I felt superior—though I've tried never to feel superior, and certainly am not. A later term would be that they were square, and I was not."

He reaped so little, wanted so little.

"You ask, 'Was there a children's fence for such things as this jewelry?' No, we'd either give it away or sell it to whoever wanted it. There was no mercenary motive behind this, except to have something you couldn't ordinarily have."

I asked him what his mother and father felt and did about his youthful misdemeanors:

"Actually, they had no control of me. I was a willful person. They did the best they could. My father did everything in his power to correct me. My mother also. My brothers often tried to help, but I just wouldn't conform. I went my own way. I knew I was wrong. I was just willful and stubborn, but I preferred to go my own way. I'd often leave the house and they wouldn't know where I'd go and what I'd be doing. I'd have to cover up by lying. They didn't want me to associate with some of the kids they saw me with. But I did, and that was that."

Specs, who was nicknamed for his freckles ("Whatever became of freckles?" he asks quizzically) rather than for the eyeglasses he eventually wore, left school forever in the course of the eighth grade. Of that period, he remembers:

"I left school and went to work at several jobs . . . Western Union, candy factory and different things like that. But I always was easily discouraged. I always wanted to do something other than what I was doing. So I'd go back to the friends I had formed, move around town with them, and revert to stealing. As I got older, it became a different thing. It became a way to make a living, a way of life."

Prohibition happened to Specs, too:

"I would have been eleven. It didn't strike our area too hard, at first. Naturally, there were a few speakeasies, people

11

making home-brew and so forth. But as it went along it did hit our area pretty good and everybody seemed to be involved in dealing in liquor.

"I was too young to go into business. But I did operate against people who were dealing in liquor. I stole their stuff, hijacked them, and made some money with that type of thing. In those days there were shops that provided seals, labels and stamps—all counterfeit, of course—and the bootlegger who brought the stuff in by boat, or made it himself, needed them to convert the bootleg into what looked like the McCoy.

"We'd procure these stamps and such for the bootleggers by breaking in, stealing them and selling them cheap. Otherwise, they cost the bootleggers a bundle. It was profitable for us."

Specs had just about severed his ties with home by this time, and apparently no member of the family went out in search of him:

"Ever since I had been a very young kid I used to stay away from home. In fact, my own brothers and sisters really didn't know me except on the days when there would be a birthday or a family gathering, something like that. I knew my own family less than I knew other people. In later years, especially since this Brink's thing happened, I've gotten to know them better than I ever knew them before."

It wasn't that Specs was mistreated as a child:

"My family were all good people. They never did anything to me that I should desert them. It was just something within me that made me do this type of thing, that made me not want to be with them at home, like ordinary kids.

"There were no whippings or anything like that. About that time my father's work kept him at the House of Correction on Deer Island—that's in the Harbor—six days a week. He was acting master, as they call it, of the place. Like an acting warden. On the day he'd come home there were many

things he had to correct, things that had happened throughout the week. There would be punishment to give out.
"So I'd leave home and stay away. At first it would be for
just the time my father was home. Then I'd stay away for a
week. After that I'd stay away for two weeks. Eventually,
I didn't get home at all, even as a young kid. I'd stay with
kids who were doing the same thing I was doing. We knew
all the teamsters and truckers and people like that. We'd
sleep in barns, just for the hell of it. It was a standard thing
to stay away from home on holidays and sleep out, on the
Fourth of July, March 17, St. Paddy's Day, the seventeenth
of June, which is a holiday in Boston, Patriot's Day. It was
a ritual. As we got older, we'd get a room. And as we got
older than that, we'd get an apartment or a hotel suite. But
as a kid I'd stay any place I could."

Specs was in and out of Lyman consistently during this
period in his life:

"My father always came through for me . . . perhaps too
much. He was a very great person in my opinion. He always
got me out of whatever trouble I'd get into. He must have
rescued me a dozen times from the difficulties of that period
in my life. For example, in reform school I'd have to make
what we called forty-five hundred points a month—work and
good-conduct points—in order to be sprung. But I never
was so much concerned about making my quota. I always
knew I would get out because of my father."

He kept his father busy.

By the time he was thirteen he had stolen, among other
things, a horse and a watch. A sociologist from Lyman, the
country's oldest boys' reformatory, had written in his record:
"Home restraint is lacking. The boy has had too much his
own way. He has had the run of the streets."

On one of the occasions when he was released through
his father's intervention, Specs quickly took up with a teen-
age mob somewhat ambitiously named the Dripping Daggers

13

and came to grips with what amounted to his first violence. While prowling with other members of the group he saw what appeared to be a drunk stagger out of a house in that seamy neighborhood and stumble haplessly down the street. The boys closed in on the man—who had accidentally shot himself while cleaning a gun and was in search of a doctor —muscled him into a dark doorway and took the $10 he had in his pocket.

The wounded man lived to tell the story and identify all who thought they were simply rolling a souse, including Specs. Specs was given another three months in Lyman.

And so it went for Specs. As he grew into manhood the size of his prisons increased accordingly:

"I got into more serious things and was sent to the Concord Reformatory. The charge was for using an automobile without authority. We were a group who would take several cars at a time and race them, kibitz with them . . . a foolish thing. So I went to Concord for one of those capers. I did fifteen months, and I was out only a short time when I was returned there for an offense for which I wasn't guilty."

I asked him why.

"I knew who had committed the offense," he explained, "but it just wasn't . . . well, it was just one of those things where you just had to take it."

Later in life, Specs was to believe differently.

Specs discovered that he could take prison as an adult as readily as he had taken it as a child:

"I suppose I had been conditioned in my mind. Jail became just one of those troubles you learn to take in stride. If it had been terrifying, well, I wouldn't be where I am today. It wasn't a breeze by any means. The inmates were usually rough and tough, and so were the guards. Things are made easier for an inmate today—but whether that's good or bad I couldn't say."

In time, Specs was destined to be arrested seventy times, draw twenty-two convictions, and live through seven or eight periods of probation and two paroles. But there was something memorable about the rap he took for a crime he never committed:

"I did forty-two months on that charge, by far my longest stretch until then. It was a bad break. You see, a bunch of us kept a house in Dorchester, a Boston district. We used it as a drop for stolen stuff until we could unload whatever we stole. When any of us wanted to use it as living quarters we'd first make sure that none of the others had planted anything there.

"The night I was arrested there, with a pal, we asked in advance whether there was anything planted there, otherwise we would have gone to a hotel. But two friends who had made a haul that day, and had put the stuff in there, assured us the place was clean—and to come ahead.

"During the night, the cops came in. It was a relief to be awakened and know you were clean. But when they searched the place they found stolen clothing all over the attic. We were charged with that offense, found guilty and sent back to Concord. I hadn't been out hardly two months.

"Well, it was like meeting folks from home, to get back to Concord. During the time I was there on this bum rap I met Pino and two others I knew slightly, and then much better—Henry Baker and Jim Faherty. We had no way of knowing it then, of course, but one day we'd all be together and bust Brink's."

One of the two men who had double-crossed him showed up as an inmate after Specs had served about half his term. Specs remarks:

"I was his enemy for a time, but of course it died out. We just let it go at that."

I asked O'Keefe why he would take nearly four years in prison protecting a man he hardly knew. Specs, shrugging, explains:

"Amongst ourselves, everybody knew the true story. Why tell the police?"

Specs' term finished early in 1931 in the pit of the Depression. He came out of Concord determined to get a job, any kind of job, and go straight:

"I couldn't find work. I don't blame the Depression. I guess I just didn't look hard enough for a job. I went back into the same groove and again started making a living the best way I could."

He was soon back in prison, this time on a year's sentence for possession of a gun. Today he classes that as a bad break, one with wryly comic overtones:

"It wasn't the first time I had been around a gun. I usually needed a gun as a kid, during those days of hijacking and grabbing an occasional bookmaker or gambler. You'd have to show them something . . . just show them you had it.

"So now I was in Worcester to grab a dice game, and that was purpose of having a gun at that time. The owner of a dice game was, to us, fair prey. We'd never bother the customers, the players, the fellows drinking the stuff in the back room. Just the owner or the manager. But I never got near to the fellow we were going to grab in Worcester.

"Foolishly, the owner and operator of the car—a legit car —stopped at the whistle of a police officer. Seems he didn't have his lights on. Imagine stopping for a police whistle! But the kid did, even though he knew we had a gun in the car and we were on parole. The police immediately came over to the car and decided we looked suspicious. There were two of them. They pulled their revolvers and marched us to the nearest police station.

"I was sick over the thought of going back. I decided to run away from them. Just outside the station house I got the police interested in the two other fellows, on some pretext, and as soon as they turned their backs, I was off. It looked like a perfect getaway. I went away from there as fast as a mouse.

"But then it was my misfortune to be hit with an awful tackle that brought me down. Of all the cops in town, I was

16

unlucky enough to have drawn the one who had been a star end on the Holy Cross football team . . . Those little things happen, to change a picture."

Specs didn't like jail in Worcester, and so he decided to leave:

"I made myself obnoxious. I just didn't like the inmates or the prison personnel. They were a strange bunch, the inmates. They'd run to The Man if anything happened. So I picked a couple of fights; I was nasty and surly to the officers, and so forth. It worked. They sent me to a place I knew better, Deer Island."

Specs pulled the only prison break of his long criminal life while at Deer Island serving the remainder of his Worcester sentence and an additional two-year term imposed on him, while in Worcester, for an old charge involving the theft of ten overcoats. Specs has reason to remember his flight:

"There hadn't been many escapes from Deer Island. It was awful difficult to leave. But I figured I had two more years to serve and, being young, I figured that now was the time to go away and try once again to start a different way of life. Try it some place far away from Boston. So a kid and I figured out a plan.

"Deer Island is divided by a wall. On one side is the House of Correction, where I was, and on the other side was Government property. There had been gun emplacements there at one time and another . . . an old fort of some kind. That part had a pier, and an old rowboat. I had gotten a job as a kind of teamster, working in and out of the prison store as a delivery man. I was naturally interested in what was in the store, particularly after I decided to leave that place.

"The store had what we needed most, a pair of oars and locks. The old man who ran the store was a great old guy, careful, cautious and smart. He must have noticed that I had taken one of the many keys off the big key ring he carried. On the evening of the day I took it—it was a key to a side

17

door of the store—we watched him check that particular door. We saw him discover that I had left the inner lock, a bolt job, 'open' so that all that I'd need to do was slip the stolen key into the regular outside lock and go in.

"That meant we had to make a different type of entry, and we did. We got in through a window after breaking a screen, got what we needed, went over the wall to the Government side and started for the pier. It was early night, and cold. December 28, 1932.

"Why wasn't there an alarm sounded? Well, we had thought of that, of course. There at Deer Island we didn't have to be in our cells until nine o'clock each night. For a few weeks in advance of leaving there, my friend and I would delay going into our cell. First we'd be a minute late, then a couple of minutes, then five minutes, and finally we had it up to fifteen minutes. The officer would be hollering for us, of course, to get in there and be counted. But he got accustomed to our being late. You have to plan things."

Specs and his partner needed those borrowed minutes. They had not counted on the tide being as low as it was. In the confusion and hurry, Specs, who was lowering the heavy rowboat by means of a rope twisted around a girder, let the boat drop through the last ten feet. It half filled with icy harbor water.

"I can't swim," his partner suddenly realized, terrified.

In the face of possible shipwreck, Specs had to make the hard decision. He yelled, "We've committed ourselves. We've gone this far, we've got to go on."

It was a short but grueling voyage. At its nearest point to land, Deer Island is separated from the mainland by a seething nest of whirlpools named Shirley Gut. It had defeated and drowned more than one man who sought escape:

"The current kept fighting us, even though we took the long way around to shore. We needed all of that time we had arranged for by conning that guard into thinking we were just fellows who could never get back into their cells

18

on time. But we made it to Winthrop before the alarm spread.

"Winthrop practically adjoins the island, so we got out of there as fast as we could. We went up the narrow-gauge tracks to East Boston, caught a cab and came into downtown Boston, where we split up, as we had agreed.

"I looked up a bootlegging friend of mine who knew what I was up to. He had some money for me and some clothes, and a ride to Hartford. From there I took a train to New York."

Joseph James O'Keefe almost found redemption in the Big Town.

When he first arrived, to earn a daily living he joined with small groups of thieves specializing in stealing suits from exclusive men's shops. In seemly atmospheres, such as that of Abercrombie & Fitch, while a confederate was discussing the relative merits of a suit with one of the shop's princely salesmen, Specs would select a suit from a rack behind the salesman's back, fold it swiftly and neatly into the flattest possible package and hide it in the seat of his trousers.

Then he met Mary Gerst, an Ohio girl who had come to work in New York as a domestic. They fell in love and —Specs having long since fallen away from the faith of his boyhood—were married in City Hall. There was no religious service. Franklin Delano Roosevelt had unveiled his New Deal. Specs O'Keefe, with the first real responsibility of his life, was determined to espouse a new deal of his own:

"I lied to Mary, of course, about how I earned my living. But the more I lied the more I realized that what I was doing in New York was distasteful and hazardous. I wanted a job. I wanted to get myself located, wanted to try to be legit. So we packed what little we had and went to Ohio. We lived in and around Defiance for six or seven months. I worked for various farmers, doing odd jobs. The wages were rough—a dollar a day, usually.

19

"We moved to a little crossroads town named Jewel, Ohio, and I got a job in an A. & P. in Defiance. It was long, hard work, and my take-home would be a buck or two. Still, I might have stuck it out if I hadn't received a letter from Boston. I had sent my Ohio address to Vinny Geagan . . . Vinny made Brink's, too. Vinny wrote that he and a few others were going to grab a shoe factory payroll and he had talked them into letting me in on it.

"I was never good enough for Mary and I never will be, and I proved it the day I got Vinny's letter. I did a terrible thing. I told her my father was ill and that I had to hurry home for a time.

"As soon as I reached Boston I went to Vinny's place. They had already lined it up. Usually, those payroll jobs go on a Friday. But it wasn't ready for the first Friday, so I sent word back to Mary that I'd be delayed. It finally went the third Friday. Meantime, I stayed in Boston and in order to live I grabbed a few bookmakers. That's no heinous offense! I always figured that any way you figure out how to beat a bookmaker you're entitled to do it.

"So we finally grabbed the shoe company. It was a factory on the fourth floor of a building. The fellow who steered it had access to the building and it was legitimate for him to be in there. He was paid to give us the "office" as to when the money was in the place where we wanted it to be. And he did. He came down past where our car was parked and tipped his hat. That was the signal. We went in.

"The money wasn't in the place we wanted it to be. There were sixty or seventy shoe workers in that room. They knew something was wrong but they didn't know what. We wore old clothes and had handkerchiefs or pieces of paper against our faces. Then we showed the guns, of course. Just then, when we were wondering what to do, we heard footsteps.

"Two girls were coming up from the third floor with the payroll. The poor things walked right into us. The money was in trays. We took the trays from them and started out.

But there was a hitch. The shoe workers were so sore at seeing their pay taken from them that they wanted to fight us for it. They started down the steps after us and wouldn't stop until one of the fellows with us fired a shot into the wall. That stopped them. We got out, jumped in the car and left. "It was a fair score . . . not much. By the time we paid off the steerer—we paid him more than he deserved, but we wanted to keep him happy—my bit came to about $1,250.

"I know it sounds crazy but I decided to use that stolen money as a stake to go honest. I drove back to Ohio, picked up Mary, and we went on to California. I looked for a month for a job. The money ran out. So we headed back to Ohio and wound up in a Cleveland rooming house."

It was a wrong move for Specs. Cleveland police arrested him:

"One of those long shots. I had been away from Deer Island for two full years by now, and I had another name and was legit. But I got grabbed anyway.

"It's the little things, the strange things, that work in favor of the police. One day I drove our landlady downtown to do some shopping. I parked outside a store and was waiting for her when two police officers walked over to the car. I found out later that they were notorious for finding people like me. They seemed to have built-in radar, or something.

"This day they were looking for some crazy guy named Robertson who had kidnapped a child in Chicago. My car had Illinois license plates. They wanted to see my license and everything else I had.

"All my credentials were in the name of George Hendricks, one of the two names I was using. I had had letters written to me in the name of George Hendricks, and produced several of them. My car was registered in that name. I even had an insurance policy in that name.

"I told the Cleveland cops I was a novelty salesman, in town on business. Well, the story was going real good and they looked ready to go on their way when the landlady came out of the store and tossed her packages in the back seat of the car.

" 'Do you know this man?' one of the officers asked her.

" 'Certainly,' she said. 'His name is Pat Kennedy.'

"That was my other name."

Specs was taken to headquarters. Nobody there believed his story that "Pat Kennedy" was just a name the landlady called him. He was held on suspicion until his fingerprints were checked with the FBI in Washington. When his true identity was thus revealed, Specs waived extradition and was returned to Deer Island prison to serve out the two-year sentence he had so drastically shortened by escape.

Mary went to Boston with him, found work in a factory, visited or wrote to him every day, saved a little money against the day when he might make another effort to earn an honest living. Memories of that period stir strongly in Specs:

"Mary was always a very decent, a very clean girl, just too wonderful for me. It's just that we differ in nature. That's why we're not together today. If I had been a more thinking person, a more decent person, I'd still be with her today."

At Deer Island, during those two years, Specs either met or heard from all the men with whom he was to rob Brink's. By the time he was released, in 1936, he was an accepted part of the team.

3

Now the core was hardening. If there was a leader of the slowly developing band of robbers it was Tony Pino. He had grown so fat and gross by 1936 that the others privately referred to him as the Pig. But all agreed that he had no match as a man who could case a place and render the proper verdict on whether the risk would be worth the harvest.

Around him he had gathered Baker, his brother-in-law Vincent Costa, and a tough, good-looking young hood named Adolph Maffie, who was called "Jazz." Vinny Geagan, who was later to join them, had just gone up for twenty-eight to thirty years for armed robbery and attempt to kill a police guard.

For Specs, it was like graduating from the minor-league bedlam of Deer Island to a postgraduate school of crime:

"They had a variety of things going for them—a payroll here, then a change of pace, then another payroll. We mixed them up. And we kept learning. For example, Pino claimed efficiency at being a safecracker. Used to keep telling us what a great Pete man he was. A Pete's a safe. We kidded him a little, I guess. I told him that safe-cracking wasn't anything but bull strength, rough mechanics. So he insisted on showing us what an art it is. He invited an old fellow who called himself the Maestro to come along with us one night. His age made the Maestro passé, but, anyway, there we were—I for-

23

get the name of the place—being given a lesson in safe-cracking.

"When he showed us how to do it I couldn't resist laughing out loud. I said, 'Christ, you've been living under false pretenses. It doesn't take a maestro to do that. A kid could open it.'"

In time, Specs developed the uneasy feeling that Pino was pressing his own and the luck of the others around him:

"I had been working on the side with some people downtown and making a living. I wanted to get away from that dangerous type of thing, and do the less dangerous things they were doing in the other crowd. So I tied up with Dave Green. Beeno, they called him. Later on he was shot by a New York fellow, an infamous murderer, a murderer for hire —a fellow they called the Chicken.

"Beeno and I were very friendly. We worked well together. Beeno was a money-maker and a real good guy. We made good money grabbing bookmakers and breaking up gambling places . . . even did a little bookmaking ourselves.

"But I got itchy feet again after a year and went out with some different people in a different part of town. It was just general hustling and stealing. Enough to keep me going and safe enough to keep me from being pinched.

"Mary didn't condone any of this. Our relations became so estranged that I would go home only on weekends, especially after I moved her to a house in Stoughton, about sixteen or seventeen miles out of Boston.

"I even tried working again. I took a job in a liquor store. The job was legit enough, but I wasn't. To round out my living I'd go out and do things once in a while. My associations were such that, being located in a liquor store, I was subject to all kinds of bites. I never refused anybody. As the bites mounted, I needed more income. So I'd go out and steal."

24

It went that way in 1943. One night Specs and a pal got half a can on and went to the Boston Garden to take in the fights. The main event ended abruptly and the only thing Specs could think of to do with the time on his hands was to prowl around the city in search of something he could turn into the cash he needed.

"I got pinched by, of all people, probably the most honest cop in the world. His name was Frank Collins, an ordinary guy but a real fine guy—but honest. He nailed me as I was going into a fancy men's clothing store. I had a crazy notion I could get away with forty or fifty or sixty suits. But, as I say, I wound up with the honest cop. Half stiff.

"That was a troublesome thing. I had to do something to overcome this trouble. So I volunteered to go into the Army. Mary signed a waiver—with relief, I guess. But they wouldn't take me in the Army. They discovered that I had a heart murmur, something I didn't know I had. So I went to the Navy, and tried to pull a fast one on it. I met a recruiting officer who was a pretty good guy and he offered to help me get in, in spite of my record and the heart murmur. He sent to the Bureau of Records, Inquiry Department, State Police, and asked for the record of 'Joseph James.' When the Bureau wrote back that 'Joseph James' had no police record, he simply added the word 'O'Keefe' to 'Joseph James.' Now 'Joseph James O'Keefe' had no record, at least so far as the Navy was concerned. Simple as that.

"Next, we had to do something about getting past the medical. We lined up a friendly doctor and were halfway through his examination when his superior came into the room and sent him out on an errand. Of course, the new doctor wasn't friendly at all. He found the same heart murmur and turned me down."

Specs was desperate to get into uniform, but not for reasons then widespread in the United States. He made it, too. He wangled seaman's papers enabling him to enter the

25

Merchant Marine. Though he couldn't cook an egg, a friend arranged for him to be listed as a chief cook, with all the rights and privileges pertaining thereto.

Specs went to sea in the Liberty ship *Webb Miller*, named for the first U.S. war correspondent killed in World War II. Through the winter of 1943-1944 the *Webb Miller* plowed back and forth between British and North Ireland ports, with an occasional ocean voyage in a convoy. It was Specs' longest honest stretch in years.

On June 3, 1944, pier hands near Cardiff, Wales, loaded the *Webb Miller* with a huge store of supplies of food, medicine, half-tracks and spare parts for assorted vehicles and elements of the 82nd Airborne Infantry. By the fifth of June the ship had joined hundreds of other vessels of the invasion fleet in Bristol Channel. On the early morning of D-Day it took its place off Utah Beach.

Specs, rejected by both Army and Navy, took a small but necessary role in the invasion of Festung Europa. With its men and cargo discharged, the *Webb Miller* was about to return to its port for more supplies when a twin-engined Luftwaffe bomber broke through the Allied air cover and dived for it. The bomb hit another Liberty ship scarcely forty yards from the *Webb Miller,* penetrated the No. 5 hatch, exploded and killed sixteen Merchant Marine personnel.

On D-plus-5, on the *Webb Miller's* second trip to Utah Beach, Specs and a seaman named Mahoney, also from Boston, went ashore and headed inland toward the intense fighting:

"We weren't dressed like soldiers, so we didn't get far before a soldier stopped us. 'Where the hell you guys think you're going?' the guy yelled at us. I said, 'Aw, we're going up to see what's happening.' He said, 'For Christ sake, are you crazy? Go back on the ship. Or stay on the beach.' So we did. We saw tanks that had been hit, and it was incredible. The metal would be almost two inches thick and yet it would be torn like a newspaper."

Specs saw no action in France, but to his surprise and delight he found some in England.

He and a fellow crewman we will call Davy O'Neil, both drinking a bit, missed the *Webb Miller* on one of its recurrent voyages from Southampton to Utah Beach. That night they stayed at a Red Cross hostel and in the morning reported to the War Shipping Board, the U.S. Navy and the local police—which was the routine in cases of that nature.

At the War Shipping Board, Davy gave Specs the "office" to take the attention of the girl receptionist away from him. Specs did, and Davy came up with a handful of ration books good for the purchase of clothing. The unsuspecting girl, in turn, directed the two of them to a pier at which they could catch a ferry to the Isle of Wight, where the Navy would handle the next step of their return to their Liberty ship. They didn't get to the ferry. Specs tells why:

"There were a series of booths, guard points I guess, or check points, on the way to the ferry. We got as far as the third booth and there's a little old guy in that booth handling a lot of money. So I said, 'Well, this is as far as we go; to hell with the Navy. This guy's got to go out for tea after a while.' We waited, and, sure enough, he goes out for tea. And crumpets, I guess. So we popped the door, went in and scooped up all that cabbage and blew."

The loot amounted to $1,300. It lasted them four happy days and nights in London. Then they worked their way to the Isle of Wight and sneaked aboard their ship without detection.

The *Webb Miller* pulled anchor that same afternoon and sailed to Southampton. The pier area there swarmed with police. Newspapers brought aboard ship still shouted about the robbery. Specs and O'Neill were questioned as to their whereabouts during the week. They explained blandly that they had stayed at the Red Cross, mostly. When they were confronted a bit later with Red Cross registration records, they shrugged and said they had been stiff. Specs was delighted with one of the British news accounts. It stated that an "opportunist" had detected the old man counting the money in the Southampton booth and taken advantage of him later.

"Opportunist?" Specs said to O'Neill. "What an interesting name for a thief."

Specs' part in the war was coming to an end. Several other aspects of that conflict, including the defeat of Hitler and the leveling of Hiroshima and Nagasaki could shift for themselves. Specs signed a separate peace. When his ship returned to the States, he went ashore at Boston, turned in his card, rejoined his wife and with his savings bought a loose partnership in a small real-estate office. Specs' contribution to the lore of the realtor's art was sketchy. He let his partner run the real-estate end of the shop. Specs, who had held up so many bookmakers in his time, became a bookie of horses and dogs and was heard to take a dim view of any thief low enough to rob that profession.

It was during this period that he gave an example of the whimsical humanitarianism that occasionally interrupted his good steady life of crime. The seamy hotel in which his office was located was visited every day by a girl wheeling an infant, a boy. Specs, always interested in children, noticed that the child was badly cared for, and would lecture the young mother at length on her indifference.

"Why don't you take care of that kid?" Specs asked the girl sharply one day.

The mother bristled. "I take good care of this kid."

"Look, the kid don't even look good," Specs insisted. "I tell you what: I'll take it home with me."

"Oh, no you don't," the mother said. "Nobody's taking my baby anywhere."

But a few days later, while having a drink at a hotel bar, O'Keefe received a phone call from his partner.

"Joe, you can take that baby if you want it," the partner told him.

"Okay," Specs said. "Take it out to the house right away." He had a few more drinks, apparently, because when he called to tell his wife he had a little surprise for her, she said, "Joe, you'd better get out here fast, and bring some Pablum and the rest of the stuff kids need."

Upon arriving home, Specs' first act of foster-fatherhood was to call Dr. Joseph Lasserton, a police department surgeon, and give him a blanket order to give the baby the best care obtainable.

"He was great, but it was Mary who brought the baby around," Specs recalls. "She devoted day and night to the child. The only time we ever left the baby was to attend the funeral of a friend of ours. We had parked him at my sister's house, and when we came back to pick him up he was crying. He had cried the whole time we were gone. Mary said then, 'I'll never leave him again.' And she never has."

There was another momentous happening during Specs' "real estate" phase. He met a young man who was destined to have a considerable effect upon his life. In fact, he was the person who brought Specs into the Brink's robbery.

4

JUST BEFORE THE END OF O'KEEFE'S SHORT-LIVED CAREER IN the real-estate business, and its allied interests, he received a call from an acquaintance who was in search of a locksmith. The friend was part of a small group whose collective eye had fastened on a Brockton, Massachusetts, bank truck. They needed a key to the garage where the truck was kept.

Specs was happy to co-operate, but he told his friend that there might be a small charge for overtime, in case the locksmith (who had done work for him before) was employed beyond his regular working hours. The charge of the locksmith for overtime was $20, believed to be one of the first incursions of organized labor into the ancient profession of robbery.

The smithy stayed at his grinder for two nights without a key to shape. On the third night, Specs was visited by Stanley Albert Gusciora, a younger man he was to know much better and admire greatly. Gus brought with him the cylinder of the lock for which he had no key. Specs had his locksmith whip up a key in short order. Gus was impressed. Specs was flattered.

"It seems that he knew me, at least by reputation. From the time he was fourteen he had followed the same groove, the same rut I guess you'd say. He was from the same neighborhood I was. His people were good people, industrious, God-fearing people, but he was a black sheep—same as I was.

30

"Gus heard about me while he was in state prison. He was one of the youngest ever to make it. He had gone to Lyman, just as I had, and he had escaped along with a couple of other kids. In escaping they had to injure a guard, a master as they are called. The man died. Gus was caught and was given from fourteen to eighteen years on a manslaughter charge. He was just a kid . . . fourteen years old.

"Gus did ten years between the old state prison at Charlestown and the State Reformatory at West Concord. Just before he got out—this was during the war—he volunteered to undergo an experiment. Some doctors had decided that perhaps the blood of animals could be substituted for human blood, then badly needed for transfusions. It was a rough injection, and there was no antidote for it if something went wrong. Gus was about to be released in a couple of months and the doctors were surprised that he would take such a chance. One of them asked him why. And Gus said, 'Well, I've lived a rough kind of life and I've never done anything constructive, nothing good. Maybe this will clear it up a little bit.'

"Gus was such a good kid. But he was also an inveterate thief. He was born one. When he came out of prison his older brother, a lieutenant in the air corps, interceded with a colonel in Boston and got Gus in the Army. It was tough but they made it. Gus was so bright they wanted to send him to officers' training school, but he'd have nothing to do with that. He went into the paratroops and saw a lot of action in Europe. But he never forgot something he had heard while he was a kid in state prison. He had heard about me and some others and he wanted to do the same kind of thing. I know it's crazy, but that's what he wanted. He loved to steal.

"By the time he came to me, about the key, he had already met Pino. But I seemed to be the one he wanted to work with. I wasn't too stuck on going out with him, but eventually we got together. Gus was something. He wanted to put

31

things on a production basis. He wanted a nine-to-five and longer stealing routine every day, including Sundays. He wanted to make a lot of money. A real hustler. He'd get me out of bed at six in the morning, five in the morning. I wasn't quite that ambitious, but Gus was a forceful guy. We went out hustling, and we made a lot of money.

"I found myself doing the same things I had done twenty years before. Just because of Gus. You see, he hadn't done them before. It was rough on me; I was getting too old for that sort of thing. But he was such a good fellow, in my opinion. Wild, sure, and cared for nobody. He had a terrible contempt for the police. I tried to explain to him that you can't be like that, if you're going to be working all the time. You've got to respect police. They're a danger to you, I'd tell him. You can't oppose them openly.

"But he was a bad kid, that way. He didn't care for them and he expressed himself that way. He had such a cynical contempt for most everything. Also, he used to hold onto his money, too. I don't know what he was saving it for. He was a close guy with a buck. He was a grinder. When I'd go to him for a touch he'd say, 'I'll give you nothing, you've got to earn it. Take me out tomorrow morning and we'll earn it.' It was wonderful, and terrible, too.

"But if it came to trouble, of course he'd spend anything to square it. He wasn't cheap that way. He just respected a dollar. And nothing else."

Specs is convinced that Gus, in time, would have invested his stealings in a legitimate business and probably have lived happily ever after. He is not sure that he himself would have done the same. But he did try operating a legal business, shortly after the war, and found the experience unnerving:

"I made a score from a bank truck, with Faherty and two others I can't name. We had made a pretty good study of this truck and the two guys who manned it. One of the guys looked like General Patton, right down to that big pearl-

32

handled gun. We figured he could keep that; we'd figure how to get what we wanted some other way.

"After casing the truck for a while we decided that the best place to grab it was during its regular stop in front of the U.S. Bank in Scully Square. They'd both leave the truck at that stop, probably because it's one of the busiest places in Boston, and go into the bank together for whatever business they had to do there. I guess they felt safe because of all the people milling along the streets, and the cop directing traffic at the corner, just a few yards away.

"So we decided we'd nail the truck there and take it away. We couldn't take the contents because there were so many people around. The plan was that whoever was closest to the truck, as the two guys went into the bank, would step in and drive it away. We had keys for the ignition, of course. We had gotten into the garage where they parked the truck each night, and had keys made from the impression we took.

"This little guy who was with us happened to be closest. He put on a hat like the guards wore—we had to think of that, too—and off he went with the truck.

"He got thirty feet. Just as he neared the busy intersection the big traffic cop held up his hand, blew his whistle and motioned for the side-street traffic to go by. The armored car naturally had to stop.

"Moments like that can be torturous. Now the rest of us moved up to the bank door. The big stiff with the pearl-handled job would be coming out any second. We didn't have any guns, but we'd have to do something to delay him. If he and his partner made a run for the armored car—which was still there at the corner, waiting for that damned cop to give the signal—we would trip them, or something.

"Well, it seemed like a lifetime, but the cop finally gave the truck the nod just before the two guards came out, and our little guy drove right past him and took it to a pre-arranged spot, a quiet street near the Charles River where the foliage would more or less hide it while we cleaned it.

33

"The money we expected wasn't there. There was only twelve thousand dollars. There should have been much more. It was just a bad break. With my share I went into the grocery business at 413 Columbus Avenue. It was a good location in a productive area but, as it turned out, it just wasn't for me. I tried hard enough to make a go of it. I'd be there from early morning until late at night, when I'd flop into bed dead tired.

"If I had taken action in the store—you know, like horses or the numbers—I might have become a wealthy guy. I tried to stay right, and I might even have made it except for a crazy thing. The guys I had known all my life heard I was open, of course, so they began congregating at the place every day. Sometimes a legitimate customer couldn't get in the door, there was so much riffraff hanging around. I fixed up the back room real nice for them, with a card table and things like that. But they'd have none of that. They wanted to stay out front to see what was going on. And eat.

"It got to a point where I had to go out and steal *groceries* to keep the joint open. Jeepers, what a rigmarole! I found myself prowling around the wholesale markets, stealing a bag of potatoes or a crate of oranges. But I did worse than that. I did a terrible thing to another poor guy in the business. He had a fancy delicatessen across from the Copley Plaza. A real nice place, New York style. I'd go in there early Sunday mornings and I'd clean him of his expensive canned goods, fine cheeses, things like that. I'm ashamed of that. Then I'd take the stuff over to my place and put it on my shelves.

"The next day those bastards would eat it.

"I got out of the grocery business. A guy came along one day—a friend of mine who had been a bondsman—and said he was sure he could make a go of the store if I gave him the chance. He had been in the wholesale grocery business years before. So I made a deal with him. He was to run the store, and not run up any bills, and when I could sell it I'd

34

give him half. Finally I did sell it. My end came to only eight hundred dollars. Most of that went the following month, when the bills he had run up came in. Seems he was a compulsive horse player."

Specs called Gus. He had to go back to work. He knew that Gus had graduated into increasingly muscular robbery, while he himself was perfecting the theft of potatoes and oranges. Gus had some interesting and arresting stories to tell. He had been working with Pino, Richardson, Geagan and one or two others who were to became immortal in crime annals. There had been a number of fairly important capers, including the grab of a shoe factory payroll of nearly $40,000, out of which Gus received $6,000.

The size of their operations appealed to Specs, but he had reservations about the personnel involved. Especially about the man he had known most of his life:

"Pino was the kind of character who would plan things, and insist they be carried out as planned, but he never wanted to participate in the immediacy of the robbery. He might be the driver, but preferably he'd be the arranger. Very bossy.

"I'm a rebel. I don't want to be arranged by anybody. I resent anybody telling me to do this or do that, and when. If I do something, I do it on my own good time. Pino wanted to move us around like he moved checkers. That, to me, was out. I couldn't go along with that.

"But the others certainly could: Geagan, Richardson, Maffie and Costa. Costa wasn't much. He never had the guts. He'd be cut in because he was Pino's brother-in-law."

It was a well-balanced mob. Pino was extraordinarily adept at casing a proposed job, figuring the chances and rounding up the guns if needed. Geagan and Richardson were what O'Keefe calls "strong guys," and Maffie "had a head on his shoulders."

Most of them worked at regular jobs. Maffie was winked at by Boston police as a bookmaker. Geagan and Richardson

35

worked steadily as longshoremen. The police regarded Geagan and, to some extent, Richardson as two toughs who had had their brushes with the law, had served their time, and now were hard-working men following the straight and narrow. Whenever a trail seemed to lead toward them, after a holdup in which they actually did take part, the police would run into the same blank wall: Geagan and Richardson "quit ten years ago." Their standard of living appeared to be a living testimonial to their redemption.

O'Keefe remembers:

"They would never change their mode of living after making a score. They weren't the kind of guys to go out and buy a cabaret. They'd just go along, pace themselves. I guess they were out for more than the money concerned. They wanted the thrill that goes with pulling off a well-managed job."

O'Keefe readily acknowledges Pino's artistry as an arranger:

"He'd tell us what to do, the part each of us would have to play. He'd brief us on the building we were going into, the people we might expect to find there, the location of the stuff. On the day his people—us—went to work he'd arrange to have your gun here, my gun there, under a newspaper in a gutter or behind a fence post. We'd walk toward our guns looking like working stiffs, or slobs, or even rag pickers, pick up the guns, converge on the place at the proper time and nail it."

One of Pino's better jobs, before the classic Brink's grab, was the robbery of the B. F. Sturtevant Company of Hyde Park, a Boston suburb. The manufacturer of air-conditioning equipment had a payroll of $110,000. Specs was not invited to participate, but he knew about it and he found himself curiously involved. He says:

"Pino at that time had several places on the fire concurrently, including the American Sugar Company, where there was supposed to be sixty or seventy thousand dollars waiting

36

to be taken. So, magnanimously, and I'm kidding when I use that word, he turned the sugar company over to me, Gus, Faherty, Costa and a fellow who has since been killed—his name doesn't matter here. He got belted out a little more than a year ago for some other action.

"American Sugar was ready to go any Friday. But the Sturtevant job had priority, and for a time I couldn't figure why. We'd meet with Pino, and one of us would say, 'Hey, why waste time? We're going down there Friday and get this thing over with—grab it.' But Pino would shake his head. 'No,' he'd say, 'don't work this week. Let it go another week.' So it went that way for a time, and suddenly Sturtevant's went, on a Thursday. They banged it—and oh, what a beef in the papers! Terrible. Everybody was up in arms over a big score like that.

"That night those of us who were ticketed for American Sugar met Pino and his people in a park, and Pino said, 'Why don't you grab American Sugar tomorrow?' So we grabbed it. There was about $27,000 there. It was a hard one. We had to tie up their cop, to start with, and worry about a lot of sugar workers. The timing was tricky, too. We had to do it between the arrivals there of two armored trucks, each with fellows with guns. Brink's truck would come first to drop some money and then, some minutes later, U.S. Armored would pull up to deliver or pick up, I forget. But Pino had figured the whole thing out so that we had to grab the payroll in between those two trucks.

"It was a morning job. We needed a car, so we had grabbed one from a funeral director, a big black Buick. We planted it where it wouldn't be too conspicuous, in the parking lot of the Veterans' Hospital, and changed the plates.

"We must have looked a sight when we walked into American Sugar. I was covered with one of those Army foul-weather outfits, a kind of parka, which hid most of my face. Gus looked about the same. Just Gus and I went in. Faherty and this other bum stayed outside—I don't know why; they sure weren't much help. Pino had planted Costa in a hot car, a Plymouth, at a spot outside where he could follow the Buick, if the getaway was close, and stall his car in one of those narrow streets. That would block the cops, of course, and give us the little time we needed—if it turned out we needed time.

"First we had to grab the cop. He was a Keystone guy, not a Boston police-force man. Just a fellow in a uniform. He had a gun but he was slow with it and we had ours in his ribs before he knew what was happening to him. We took him in an office and tied him up. Then we had to worry about a dozen or so sugar workers who had come down to this office section of the plant to pick up their pay. Rough bastards, they were. They objected like hell when we rounded them up in another little office where they wouldn't be any bother. I tried to reason with them. I said to them 'What's wrong with you guys? This ain't *your* money we're taking.' You should've heard them howl.

"We didn't know it at the time but there was a girl on the phone in the back of the larger office room, calling the police. But things worked out for us. Faherty and the other bum came in and we dragged the money box out of there. We had still another car, a legit car, parked on a quiet street not far away. Pino's plan called for us to transfer the box from the Buick to this legit car, abandon the Buick and split up, after which Gus would drive the car with the box to the place out of town, where the money would be split up.

"But the Buick was so fast we decided to stay with it, after we transferred the box, just in case we needed some speed. As it turned out, we didn't. Just as we pulled away from the legit car, in the Buick, we noticed a Boston police department patrol car right ahead of us. The officers in there must have just then gotten the flash, for suddenly they threw their car into second gear and pulled away from us at full speed, siren going. We made a right at the next corner, abandoned the Buick and went to a movie."

Gus drove the legitimate car to the split-up point later that day. O'Keefe got his share, but when he learned that Pino was in for $3,000, as a kind of steerer's fee, he made so bold as to blast the arranger.

"That was a stupid thing we did today," Specs said when the money had been divided and Pino's bit set aside. "If we had gotten nailed we'd have taken the rap for yesterday's thing at Sturtevant's, sure as hell."

"What the hell are you talking about?" Faherty demanded. "It was handed to us on a silver platter, wasn't it?"

"No," O'Keefe corrected. "We had to go in and get it. We were used by Pino—can't you guys see that?" They couldn't.

Neither case was ever solved, and the statute of limitations has long since set in. At one point in the bewildered police inquiry, Police Commissioner Sullivan declared that it was his opinion that both places had been burgled by "farmers." Asked to explain, the elderly commissioner said he had been informed (by a phone call from a friend of O'Keefe) that in the Sturtevant stick-up one of the robbers yelled, "Where's that lettuce?" And that at the sugar plant, a gun-wielder had demanded, "Where's that cabbage?" Sullivan's point was that no self-respecting urban thief uses such corny names for money.

With two big scores in twenty-four hours to his credit, and the kind of manpower he wanted and needed, Pino set out to fashion his—and their—masterpiece.

5

THE ROAD TO BRINK'S WAS LONG, DEVIOUS AND PAVED WITH bad intentions. The better part of two years of reconnaissance, research and hard work—fraught with danger to the eleven participants—was a prelude to the greatest stick-up of them all.

Three of the eleven participants are dead, Gus (Stanley Albert Gusciora), Banfield (Joseph Sylvester), who died before trial, and Henry Baker, who succumbed to pneumonia, in prison, on February 13, 1961. Seven others are serving life terms, plus. Specs, currently free as a lark but hardly a man given to dreamless sleep, tells of the seed of what became a massive operation:

"In 1947, a month or two after the Sturtevant–American Sugar bits, Pino sent word that he wanted to see me. He had outlined what he had in mind to Gus, and invited him to be a part of it. Gus told him, 'If you want me to work, Joe has to work, too.' Gus didn't know how I felt about those guys or, if he did know, he figured the size of the scores we could get by working with an arranger like Pino made everything else unimportant. Gus must have been right, because I went to see Pino.

"I met Pino over on the beach and he came right to the point. He asked me if I'd be interested in a score—a big one. I told him I didn't know. We met half a dozen more times before he'd give me any further information. 'It's about

40

forty payrolls,' Pino finally said. I couldn't think that big. 'That would be rough, wouldn't it?' I asked him. But he said, 'No, we got it lined up pretty good. You interested?'

"I still couldn't make up my mind.

" 'Gus is going,' he said.

"So I said okay, I'd go along."

The next morning, before dawn, Pino took O'Keefe down to Federal Street in Boston and walked him swiftly past the repository of the "forty payrolls."

Specs whistled softly.

It was Brink's!

Every robber knew Brink's as a score both wondrous and unattainable. What must have gone through Specs' mind that morning was later expressed in a book by R. A. Seng and J. V. Gilmour, entitled *Brink's: The Money Movers*, published by Lakeside Press:

> . . . By modern standards Brink's is not a giant corporation, yet it has a peculiar impact upon the observer. It seizes the imagination because it has some of the qualities of Fort Knox, of the Federal Reserve Banks and the United States Mints all rolled into one. For Brink's is the great money-mover of this or any other time. Its comparative handful of employes—less than five thousand all told—handle a daily average of about one and one third *billions* of dollars in currency, coin, checks and commercial paper—more in a day than the monthly gross of giant General Motors; more in a day than the yearly gross of all but a few dozen United States companies; more in a year than the total of the national debt.
>
> . . . This is a national institution of the broadest scope that serves not only banks, corporations, companies and individuals, but Federal, State and local governments and their numerous instrumentalities. Its activities are closely associated with law enforcement agencies and have a real bearing upon the welfare, safety and peacefulness of cities and towns. It delivers—and in many cases, disburses—thousands of payrolls each week; handles church collections and

41

the receipts and change requirements of filling stations, chain stores, department stores, neighborhood stores, theaters, restaurants, sports arenas, race tracks and one-man businesses; safeguards not only bills and coins but the vital though uncashable cancelled checks that flow through clearing houses back to the issuing banks.

Through months and months of 1948, the group cased their coveted goal. And then at long last they had their plan of action and were perfectly schooled in it.

They knew exactly when a large hamper of payrolls would be brought down by elevator from the fourth floor of the building, trundled to a rear door and then passed or tossed from man to man and finally into a Brink's armored truck which was backed into position.

Part of the group was to seize and tie up the truck guards. The rest, four or five, would go in the back door and wait for the arrival of the elevator and its cargo. The group's car or truck was to pull up abreast of the armored truck. There would be no trouble with the four or five men on the elevator. They were certain to "freeze" long enough—upon opening the door of the lift and seeing themselves confronted by a row of menacing guns—to forfeit any opportunity to close the elevator door or shoot. When they were disarmed, bound and gagged, the group would dump the hamper into its car or truck and drive off.

It never came off.

Just days before the tediously rehearsed strike, the men read a flabbergasting news story in their papers.

Brink's had moved! The whole operation, its employees and treasure, simply moved away from Federal Street. The better part of a year's work in the realm of sophisticated crime went down the drain.

The months of association with what became the best-known robber band in the annals of crime in the United States had given O'Keefe an opportunity to study his associates and evaluate them in his incisive way:

42

"Pino is, well, I have to be prejudiced because of what happened . . . he always was a pig. Obese, sloppy, but thorough and smart in protecting himself and in arranging things. A great angle man. Pino had an avid hunger for money. And possessions. As kids we used to steal coal so the family could stay warm during the worst part of the winter. Every kid in our section of Boston stole coal. The more timid of us would pick it up from the railroad's right of way, near where it was loaded. The more ambitious would take it right from the coal cars, sometimes dragging it home on a sled over the snow. Where the ordinary kid was content with a season's total of, say, a couple hundred pounds of coal, Pino filled his family's cellar with it. You couldn't get down the stairs. He stole coal like it was going to be cold forever; like he thought it was Russia, or something. That's the kind of kid he was, and the kind of man he became.

"His family? Nice people. His father and mother were immigrants from Sicily. They brought him here as a baby in arms. He never went through the process of becoming a citizen. He didn't think it was necessary.

"He was an actor, as he grew up. He could make himself cry or sweat on order, like a big fat actor. He was always a pig. Once, as a kid, he found the 'plant' of his uncle. The uncle had a habit of saving his dimes and quarters until he could change them into a twenty-dollar bill, then he'd stash the bill away with other twenty-dollar bills he had saved over the years. Pino nailed the whole bundle and went out and bought himself a pony and cart—and you can imagine what that was like in the tough neighborhood we lived in. He took all us kids into a resturant and blew us to whatever we wanted. He couldn't take just an occasional twenty, or forty, which wouldn't have been noticed. He had to nail the whole bundle. He was a pig. What he did as a kid may be indicative of his actions in the Brink's case.

"McGinnis was separate and distinct from us. His type of life was rough. He's a real cold fish, a rough egg. He was a

43

successful man at the time of the Brink's. He got his start through a madam who liked him. Jean Parker. She was a good enough person, I suppose. Most of them are.

"Joe was a young guy at the time—this was around 1924-1925—and she was stuck on him. When they split up, Jean gave him about fifty thousand. He went in business, first a café—she helped him with that—then a liquor store and a few other operations. Like stills. He developed a wide connection of friends from hoodlums to politicians, racket people and legitimate people. They all began coming to him for help, one kind or another. He could bull his way ahead for you, if you meant something to him. Financially, though, he'd never give you a nickel. He's the tightest fellow in the world, I'd say. His god was, is, money. Wouldn't give you a dime or a drink of whiskey if your life depended on it, or your tongue was hanging out. Never sprang. I never saw him dressed in a full suit of clothes, or suit and pants that matched. I think of him as a guy in a black sweater with chino pants and Navy shoes. How much are Navy shoes—four dollars? His place to eat would be some place like Bickford's.

"Now take Maffie, a clean-cut type. If you didn't know him you'd tag him as a real smart guy. But after you got to know him, you'd come to the opposite opinion. He was a good gambler, though, Always made a pretty good living with horses, dogs, dice, things like that. He was a fairly successful bookmaker, too. But here's where he was dumb. He always lived beyond his means. He always wanted to do the things a rich guy does, so he had to supplement his own income with money he got from going out on Pino's jobs. His strength, so far as the group was concerned, was as a 'heavy.' He'd go in with, let's say, Geagan, and bust the situation, get control of the people in the place, the people around the payroll.

"Jazz Maffie was a kid who was sent away early. Came from a good family. He was a likeable guy, free with a dollar. I was very friendly with him. You'll see . . .

"Geagan was a different type, though he worked well with Jazz. Geagan was a morose guy. Never talkative. Always lived within himself, but a strong guy in this type of business; really on the ball. Fast, capable.

"He should never have been in the business, Geagan. He should have stuck with regular work. He was always unlucky. He was a lineman with the telephone company, a job he got through his brother—a real decent, hard-working fellow. But he got hooked up with a group that went down to Brockton, Massachusetts, and took a payroll from the city hall. In taking it, one of the guys shot a cop; not bad, but he was hit. Vinny got away from it clean, but then got pinched for speeding later that day in Boston. One of those crazy things: twenty-six miles an hour in a twenty-five-mile zone, something like that. And there he was, with some little evidence of the Brockton job in his pocket or the car. He got one of the biggest sentences: twenty-eight to thirty years on the armed robbery and seven to ten on assault to kill.

"That was 1935. While in the can he went a little religious sour, went on a religious kick. Whether you could say he was wacky, I don't know. It was strange, to us, that he should go that way, because we always thought of him as very strong. When he finally got out, he became a longshoreman, and most of the people who knew him thought that was that. But Pino was still in his background. Pino had an almost hypnotic control over him, over not only Geagan but most of the rest of us. He could tell them to sit down and they'd sit down, and never question him. A strange thing. And, in turn, McGinnis had the same kind of control over Pino, because Pino's life's ambition was to be another McGinnis.

"Henry Baker was the only Jewish fellow amongst us. He was very intelligent and an inveterate prowler. He could go into a place and actually smell out where the money was, or where was what we wanted. I'd have to waste an hour looking around for what Henry could smell in a minute. Whatever he devoted himself to, he did well. For example, he decided to learn Spanish—while we were waiting for the big one—and learned to speak it well. Learned to write well, too. In prison, before he died, he studied dentistry, something he'd been interested in since he was a kid. I was always fond of Henry, though once I had to take a shot at him. I helped him jump bail after he got mixed up in hijacking a truckload of tires late in the war; helped him go to California and get set up in business as a dental technician; helped get him a new birth certificate (I think his new name was Thompson and he was vain enough to ask us to knock a couple years off his age) and a draft card—deferred. A bright guy, but, like a lot of us, he made the mistake of overexposing himself.

"Richardson? Now he's an old man, but in his younger days he was a pretty lively drinking sort of guy who worked with Geagan on the docks. I'd say he was a working fellow. A slob.

"Costa, well, Costa was just Pino's brother-in-law. He was completely under Pino's thumb. If Pino told him to stand on his head, he'd stand on his head and never wonder why.

"Banfield was McGinnis's man. He worked around McGinnis's stills, drove for him. He was a bottle man but never drank on the job. A good fellow.

"Jim Faherty should have been any of a number of things. He was a longshoreman, a bartender, steam fitter, electrician, clerk, and once he actually had a job as custodian of a school. But he was a compulsive thief, like the rest of us. And an unlucky one. He was always getting caught. Got twenty to twenty-five years for armed robbery with a machine gun, back in the thirties.

"As for Gus . . . Gus was the best."

If the Brink's robbers had chosen the site of the new location of the money-handling organization's Boston office they could not have found a more ideal location. Brink's had selected a large garage at the corner of Prince and Commercial streets, a garage which incidentally had seen much

46

service during bootlegging days. A portion of it was soon renovated into offices, counting rooms and vault rooms.

Pino was jubilant after his first prowl of the new place. Specs was mystified by the ease of his first of many visits to the place:

"We—Gus and I—went in through the garage. Getting into the garage was as simple as getting into your own home. I opened the door with an ice pick and instinctively we waited for an alarm to sound. There wasn't any. The door wasn't even bugged! We couldn't believe it.

"Nobody was around. We went across the garage like a couple of mice and came to the door that led into the office section. I opened it with a piece of celluloid. Still no bug! And not a soul in sight—at nine o'clock at night! It was delightful. It was made for us. A forty-dollar dog, hell, even a mongrel, one that could bark, would have stopped us cold. They've always been tight with a buck, those Brink's: pay their help next to nothing, considering the responsibility they put on them. Just a little expense would have saved the whole joint for them.

"At last we found a bug, and of course it was in a place where it meant trouble for us. It was on the main vault. The two of us had seen a few alarm systems in our time but this was strange to us. We'd do something about that later. There was a lot we had to learn about the place in general, first. The amount of business in the place, for example. There were the figures, big as life, right on a clip board hanging near the vaults—just how much money was in, down to the penny. It was crazy. Later, and before the big grab, Gus and I would drop in there at night, if we were in the neighborhood, just to look at the clip board and see how our business was doing. 'How about them cheap bastards,' Gus said one night, studying the board. 'Only three hundred thousand in there.' "

Pino accompanied O'Keefe and Gusciora the next time the advance pair went in. Eventually, all eleven participants

47

in the fabled robbery prowled in and out—utterly un-detected. O'Keefe, rated the surest of the entry men, esti-mates that he personally was inside the premises between thirty and forty times during the long months of the research and development of the holdup. In short, the three-story building at 165 Prince Street in North Boston became one of the most frequently visited buildings in the city—at least after working hours. It is located in what amounts to an Italian immigrant ghetto, and its inhabitants more than shared the general opinion that Brink's was as impregnable as Fort Knox. Thus they were completely free of a sense of suspicion, if indeed they ever saw the robbers-to-be coming and going in the area.

Having clearly established the vulnerability of the rear en-trance, the men set about the task of getting keys for all other doors in the place, including the main door on Prince Street. This was accomplished by removing lock cylinders, rushing them to a key-making wizard and getting them back to Brink's and into their assigned slots before there was any chance they might be missed.

Pino could not believe that a company which dealt with so much negotiable currency would be as feebly guarded as it gave every indication of being. So he assigned O'Keefe and Maffie to spend a full night in one of the Brink's armored trucks in the garage and study any movement by watchmen or guards. At 4 A.M., after an uneventful vigil that had begun at nine o'clock the previous night, Jazz said, "Oh, to hell with this. Let's go get a drink." He didn't have to repeat the invitation.

However, the bug on the main vault worried the group; how to get around it was the chief topic of many a seminar. Specs recalls:

"What could we do with it? If we could disconnect the bug we could burn the big vault, burn a hole in it and open it that way. But this was a bug that was strange to us. We didn't know how far we could go with it before it sounded an alarm.

"Now here's where a fellow like McGinnis was valuable. He had so many connections in so many fields. For instance, he had a fellow named Sullivan who was a guy who knew about electrical installation. McGinnis sent Sullivan to Washington, to the Patent Office, to study the patent applications, specifications, drawings and things like that. But even that wasn't enough. We had to know how that particular bug was wired and what it would report to its people—the American District Telegraph Company, a protective organization—if we messed with it.

"So Gus and I went down to ADT's place one night to see what we could find. We got in through the back door with my 'loid. We padded in and went through the basement in the dark to the edge of a big lighted room that was filled with uniformed guards, all armed. There were about twenty of them. The walls of the place were kind of instrument boards, with lights showing that all was okay at this or that place which was under ADT protection. I said to myself, watching them, 'What the hell are we going to do about these guys? They'll be on us like a ton of bricks, if that bug at Brink's tips them.'

"We went up to the main floor of the building, looked at the office board near the elevator and found that the main offices of ADT were on the third floor. So we walked up the back way and went in, like going into your own house. Well, we were almost as good as Henry Baker that night. There was a row of file cases against the wall of the first office we went in. I walked over to it, pulled out the drawer marked 'B' and there it was, under 'Brink's—Commercial Street.' A nice neat folder detailing just how the joint was wired, and a lot of nonsense, too, like how to save a cent and a half per something or other using a certain kind of screws. Maybe that's why they got robbed, worrying about little things like

49

that, and all those guys in the basement never knowing that we had been in the next room looking at them."

Specs and Gus took the dossier to Pino's house, and a general council was convened to harvest all useful information from this prize. To their disappointment, information on the bug itself was sketchy. But the men noticed with grunts of satisfaction an item which stated that Brink's was insured for $5,000,000.

The papers in the dossier were carefully put back in their proper order and sequence. The next night Specs and Gus returned to ADT, re-entered the place while the company's army bivouacked in the cellar, and put the folder back in its file cabinet. Acting on a cross-reference mentioned in the dossier, the two men then moved on to the offices of the company engineer, searching for blueprints that might be a kind of Rosetta stone in their quandary. But their luck, or sense of "smell," ran out. There were hundreds of rolls of blueprints stored in racks that reached from floor to ceiling, none of them marked in a way they could understand. With mounting distress they examined roll after roll after roll until suddenly both men froze. Someone was approaching down the hall on which the engineer's office fronted. The sound of footsteps was like a burning fuse, what with the presence of the armed guards below. Specs and Gus had to gamble, and they bet correctly. They moved from the engineer's office into the office next to it. They watched the silhouette of a guard or watchman pass across the clouded glass of that office door. The man entered the room from which they had departed seconds before. Specs and Gus went quickly into the hall, and out.

The fruitless search and the inadequate information on the bug meant that if the job was to be pulled off it would have to be a holdup. The vault could not be safely burned. They had learned enough about the bug to know, or at least suspect, that the snipping of one of its wires or any other kind of tampering would set it off. Still, the prospect of burning the vault held so much attraction for the men that they continued to discuss all kinds of alternatives that would permit them to go to work safely with their cutting torches. For a time they even considered storming en masse into the ADT's guard room, disarming that armed and muscular group, tying them up, then going on to Brink's—where the vault could be burned with a certain degree of leisure. The vision of a roomful of roped and gagged guards, staring helplessly at the flashing red lights on the wall panel, and struggling vainly against their bonds as they listened to the alarm, was a pleasant dream for the robbers. It was Specs who discouraged this one.

"Geez, that's too big a proposition, grabbing all them bums and tying them up," he complained. As an afterthought he added, "And so much work." That apparently was the clincher that swung the majority.

They next considered a plan to hack through the big electric conduit leading into the ADT building, thus paralyzing the company's contact with the hosts of clients subscribing to its protection service. Proponents of this plan argued that it might take days, weeks, even a month before the conduit's jungle of fine wires could be replaced or repaired. And during that time they could move in and crack the Brink's vault while its bug was still mute.

That plan was discarded on the grounds that any such brutal treatment of the conduit inside the building would surely alert not only ADT but beef up the Boston police and make the task measureably more hazardous. An interesting alternative emerged from this discarded ploy, however. They examined a nearby sewer through which the conduit passed and decided that it might be destroyed in a way that perhaps would not arouse a hue and cry. They would drop several incendiary grenades into the sewer and destroy whatever was in there, including ADT's life line. It might look "natural," most of the men agreed.

But a curious dissent was sounded by O'Keefe, who had

whiled away his spare time during bygone sojourns in prison by reading American history.

"It's too risky," he said, just as the proposal was about to be adopted. There was a babble of curses and denials, and finally a demand that he tell them why.

"The fire might get out of hand and spread to Faneuil Hall; it's not far from that sewer," Specs said with a commendable note of patriotism.

"What the hell is Faneuil Hall!" Pino thundered. He apparently had played hooky the day his class was taught about "the Cradle of Liberty."

They toyed, too, with the ambitious notion of invading Brink's in force early in the morning and then seizing and tying up each employee as he or she arrived for work, a massive endeavor whose climax was to be the capture of the manager. At gunpoint, and after the bug had been rendered inoperative, as it was at the opening of the day's business, the manager would then be forced to open the vault.

After much consideration, this plan was discarded because it involved possible physical harm to the manager or other employees. If arrested in the wake of such a situation, each robber would be liable for additional years in prison.

Most of the reconnaissance in the Brink's area was called off in the late winter of 1948-49. The days were getting longer, and that presented a serious seasonal obstacle. Their studies had convinced them that the Brink's had to be hit shortly after 7 P.M., if the best possible conditions were to prevail. It is broad daylight in Boston at that time during the long spring, summer and early fall, under daylight saving time. And so they had to shelve their heady dreams for many excruciating months through 1949.

But they had refined their ultimate plan by now: they would strike while the vault was open and attended by the fewest number of employees. The last activity around the vault, they had discovered, was between seven and seven-thirty each working night. Then that skeleton staff went home, after closing the vault and handing its fortunes over to the ADT bug. Thus the robbers needed a certain set of circumstances: an open vault, a minimum of vault defenders, and a time of year when 7 P.M. offers the shield of darkness.

Through the long enforced waiting period they stole discreetly, careful not to take risks that could boomerang and knock them out of the big one. And they further refined the master plan as day trudged after day.

To supplement their increasingly rare prowling through Brink's, after hours, Pino went shopping. Legitimately. He bought a $75 telescope from the finest store of its kind in Boston and assigned his servile brother-in-law, Costa, to man it as inconspicuously as possible from a rooftop along a row of four-story tenements that faced Brink's. There were some optimistic thoughts expressed by members of the group that perhaps Costa might even be able to pick up the combination of the vault, through the spyglass. Pino was of a mind to settle for some less spectacular but thorough-minded revelations: the movements, mannerisms, size, age, demeanor of the late-hour crew with which they must eventually deal.

It did not work out satisfactorily. Brink's windows were dirty. ("Cheap bastards, they wouldn't even wash their windows so we could see something," Specs was to complain later.) Pino, a thrifty soul, returned the spyglass—using his wife for this chore—and got his money back. (Some years later, its then owner, a sedate bird watcher in California, found himself embarrassingly connected with the great robbery's side issues. He was distressed to learn that the self-same eye-piece that had brought him many an enchanting close-up view of the yellow belly sapsucker had been found wanting in the quest of what turned out to be a treasure of $2,775,395.12.)

As the days of extended daylight waned in the late summer and early autumn of 1949 the most concentrated planning began. Pino ruled that masks must be worn: foolproof masks. In most of their previous jobs the robbers had been content in the main with a down-thrust hat, turned-up coat collar, a hand or handkerchief over the face. But this was to be special. Pino, who read comic and adventure strips in the Boston newspapers, discovered that novelty stores were offering plastic or rubber masks of a number of his cartoon heroes. He chose masks in the image and likeness of Captain Marvel and his cowlick zombie son, Captain Marvel, Jr. He made a trip to Chicago principally to buy the masks.

It was Pino who decided that the uniform of the night for the seven who would perform inside Brink's would be chauffeur's hats, Navy pea jackets (clothing traditionally worn by Brink's guards and drivers) and rubbers—to deaden footstep sounds. Specs, who resented being told too many things to do, decided to be a nonconformist on the latter. He wore a pair of crepe-soled shoes.

Two vehicles were stolen for the occasion. First, Pino and Gus selected a new green Ford truck. It was to meet several specifications not anticipated by the manufacturer. It had to be large enough to hold nine of the eleven robbers but small enough to fit as inconspicuously as possible into Prince Street. It had to be strong enough to hold the men and the treasure, but light enough to be rocked up partly on the pavement, if it should prove to be a menace to the flow of traffic in Prince Street.

The men turned their three-quarter-ton "rib and canvas top" truck over to Banfield, the gang's handyman. He made certain alterations calculated to save what might be precious seconds. He fashioned a door (and opening in the canvas) in the side of the truck that would face the Prince Street door out of which the money would be brought. This would permit faster loading than could be accomplished by means of the drop-gate in the rear of the truck.

The second vehicle, an almost new Ford sedan, was stolen by Specs while its owner was being beguiled by a Brahms suite at a concert by the Boston Symphony. Costa had complained that the car which had been assigned to him—to get him to the scene ahead of the others and to protect the get-away, if necessary—was not in good working order. So Specs stole him a good one.

"Find some fault with this one, you jerk," Specs cheerfully challenged Pino's brother-in-law as he turned the music-lover's car over to him.

The men made five tense dry runs on Brink's before the big strike.

On each occasion the involved machinery was set in motion; it worked perfectly, only to break down just short of the pay-off.

On each occasion, Costa went on ahead, parked his car in the right spot on Prince Street, entered the chosen tenement house through the rear, climbed swiftly and noiselessly to the top, padded out on the roof like a cat, tested his flash-light, then watched the condition of things in Brink's vault room and elsewhere in the building across the street.

On each occasion, too, Banfield wheeled the truck into its proper position, picked up the men, individually and in pairs, and began the advance on Brink's.

Specs says:

"More damned details. We couldn't carry change in our pockets, for example. Might jingle as we went through the place toward the vault room. Couldn't wear watches. They might tick too loud! Couldn't smoke in the truck. Somebody might wonder why smoke was coming from an enclosed truck. We had to pile out at the right place. We had to be careful that we walked casually down through the terraced street alongside Brink's, so we'd look just like the other Brink's working stiffs.

"And, after all that, then there wouldn't be any signal from Costa, which meant that something was wrong. Maybe the vault had been closed, or there was a light on in one of the rooms we had to go through, indicating people might still be working in there."

The delays so rasped the nerves of Specs and Gus they

seriously considered backing out of the plot after a particularly frustrating dry run on the night of January 16. They resented the "deadwood," too, the partners who would not be going into Brink's: McGinnis, Pino, Costa and Banfield.

They could have afforded the luxury of retiring from the conspiracy just then, Specs and Gus.

Earlier that day the two pulled one of the major jobs of their lives: the $43,000 holdup of the accounting office of Boston's big and busy Hotel Statler. Their role in that up-to-now unsolved robbery is told by Specs:

"Gus and I had watched this one for a long time, and we probably would have waited still longer if we hadn't been so edgy over all those delays on the Brink's thing.

"It was a big day for the Statler. Lots of people in the lobby, lots of activity. We went up the steps to the office on the mezzanine, steps that aren't used much. Near the top we took off our hats and put them on a step. Then we pulled a couple of brown-paper bags—with eye slits in them—over our heads, took out our guns and walked in.

"Well, they froze. We must have looked pretty terrible at that. There were some poor people at their desks, on one side of the room. They sat there like statues. There was a poor old fellow in uniform there, too, a guard of some kind. Gus stuck his gun at him, made him lie down and tied him up. A nice-looking kid, a messenger, I guess, suddenly made a break for the door we had come through. I got in front of him and showed him what I had.

" 'Don't do that, son,' I said to him, quiet. 'You wouldn't want to get hurt now, would you? You just go over there and lie down next to the guard and nothing will happen to you.'

"We scooped up the cash, told them all to stay put, backed out, took off the bags, put our hats on and quickly joined the crowds in the lobby.

"People were all excited. Some were clapping. Former

Secretary of State, General George Marshall, was coming in a door. The manager was there, bowing and showing him in. "We went out another door with the forty-three . . ."

And at last it came, January 17, 1950, the most memorable day in the life of Joseph James O'Keefe. This is what it was like to him:

"During the big day, as usual, we were supposed to go about our business as if nothing was going to happen out of the ordinary. I spent the day in my room at the Copley Square Hotel. Had some company: a girl who had a boy friend in New York she wanted to get to, and another girl I was friendly with, named Helen. The girl who was stuck on the bum in New York kept calling him from my room, and finally raised him. He told her to come on in to New York, and she blew.

"That left me with Helen. And a problem. I had to be at the right spot in Roxbury at the right time—just before seven o'clock—to get into the truck. Helen was drinking and she thought I was too. I wasn't touching the stuff; I had too much going for me. I was thinking pretty good, too. When Helen wasn't noticing, I moved my wristwatch forward, making it seem later than it actually was.

"Finally I said to her, 'Geez, it's awful late. I've got to go out for a while. I've got to get a couple hundred from a guy, so we can go on drinking.' Then I looked at my watch and said, 'Cripes, it's seven-thirty. I've gotta go.' It was only six-thirty, six thirty-five, something like that. But she didn't know.

"I shot out to the meet place, got in the truck and we drove down toward Brink's once more, sitting side by side on the floor, not talking. Banfield drove. Pino sat with his back to Banfield, his legs spread out down the middle of the truck floor, or curled up like a Buddha. Seven others of us were seated to his left and right, three and four. It was pitch-dark in the truck, but we knew where each other man was. I knew I was next to Sandy Richardson and that Geagan was on the other side of Sandy.

"Pino knew where I was. He poked me, then once again he handed me the keys to the different doors we'd have to go through. The flange part of each key had been filed in a certain way. I could tell which was which in the dark, like a blind man reading Braille.

"The weather was in our favor that night; not the worst kind of a Boston night in winter but bad enough to keep people off the streets in that crummy neighborhood. The fact that it was a bad neighborhood made it dangerous for us. A lot of people living around Brink's had served time or were little bookies or odds-and-ends thieves, and on account of that they would recognize us. Even the good people of the neighborhood were dangerous. One night Tony Shucca, the old fighter, happened to be walking down a street near Brink's just as we started walking up it. I spotted him before he saw us—I think Gus was with me—and we got out of there in a hurry. He would have remembered later that he saw us near Brink's, when we were picked up as suspects. Besides, anybody recognized near Brink's before the grab was automatically out. Through.

"Banfield stopped the truck at the usual place and we waited, none of us saying anything.

"Then Costa gave us the light from the roof.

"Seven of us got out right away: Baker, Richardson, Geagan, Faherty, Maffie, Gus and myself. Banfield and Pino stayed in the truck. They'd bring it around to the entrance a little later.

"The seven of us strolled down through the terraced playground that stretches along the side of the building, then turned into Prince Street. There was nobody around that we could see. I went for key No. 1, the key to the front door, and in we went.

"The first thing we had to do, just inside the now closed

door, was to take off our chauffeur caps and put on the masks. They were like skin rubber, fitted right over our heads and came down to the collarbone. I thought they were masks of movie actors—John Barrymore or somebody. It wasn't until later I learned, or even heard of, the Marvel boys.

"When all the masks were on we put our caps back on and started up the stairway to the second floor. Key No. 2 let us through the door at the top. Key No. 3 let us into the office area. It was dark, as Costa's signal had told us it would be. We kept going toward the vault room, me on my crepe soles, the others on their rubbers. There wasn't a sound in the place. Or from outside, either, though we knew Pino and Banfield would now be moving the truck down to Prince Street, and Costa would be coming down from his roof to get in the Ford and line it up behind the truck—in case.

"Key No. 4 let us into where we wanted to be. Where we had to be.

"It took us about twenty minutes, from the time Lloyd said, 'Oh, my God,' until we pulled away in the truck.

"There was no elation in the truck. We had been through this routine so many times that, suddenly, there was no kick —just a little satisfaction, I guess, that the getaway had been so clean.

"The original plan called for us to take the stuff to Charlestown, across the bridge, a short distance from Brink's. But that had been junked at the last minute because it was a much-too-built-up area. It was too close, too residential, and didn't offer enough cover.

"So we took it to Roxbury, instead, to the home of Maffie's parents, about a fifteen-minute drive. It's a family-type house. Jazz had and has a real good family, good parents, immigrants who couldn't speak much English. They either didn't know or couldn't understand what their son was. He had them trained, I guess. Anyway, as we drove up with the money, he went in first and chased them upstairs, out of the way.

"Geagan was on parole at the time. He was sure he'd be picked up for questioning, so he got out of the truck before it got to Maffie's place. He wanted to begin establishing his alibi as soon as possible.

"So did all of us, but there was the question of counting the money, or at least some of it, so that we could get a general idea about how much it came to. It was bundled well, which helped, but still it seemed to take forever.

"Pino, Faherty, Richardson and Costa blew in a hurry, Richardson taking $20,000 with him and Costa picking up $40,000 later. They wanted to show themselves in places where they normally were about that time of night.

"Gus and I, Jazz, Baker and Banfield went the distance with the stuff. Maffie was in charge of adding up the figures we called out. You never saw so many bags of it. Maybe thirty-five or forty. One of the first we split open—Baker did it with his knife—was marked $135,000. A nice score, he said. But when he ripped it open, out spilled a big glob of veterans' checks. We were sick at the sight of them, not so much because we knew we couldn't cash them but because this meant we had a Federal case on our hands. The FBI would come in. But we shook it off and went on with the count. At some time, I don't remember when, McGinnis came in.

"We stopped that night at $1,143,000. There was a lot left, but Gus and I had to get out and be seen some place. I saw from twelve to eighteen payrolls whose envelopes would have been too tough to count then. We put $380,000 in a coal hamper, and Baker was to take that from the place that night, so as to spread the stuff a little. We dumped the odd payrolls and a lot of loose ones, fives and tens, in a Brink's hamper we had brought along, and set that aside to be counted later.

"Then there was the 'new' money, fresh money whose serial numbers ran in sequence. That meant it was traceable. We had agreed that anything we picked up that was trace-

able would be destroyed, and by fire. That was one of Mc-
Ginnis's jobs and the argument was that it was things like
this, and his connections, that entitled him to a full share of
the loot. He never came near Brink's that night. He was in
his whiskey store establishing the best alibi any of us had.

"The 'new' money came to $98,000. We put it in a sack
and tossed it in the corner with the other junk McGinnis
was to get rid of. It was quite a pile by now. On plan, we
had cut up our pea jackets, masks, chauffeur hats, gloves,
rubbers and my crepe-soled shoes. The veterans' checks and
other checks—they came to $1,557,183.83, we learned later
—were in that pile, too. And four guns we had taken from
the Brink's people when we left. McGinnis's job was to
break up the guns with a hammer and throw the parts in
the water. Deep water.

"He didn't get around to doing a couple of those things,
including burning the ninety-eight G's."

Specs and Gus left Maffie's that night about nine-thirty,
taking none of their share. O'Keefe's car had been parked
nearby, so it was no great hardship for him to walk shoeless
to it. He had a spare pair in the car, put them on and drove
carefully to a friend's bar and grill which he and Gus often
frequented.

The Boston "fuzz," as O'Keefe calls the police, were "wild."
Their car sirens wailed through the cold, clammy streets.
An extraordinary manhunt was in full cry. Unbeknown to
Specs and Gus, Faherty was picked up on suspicion as early
as 8:40 P.M. He was hauled from his favorite bar to the near-
est precinct, questioned and released.

They were on their first drink when a kid rushed in selling
the early edition of the Boston *Record*. The headline proclaimed that Brink's had been held up for $250,000.

"What a score somebody made," Specs said to Gus.

After another drink, Specs remembered Helen.

He left Gus at the bar, drove to the Copley Square Hotel

and found the lobby "infested with all kinds of law." Something warned him to call her on the house phone rather than go directly to his room. Specs called the room, heard the receiver lifted and sensed rather than heard a man's voice whisper, "Answer that."

Helen came on the phone.

"Do you have company?" Specs asked.

"Yes."

"I'll see you later," Specs said and hung up. He walked unscathed through the lobby's police officers, went out through the bar, got in his car and drove back to his friend's grill. After another drink there he called the hotel again and this time Helen was alone. He told her to meet him for dinner at the same Italian restaurant where they had dined the night before, a place that was only three blocks from the scene of the stupendous holdup. He warned her to be sure she wasn't followed, and to take a subway and change cars from time to time, rather than come by cab.

Later editions of the *Record* and other Boston morning papers were hawked through the restaurant as Specs and his girl fenced their spaghetti and chicken cacciatore. Brink's, he noted without comment, was finally catching up with the extent of their loss. The headlines were placing the heist at a million dollars.

As he read and ate, and Helen gabbed away on some extraneous subject, three Boston detectives entered, scrutinized the customers, gave Specs and his girl a particularly hard stare, then left.

"They thought I was just another sucker," Specs reported later to his friend Gus.

So did Helen, apparently. The Boston police sergeant who had stormed her room was regularly assigned to the Hub's hotel detail. On the night of the robbery he made a routine check of the registers of several hotels and found "Joseph J. O'Keefe" signed in at the Copley Square. He went to the room and was in the process of questioning the woman when

62

Specs called from the lobby. After satisfying himself that Helen was just a "friend," and actually lived at the place where she claimed to live, he released her.

Specs asked her if the detective had shown any interest in the time of night he, Specs, had left her.

"Yes, and I told him," Helen said. "I told him you went out at seven-thirty or a little after. I remembered you told me what time it was just before you left."

Specs silently checked the paper he was reading. Yes, the robbery had been ten minutes after seven. He smiled at Helen.

"Did he ask you what I did for a living?" he asked her.

"Yes," Helen said, "and I told him the truth. I told him you were a bookmaker. Was that all right to tell?"

The man who had led the way into the biggest robbery of them all breathed happily, and yawned.

"Sure, honey," he said. "That was okay."

It had been a long day.

6

THE BRINK'S EMPLOYEES LAY THERE ON THE FLOOR, BOUND AND gagged, until they heard the last of the moneybags dragged to or thrown down the stairway leading to Prince Street. Then, as they began to stir, they were alarmed by the return of one of the gunmen, the one with the crepe-sole shoes. He apparently had misplaced his chauffeur's cap in the confusion of taking the money from the vault and the sounding of the buzzer. The robber looked around for the cap from under his garish mask, quickly and fruitlessly, then left. Soon the employees heard the front door slam shut.

Lloyd the cashier, twenty-two years with Brink's, cashier-dispatcher James C. Allen, a man of faulty vision whose eyeglasses were taken from him by one of the bandits, Brink's chauffeur Sherman D. Smith, whose glasses also were taken from him, and two messengers, Charles S. Grell and Herman E. Pfaff, with thirty-seven years of service between them, squirmed and struggled against their bonds. Muffled curses came from their taped mouths. To his indignation, Grell also had been stripped of his glasses.

Lloyd was the first to free himself. He ripped the adhesive from his mouth, got up and lunged to the nearest emergency button, hardly five feet from where he had lain. It was 7:27 P.M.

Smith was next to work himself free. He de-gagged himself and then wrenched the adhesive and the ropes from the other three men as Lloyd followed his urgent pressing of the ADT button with a frantic call to the Boston police.

No one at first thought to call the FBI. But one of the greatest and most trying manhunts in the annals of crime was under way. It would last six years.

As the Boston police and a few alert reporters and cameramen streamed into Brink's that dismal night within minutes after Lloyd's alarm, the first person they encountered was the man who had shocked the robbers by pressing the back-door buzzer. He was in his little garage office, chewing his cold supper and feeling good about his new job.

William L. Manter, a stolid soul born in Saugus, Massachusetts, forty-nine years before, felt good because Brink's had kept him on the payroll. He had been a driver for the company from 1927 to 1933, but had become involved in so many accidents by that time, he was transferred to the guard department. He served as a guard from 1933 until January 16, 1950, when, to his delight, his application for a job as a maintenance man in the Brink's garage, with regular hours from 2:30 P.M. to 11 P.M. was approved. The maintenance man who had been working in the garage stayed with Manter on the sixteenth, his first day on the job, to show him his duties.

Manter reported at two-thirty on the seventeenth and found that he would be on his own. During the afternoon he washed two armored trucks and gassed up and checked the oil on other armored vehicles that pulled in. The flow of trucks into the garage seemed to Manter to fall off completely at six-thirty that evening. Shortly after seven o'clock he thought it expedient to inquire whether any more cars would be coming in for service. He was hungry and wanted to start his dinner.

He knew there were employees working in the vault room, which could be reached by a door leading from the garage. So he walked over to the locked door and pressed its buzzer. When there was no answer he pressed it again. When there was still no answer he shrugged and walked back to the little office and opened his packaged meal.

Manter's reaction to what must have been a deluge of rough questions—the police were sure at first that the robbery was an inside job—became part of a bewildering pattern of false leads and clues in the Brink's case. He was subsequently released that night with a warning that he would be questioned further. Manter went home in a state of shock induced by the startling events of his first night alone on his new job. He left his home in his car the next afternoon at one-thirty, ostensibly bound for work. When he did not appear at Brink's at his appointed time of two-thirty, a state-wide alarm was sent out for him. His worried family guessed "he just took the day off."

Manter was picked up in Waltham, Massachusetts, on the night of the twentieth. He was wearing a kind of pea jacket. In his car was a chauffeur's cap, a roll of adhesive tape, and a scrawled note indicating that he contemplated suicide. He was rushed to Boston police headquarters, and his name was added to what became an almost endless list of suspects, a vast majority of them—like Manter—subsequently cleared.

By eight o'clock on the night of the robbery the scene in the vault room beggared description. Police, reporters and cameramen, moving from one babbling employee to another to get their stories, literally waded through a slush of currency and checks either dropped or discarded by the departed robbers.

Elderly Police Commissioner Sullivan clambered to the top of a desk, bellowed for silence and then bawled: "Get these newspapermen away from all this money."

An old reporter who knew his way around Boston barked back: "What about keeping the cops away from it, too?"

The FBI, which was to move mountains to break the case, still had not been made aware of the biggest of all cash robberies.

Shortly after 8:30 P.M., William J. West, then assistant special agent in charge of the Boston office of the Bureau, listening to a radio broadcast in his home, was electrified by the news that Brink's had been robbed of a huge sum more than an hour earlier. He quickly called the office to instruct the agent on duty to call Station No. 1 of the Boston police department (the precinct in which Brink's was located) for full details. Six agents were immediately assigned to the case.

By 9:53 P.M. a report was being teletyped to FBI Headquarters in Washington. At 6:58 the following morning the Boston office teletyped to Washington that thirty special agents were on the case. Within minutes after that message was received, J. Edgar Hoover telephoned FBI Inspector Myron E. Gurnea, then on special assignment in Cincinnati, and ordered him to fly to Boston on the next available plane to take charge of the Bureau's investigation of the robbery. By January 30, twenty-one additional special agents had been ordered to report to Boston on special, temporary assignment. Ten of these were assigned exclusively to the Brink's investigation; the others were to assist in handling other investigative matters in the Boston area. Five stenographers from the FBI were also brought in, for there would be countless words to record, to check, to sift, to assay.

The first teletype from FBI–Boston to FBI–Washington on the morning of the eighteenth of January was from E. A. Soucy, Special Agent in Charge. It read:

Neighborhood check [being made] in vicinity of Brink's today. Federal Reserve Bank of Boston and all other banks involved being contacted by agents this morning for purpose of analyzing monies turned over by Federal Reserve, for purpose of obtaining any possible identifying data. All employees of Brink's with the exception of one who was ill have been interviewed. Photographs of entire layout completed. Critical area processed for latent fingerprints. No clue yet as to details of getaway or direction in which robbers went. All roads have been blocked by the state police during the past night . . . Suggest New York City, Albany, New Haven and Newark [field offices] contact underworld sources for purpose of obtaining any information concerning this holdup.

By mid-afternoon of the eighteenth, Soucy was able to report by phone to Washington that special agents assigned to the case had already interviewed more than three hundred persons. Shortly after Inspector Gurnea arrived from Cincinnati that night he teletyped Washington:

> Check being made of all airlines out of Boston covering departures of possible suspects. Samples of moneybags, wrappers and payroll envelopes from various banks where Brink's made pickups being obtained. Serial numbers of stolen currency secured where available.

Off to the FBI's famed Identification Division were shipped fingerprints of every Brink's employee, fingerprints from the Prince Street door to the vault, the adhesive tape, binding rope and the lone chauffeur's cap which was discovered after the robbery.

The FBI formally established its legal right—and duty—to participate in the search for the robbers as it swiftly moved into the case. The crime was officially within its province: included in the loot taken was $515,100 which Brink's had picked up that day from a Federal Reserve Bank; $113,273.23 in cash, U.S. Treasury checks, commercial checks, postal notes and money orders carried by Brink's from the Veterans Administration office.

In time, the FBI file on the Brink's robbery grew to the greatest footage of any of its classic cases, more than a hundred volumes larger than the Lindbergh-Hauptmann kidnaping case, and much larger still than the Alger Hiss case, the roundup of the submarine-landed Nazi saboteurs in World War II, the Rosenbergs–Fuchs–Gold–Greenglass atomic bomb spying case, and the vicious Greenlease kidnap-killing.

No tip was ignored, however preposterous it appeared on the surface. No leaf was left unturned.

Immediately after the robbery, all field offices of the Bureau were instructed to check at newsstands where out-of-town newspapers were sold to determine if any person or persons purchased Boston papers under suspicious circumstances. A number of such purchasers were questioned, but none had the remotest connection with the robbery.

Agents who combed the immediate neighborhood came up with tantalizing fragments of information:

A woman bookbinder named Nataro, who occupied a third-floor apartment on Prince Street opposite Brink's, stated that she arrived home from work at about 5:30 P.M. on the night of the robbery. She fixed herself dinner, cleaned up the kitchen and, as was her custom, sat down at a window overlooking Prince Street to look for her brother, who often paid her a visit during the early evening hours.

As she looked out on Prince Street at about seven o'clock Miss Nataro noticed a shiny black car parked directly beneath her window. A man was walking back and forth on the sidewalk adjacent to the car. He wore a topcoat and a hat.

A few minutes later, Miss Nataro saw a group of men emerge from the playground next to Brink's. She believed that there were six men in the group. All wore Navy-type pea coats and chauffeur's caps. Two of the men were carrying what appeared to be white bags folded under their arms. The men walked directly to the Prince Street door of Brink's and had no difficulty in opening the door and stepping inside.

Miss Nataro then told the agents that she moved away from the window to attend to something in her flat.

"When I came back to the window about an hour later the shiny black sedan was gone," she said.

A woman who lived in a second-floor apartment opposite Brink's told agents that upon returning to her place at seven-fifteen the night of the robbery, after making a phone call in the neighborhood, she noticed a car parked at the curb, its motor running and a man behind the wheel.

In addition, the woman stated that there was a truck in

front of her apartment, too, and as she stood there it pulled away, then stopped directly in front of the Prince Street door of Brink's, with its left front and rear wheels on the sidewalk.

About the same time, she further told the agents, she saw a small group of men—probably five, she guessed—appear on Prince Street. This group stopped at the parked car momentarily, then stepped toward the truck. One of the men was wearing a chauffeur's cap and a pea jacket. The others appeared to her to be bareheaded and to be wearing dark jackets.

"About a minute after that," she went on, "one of the men got in beside the driver of the parked car and it backed down Prince Street a short distance to the corner of Commercial Street. Then the car disappeared, its lights out, up Commercial Street. The other men? They entered the rear of the truck and it pulled away, straight up Prince Street."

Pressed for more details, the woman said the car involved seemed to be black and "rather new." She described the truck as "the type used in moving small loads of furniture. You know, one of those with canvas on the top and sides."

A doctor assisting at the Medical Mission Dispensary, located on Hull Street adjacent to Brink's, told of driving his car to the dispensary about seven o'clock that night and spotting, in his headlights, a black sedan, parked and with motor running. A man was standing just to the right of the car, the doctor told the FBI. He described him as being about five feet five, weighing about 150 and between thirty and forty years old.

"He didn't have a hat, but was wearing a full-length coat, a white shirt and a dark V-neck sweater.

A nurse arriving at the same time described the man near the dark sedan as "about five feet nine inches tall, wearing a topcoat or an overcoat and, I believe, a cap." She also noted a stake-body truck in the area.

The first neighborhood search also produced a young man

70

named Edwin Coffin, who, with his teen-age girl friend, was walking near Brink's shortly after seven o'clock on the night of the robbery. As Coffin described it, he and his girl stepped off the sidewalk to cross Prince Street. As they did, Coffin observed a truck parked near the corner of Prince Street and Commercial Street. It was facing up Prince Street. When the couple began to cross the street the truck started up, stopping just before it reached them.

After safely reaching the sidewalk on the Brink's side of Prince Street, Coffin and his girl began walking through the nearby playground toward Snow Hill Street. Coffin kept looking back at the truck, however, he told the FBI. He said that on three occasions during the next fifteen minutes the truck pulled up Prince Street to an area near a street light. It would remain in this spot for two or three minutes, then back up to a point near the Brink's offices. According to Coffin, the last time the truck pulled up Prince Street it did not stop at the street light but turned right at Lafayette Avenue and disappeared.

Coffin said he had had an opportunity to get a good look at the truck when it nearly ran him down as he and his girl crossed in front of it. He identified it as a Ford, new, with a rack body covered with dark brown canvas.

"The body of the truck was green," he said. "There was no name on it. I saw only one person in the truck—the driver. He was husky . . ."

In New York, in the first hours after the robbery, two detectives questioned, then released, a twenty-year-old Army corporal, William G. LaCasse, of Pittsfield, Massachusetts, who had boasted to a talkative girl friend that he knew one of the men who staged the holdup.

State troopers in police cars were fanning out through a wide region around Milford, Massachusetts. A Milford mill-worker had just reported to police that "five men in a black car" had stopped his car and at gun-point relieved him of his driver's license and Army discharge card.

FBI offices in Florida, California, Nevada, Arizona and other resort centers were alerted to be on the lookout for individuals obviously possessing large sums in cash. Race tracks, dog tracks, jai alai frontons and night club managers were enlisted. So were licensed gamblers and bookmakers.

As expected, a blizzard of clues and leads inundated the authorities after the release and distribution to all sections of the country of the following FBI notice:

REWARD
$100,000

has been offered by BRINK'S, INCORPORATED, Chicago, Illinois, "for information leading to the Arrest and Conviction of Persons involved in the Holdup of the Office of Brink's, Incorporated, 165 Prince Street, Boston, Massachusetts, on January 17, 1950." The person or persons to whom the reward shall be paid and the amount will be determined by a specially designated reward committee.

If you have any information concerning the identity or the whereabouts of any of the perpetrators of the robbery of Brink's, Incorporated, at Boston, Massachusetts, on January 17, 1950, please communicate with the undersigned or with the nearest office of the FEDERAL BUREAU OF INVESTIGATION, U.S. Department of Justice, the local address and telephone number of which are set forth on the reverse side of this notice. The telephone number can also be obtained from page one of your telephone directory.

If such information leads to the arrest and conviction and/or recovery of money, the FEDERAL BUREAU OF INVESTIGATION will, if specifically requested to do so by the person furnishing information, advise the Reward Committee of the information so furnished.

JOHN EDGAR HOOVER, DIRECTOR
FEDERAL BUREAU OF INVESTIGATION
U.S. DEPARTMENT OF JUSTICE
WASHINGTON, D.C.
TELEPHONE NATIONAL 7117

The second biggest news story on the night of the robbery was an accident that befell the nation's only active battleship, the immortal U.S.S. *Missouri*. It ran aground two miles off Old Point Comfort in Chesapeake Bay as it left for its first cruise under a new skipper, Captain William D. Brown. Ten days later a man called FBI headquarters in New York with the suggestion that Captain Brown was involved in the Brink's robbery and had purposely grounded the *Missouri* in order to take public interest away from the holdup. He urged that the distinguished naval officer be given a lie detector test.

The caller was not the only nautically deranged tipster. In Mr. Hoover's mail shortly after the robbery was a letter from a woman in Greene County, Pennsylvania, which read:

> Concerning the Boston Brink robbery: Why were those fellows all dressed in pea jackets and navy blue caps?— There is a reason—My idea is: They got away in a sub-marine.
>
> It would be too suspicious to be seen in civil clothes in a sub-marine, but closely resembling the Navy, nobody pays attention.—It could look, as if they training for the Navy.
>
> I have the sure feeling they are not on land, at least not on American soil.
>
> Now I dont know much about a sub marine. I am just a wife; and mother of two daughters. But my idea is: Search the Sea. Search for a submarine. Might be a foreigner one—.
>
> I just had to let you know, as it is every good American Citizen's duty to help solve crims. And—
>
> I hope the F.B.I. is successful in arresting those fellows so I hope to be the receiver of the $100.000 dolars reward which is offered. Please do not disregard this letter.

Not many, if any, tips were "disregarded." A detailed survey was made of the Boston waterfront, considered a likely escape port for the criminals.

Four days after the robbery a man in East St. Louis, Illi-

nois, sent a telegram to Federal and local authorities in New
Orleans stating that the Brink's robbers would pass through
New Orleans en route to Jamaica. Early on the morning of
January 23 of that year the same man wired authorities in
El Paso and Edinburg, Texas, declaring that the robbers
would cross into Mexico at San Juan, Texas.

The FBI found him readily enough. He greeted the agents
warmly.

"I am a seer, a prophet," he announced. "I've been having
visions since the early 1930's and have helped the police in
many bank robbery and kidnaping cases since then."

The agents, filled with the leaden feeling that comes at
the end of a fruitless inquiry, asked him to stop sending such
telegrams.

"Really, it's no trouble at all." The prophet beamed, shaking their hands enthusiastically. "If I have any more visions
I'll report them to you right away."

By now it was a story which had spread beyond the
U.S. From Montreal, in scrawled French, came this letter:

> In what concerns the Brinks Company matter, this may be
> of interest to you. I have had on several occasions in my
> home, a transient male guest, and some time before the
> Brinks Co. robbery he told me that he had a "big deal" to
> make and that if he succeeded he would never have to work
> for the rest of his days, and if he failed it would be prison.
> This gentleman often had long distance telephone conversa-
> tions which seemed suspicious to me. He also stated that he
> had used a Cadillac car to cross the border without worry.
> All these arrangements seemed suspicious to me. If this
> should interest you, you can communicate with me for
> further details.

Brink's employees, past and present, were gone over with
the fine-tooth comb of interrogation. One aroused great suspicion for a time by refusing to take a lie detector test.

74

Threatened with arrest the haggard and worried suspect, a mousy little married man, asked to be heard in private by selected police officers. He repeated his plea of innocence to them for the hundredth time.

"Then why won't you take the polygraph test?" he was asked.

"I can't . . . I just can't," he cried. "I'm not afraid of what it would show when you asked me about the robbery. What I'm afraid of is that somehow, I don't know how, it might tell that I've been keeping a woman on the side for years. If my wife ever knew . . . Oh, dear."

Pfaff, the Brink's messenger, to his astonishment and indignation, found himself singled out for especially searching questioning. A few days after he had been seized, tied and gagged, Brink's received a letter from a woman in Milwaukee stating flatly: "The key to solving the Brink's robbery is held by Herman Pfaff."

FBI agents sped to her home.

"I am psychic," she told them. "When I saw Pfaff's picture in my newspaper I heard the 'Voice of the Little Man Who Wasn't There' tell me that here was the key."

The patient agents sighed. They started to leave. The woman led them to the door and said, "Of course, I can be wrong."

The case produced perhaps the greatest wave of letter-writing ever to hit U.S. penal institutions. Hundreds of men serving time wrote to the authorities to report on scraps of information or pertinent exchanges of confidences. Most of those questioned wanted payment, usually in time off, before telling their stories. The FBI is powerless to provide such relief.

"Are you kiddin'?" protested a Massachusetts hoodlum who was routinely picked up and questioned after the robbery. "If I knew who pulled this job I wouldn't be talking to you. I'd be out looking for part of that loot."

75

One FBI report read:

> A man of modest means in Bayonne, N.J., was reported to be spending large sums of money in night clubs, buying new automobiles and otherwise exhibiting newly found wealth. A thorough investigation was made. The man's whereabouts on the evening of January 17 was determined. He was not involved in the Brink's robbery. A wealthy New York homosexual was his source of additional income.

The estranged wife of a well-known South Boston hoodlum called the FBI on January 20 to report that she suspected her husband of being involved. Though separated from him she had seen enough of him since the robbery to note that he seemed suddenly in the chips. FBI agents made an exhaustive check on the hoodlum's activities on the night of the robbery and thereafter. Then he was checked off the lengthening list of suspects. His fresh money was coming from another Boston woman, with whom he had taken up residence.

An old-time underworld associate of a Boston gunman reported that the gunman was broke during the latter part of 1949 but late in January of the following year could afford not only to go to Florida but also to buy a $60,000 bar in Miami. The Miami Bureau went to work immediately, and another bubble burst: the gunman did not own a bar; he was being supported by his wife, a waitress; he had been in Miami and remained there since early January.

A Las Vegas gambler whose life would be in jeopardy if his name were even now revealed led the FBI on a fruitless and expensive search. He told agents a detailed story. He had made the acquaintance of a visitor to Las Vegas from Florida, he said, a businessman who had surprised even the case-hardened croupiers and stickmen along The Strip with the size of his bets. Late one night while drunk the Florida businessman told the gambler—the gambler stated—that he was using Brink's money. The whole robbery was planned by Willie Sutton, it was said. Sutton "sold" some of the money to a Florida bookie, who in turn let the Florida businessman have a sum of it, for a price.

Continuing his story, the Las Vegas character also implicated a well-known Providence hoodlum and a Detroit bookmaker.

It was completely cock-and-bull, but it kept agents jumping from Nevada to Rhode Island.

A convict freshly released from the Chillicothe, Ohio, Reformatory ignited another extensive investigation by informing the FBI that while confined in prison he had overheard a group of fellow prisoners, several of them from New England, plan the Brink's robbery. It was of course not true. Simultaneously, agents checked out a New York mobster who had moved to Ohio shortly before the robbery and had been absent from his job on January 17. He proved without question that he spent that day and night in Cleveland.

In addition to the rope and adhesive tape, the robbers had left behind them a chauffeur's hat. It was quickly determined that it was made by a New York firm named Allerhand and Landy. Hundreds and hundreds of man hours of work were expended on this check-out. The hat departments of many U.S. stores were visited and questions asked. But nothing came of this tedious labor, nor did the rope and adhesive lead anywhere. The Brink's employees who were tied and bound agreed after some debate that the bandits had worn Captain Marvel or Captain Marvel, Jr., masks. The manufacturer, Regent Rubber Creators, Inc., New York, yielded its list of retail clients. A coast-to-coast search elicited no information that could be associated with the robbery.

Continuing inquiry was made of the Brink's neighborhood for information concerning the vehicles used by the robbers. As was the case in so many other investigations, this led mainly to dead ends.

Dozens of known hoodlums who lived in the tough area

around Brink's were hauled in and questioned, when police and FBI temporarily agreed that it might have been a neighborhood job. There was still another period when police concluded that the Brink's coup was too big, too daring, too imaginative to have been pulled off by homebred talent; that it must have been the work of big-time New York mobsters or the remnants of Chicago's Capone or Detroit's Purple gangs. Dozens of nationally and even internationally known racketeers thus were questioned, with what the FBI calls "negative results."

Within forty-eight hours of the robbery, all eleven men who pulled it were questioned.

O'Keefe and Gusciora acknowledged they were together that night, but only for the purpose of having a few drinks. This was confirmed, and loyal barfly friends were sufficiently vague about the time they saw the two.

McGinnis was able to present an impeccable alibi. It was incomprehensible to the police that a theft of this magnitude and painstaking perfection could be pulled off in Boston without the knowledge of this dominant figure in the Hub's underworld. McGinnis proved beyond question that he had left his home shortly before seven o'clock and had gone to his nearby liquor store. There he met Lieutenant Jim Crowley, a veteran and respected Boston police officer. Crowley had dropped in to ask McGinnis if he had any idea about who might have held up the Statler Hotel's accounting office the day before. While giving his learned estimate that it probably was an out-of-town job McGinnis briefly excused himself and made a quick, quiet phone call. Within minutes, a customer entered the liquor store. It was Pino.

Later, Crowley was put in the position of substantiating McGinnis's alibi. He absolved Pino to a slight degree, too, though he was admittedly confused as to the precise time of evening it was when Pino entered the store.

Maffie, questioned late on the night of January 17 after he had left his parents' home, was elaborately vague about where he had spent the evening. Baker, when picked up and questioned the day after the robbery, told police he had eaten dinner with his family the evening before and then, at seven o'clock, had left the house for a two-hour walk. No, he met no one nor did he speak to anyone during his walk. It was a bad night, Baker explained.

Costa's story, when queried, was that he had come home from his job in a motor terminal and had dinner with his family. At seven o'clock he went back to his job and worked there until nine.

The others all appeared to have been doing something else between seven and seven-thirty that night. Except perhaps Banfield. Banfield's chuckling alibi to police who questioned him in February of that year was that he had gotten drunk on New Year's Eve "and stayed drunk all through January." A disgruntled former girl friend volunteered the information that Banfield was cold-sober on the night of January 17. But others questioned said they had not seen the man sober in months, even years.

And thus did they pass their first test.

7

SPECS WOKE UP WITH A SLIGHT HANGOVER ON THE MORNING
of January 18, 1950. He showered, shaved, read the sensational accounts of the robbery, then breakfasted leisurely.
He was an hour or so late for a scheduled noon meeting at
Maffie's place in Roxbury.

They were all there. There was more counting to attend to.
McGinnis expounded at some length on a process whereby
money could be aged a bit, to offset what was certain now
to be a heightened suspicion of crackling new bills, particularly of large denominations.

All through that afternoon the men went carefully over
their colossal haul, looking for pencil markings or other
notations on the currency which might make those bills
traceable to Brink's. They mutually pledged, as they had
before, that if anybody "muffed" he would be "taken care of."
They did not have to add "killed."

Night had fallen before it was agreed that until the assorted payrolls and small change could be straightened out,
each man should take $100,000. Specs and Gus wrapped
theirs in a single brown-paper bundle and took it to Specs'
1947 Pontiac, parked nearby. Here's Specs:

"We put the package in the trunk and drove to the Veterans' Hospital. They've got a private parking lot for the
patients and doctors. It's a good place to put a car that just
possibly could have become hot, even though it wasn't regis-

tered in my name. Patients sometimes leave their cars there for days, weeks.

"So we parked it. I locked the doors and put the key in a little magnetic container and stuck it underneath the front of the car on some metal near the shock absorbers. That meant that either he or I could take the car away, if something happened to one of us.

"It wasn't a very ideal way of hiding the money. Originally, we planned to take it to the house of a friend of Gus, in Dedham, Massachusetts. But he decided it wasn't safe, or maybe he phoned the guy and the guy didn't want to accept the responsibility. So we parked it.

"The next night Gus and I went back to the hospital and picked up the car. It had begun to snow and I was afraid it might get snowbound there in the open lot, or we might have trouble driving it away in a hurry, if we had to. I didn't have any chains. So before the snow got too heavy we drove into a garage on Blue Hill Avenue in Boston and handed it over to the attendant. The two hundred was still in the trunk.

"We got busted—arrested—the next day.

"Gus had planned for some time to visit the grave of his brother, who was killed on the Ploesti Raid. Now he figured this would be the best time to go. The brother is buried in a veterans' cemetery in Jefferson City, Missouri, in the same casket with another crew member. The bomber crashed so hard when it was shot down that the body of Gus's brother couldn't be separated from that of a boy who was next to him in the plane. The War Department suggested, and the parents agreed, that the bodies should be buried in some cemetery near the middle of the United States. You see, the other kid was from California.

"None of the family had ever seen the grave, so Gus decided to take his father and mother and some other member of the family. He picked up the train tickets and everything was set. I was to drive them to the railroad station.

"I picked up his car, a Buick, leaving my car and the

money in the garage in Boston, and drove out to my house in Stoughton, Massachusetts, where the wife and the boy were waiting for me. I picked them up and started for the farm where Gus's people lived. It's only a few miles away.

"On the way over there I noticed a car, a gray business coupe, with two guys in it. It was in front of me and headed in the same direction of Gus's place. There was just something funny about it, so I took a right onto an alternate road.

"The farm and the farmhouse looked okay when I drove up, though I did notice there were a couple of fellows working at the top of a telephone pole nearby. Linemen, I thought. But actually they were dicks. How would I know just then?

"We went inside and couldn't have been there ten minutes before the whole joint was surrounded by the law. They swarmed in: state police, Boston police, even local police from the little town. They searched that joint like nothing you ever saw, from top to bottom and all around the land. The old man had twenty or thirty hives of bees, and they searched those, too.

"The whole thing could have been blown up then and there if one of them had sense to look on the top of the visor in the Buick. They looked everywhere else in and under that car. The ticket, the receipt, for my Pontiac was sitting on the visor. If that had been found they would have gone to the garage, searched my car and found the two hundred thousand.

"After three or four hours of search—which meant Gus and his people blew the train—they lugged Gus and me into State Police Headquarters at 1010 Commonwealth Avenue. All the brass was there: state and Boston police and, I suppose, the Federals. The questioning began about 3 o'clock. At six or seven they did something that surprised us. They took us across the street to dinner in a public place. About eleven or twelve that night I finally said, 'What the hell *is* this; what are we held for?' One of them said, 'Oh, you're not under arrest.' So I said, 'Well, for Christ sake, if I'm not under arrest I'll see you later. I've got a lot of things to do. I'm a busy man.'

" 'You can walk out any time you want,' one of them said, 'but if you walk out, the Boston police will arrest you.'

"They were pretty well fed up with us, particularly me. Gus and I had had an agreement for a long time about answering police questions. Gus was a voluble guy who didn't need a minute's notice to make up a good story about why he might be in this place or that, if caught. He came up with one for this occasion, of course, but it became a burden to him later. He couldn't remember precisely what he told those guys.

"I had another system. I'd just give my name. That's all. Before they started in on me that day I was kibitzing in an office with a couple of successful police lieutenants I knew —Jerry McCarthy and Andy Trodden—and I told them that I wasn't going to answer anything. They tried to convince me that that was the wrong thing to do, so far as I was concerned. They said that if I was being accused wrongly the natural thing would be to deny it, not clam up. I said, 'To hell with it. Should I spend the rest of my life denying charges? I'm just not going to respond to anything. I'll be an unnatural guy.'

"The questioning of me was under the direction of Captain Frank Wilson. He was a very gentle guy but persistent and smart. He was a Negro but he was so outstandingly honest he rose eventually to deputy chief. He became a big factor in the case as it went along and must have questioned me alone thirty or forty times, and later they called him 'The Man Who Broke the Brink's Case' in an article in *Ebony* magazine.

"Wilson had his stenographer, Bill Shanahan, with him and eight or ten police officers. I said to him, 'Captain, I'm not going to answer any of your questions. I'm just going to give you my name. It's Joseph J. O'Keefe.'

" 'Where do you live?' Frank asked in his patient way.

"I told him I couldn't go any further than my name. He shrugged and said, 'Well, I've got a lot of questions to ask you, so I'll ask them anyway.' And he did. There wasn't any direct question about Brink's, but any of the ones he asked might have led toward the robbery if I answered. So I choked up on him.

"There was a young police sergeant there—wise-guy type I had had trouble with before. He got hot at me and yelled, 'Listen, why don't you answer the captain's questions? I've got to get home; I've got a family.' I said, 'Well, for Christ sake go home then. Who cares? Screw. I'd like to go home too. I've got a family.' That ended the interrogation.

"After Gus told his long story they lugged us down to the Boston police headquarters on Berkeley Street and we were booked on suspicion. They brought along two others they had been questioning the same night: Jake Dana, the fellow who made our keys for us, and a kid—a little Irish waiter—in whose name the Buick was registered. Gus gave him fifty bucks or something to let him use his name for the car. The questioning started all over again. A Boston police lieutenant who had been very active against me, a fellow named Arthur Tiernan, took me aside, nodded at Dana and said quietly, 'Joe, do you think that guy might be the key to the whole thing?'

"I laughed at him. 'Who knows?' I said. 'Keys are his business, aren't they? But how the hell would *I* know anything about this case?'

"Tiernan said, 'Geez, I'd love to do something with this one . . . bust it. It's a big one.' Like a lot of others, he was thinking of the promotions that were bound to hit any officer who cracked the case.

" 'I wouldn't know how to begin,' I told him.

"He didn't figure on me at all. Of what he knew about me he figured I wasn't big enough.

"They threw us in the city prison on a charge of suspicion or 'consorting,' something phony like that, and we were in

84

custody for two or three days. The next morning the questioning started again and it didn't stop until they let us go. All during the time they had him, Jake Dana wouldn't take a glass of water or a bite of food. He was afraid there might be something in the food or drink that would make him talk. I felt sorry for the poor son of a bitch. He was in a trap. He *was* the guy who made the keys we used at Brink's, but he didn't know he made them for that purpose. It was just another job for him. But subconsciously he probably knew he was on the edge of trouble. He had been arrested once before with Pino and didn't want to be again, and I don't blame him.

"They let him go finally, and they threw the Irish kid out, too. But they held onto Gus and me. Lieutenant Crowley wanted to talk to us after he got back from New York, where he had gone to check on one of the crazy leads.

"Crowley was in charge of the case, I guess you could say. He was on the Boston police department's robbery squad. There's a skein of Crowley all through the case. He was the unwitting alibi witness at McGinnis's store the night it happened. And many years before he had taken a stand for Pino in rendition proceedings between the states of New Hampshire and Massachusetts. He testified at the extradition hearing that he saw Pino twenty-five minutes before a robbery fifty-five miles away happened.

"The reason he happened to be in McGinnis's store on the night of the big one was that he was investigating the holdup of the office of the Boston Statler the day before. But both McGinnis and Pino were able to use him as an alibi witness. I've never known anything like that in all my years in this business. I suppose it's okay to use a police officer as an alibi witness once in your life, but how could you put a guy in a box twice?

"Crowley came in boiling from New York. He approached me in anger. He was angry with everybody. You know, normally there's no anger connected with a pinch, but there was this time. He told me he was going to break this case and he didn't care who got hurt. He told me that in previous years he hadn't pressed me too much, that he had been friendly with me ever since I had been a child, really. We were brought up in the same neighborhood. Now, he said, he was going to go all out, and that it didn't matter how long we had known each other.

" 'I want a lot of help on this thing,' he said to me.

" 'Jeez, Jim,' I said, 'I was just thinking that you could help *me*. Get Gus and me out of here so we can go back and make a living. We've got a lot of things to do. We're going in debt by being in the can. We've got to get out and rob somebody.'

"Oh, he was so mad. He said, 'Listen, I want to hear from you and don't you forget it.' I said, 'You're not going to hear from me, Jim. What could *I* do for you? This case was a bolt from the blue. Who the hell knows what happened?'

"He, too, didn't figure me for it."

The little matter of their $200,000 naturally bothered O'Keefe and Gusciora during this painful sequence of days. They agreed that it would be best to get the money to a safer place. Specs, who had obtained permission to make several telephone calls, called Jazz Maffie and asked him to visit them in city prison. Jazz did so and was told about the garage ticket on the visor of Gus's car. He picked it up, got the O'Keefe car out of the garage and turned the $200,000 over to McGinnis.

Of that maneuver, Specs says:

"McGinnis took the money. He had trucks, transportation, places to plant it. He had the means and, after all, it was his job to facilitate everything after the robbery. He wound up, too, with the $380,000 Baker took away the first night for safekeeping. There was so much heat around town that the people Baker took it to wanted no part of it. So Baker brought it back to McGinnis.

"McGinnis was agreeable, but he announced after Baker dropped the bundle on him that it was $35,000 short. That

86

was a blow to us. Who the hell got it? Thirty-five thousand is a good score. We'd go out and take the chances on robbing a payroll for that much. I had a bad feeling about this; that something bad would develop over it. It also occurred to me that the old saying about honor among thieves had been pretty well disproved. Did Baker get it? Did the people he took it to in the first place get it? Whatever, I felt he should be responsible for it."

In his deep concern over the Brink's case, Crowley inadvertently did Gus a favor. O'Keefe was the intermediary. Both were about to be released on this occasion, for want of evidence, when it developed that Gus was wanted on a charge that he had been involved in a minor accident while driving home the night after the Brink's robbery and had not been able to show a driver's license when police appeared at the scene. He didn't have one, actually. Specs mentioned this matter to Crowley in the course of their talk and Crowley took care of it and went on to bigger questions.

The two were released together. They found the city in turmoil. The Boston newspapers, radio and TV were in an absolute tizzy. Brink's jokes were beginning to appear, and in Portland, Maine, a Brink's guard had a nervous breakdown when—as a gag—a friend poked his finger in the guard's back and muttered, "This is a stick-up!"

It wasn't safe to collect from McGinnis, Specs and Gus felt. They had no immediate need for cash, what with the Statler and other money either in their pockets or planted. (Gus maintained a modest bank account under his own name, but neither ever had a safe deposit box. "Not safe," Specs says, dismissing the entire system with a wave.) So they let McGinnis hold their money for the better part of the next month while they lived the lives of deacons.

But something had to be done about it eventually. Specs called Maffie, and in the course of their meeting it was agreed that Maffie would plant the money. The actual transfer of the cash was made at an obscure roadhouse near Stoughton.

McGinnis drove up to the place with Banfield at the wheel of the car. Specs and Gus were in Gus's car in the parking lot. The other car, also a Buick, came in swiftly and McGinnis handed over two suitcases, which were put on the rear seat of Gus's car. It didn't take a minute. The cars went their separate ways.

Specs:

"We drove on to Maffie's farm place for a little while, then into Boston and met Maffie and a fellow named Dee Daly, a friend of Jazz. I gave Maffie my suitcase of money. Gus kept his. His money has never shown up. I don't know who ever got it, if anybody did. It could be rotting in the ground right now.

"I didn't know the exact location of the plant Maffie had in mind for my money. It was to be in New Hampshire, where his wife came from. They knew somebody there who had a farm and, as I understood it, the dough was to be buried at the bottom of a dry well.

"I wasn't worried about what would happen to it. Maffie and I were really friendly. It never crossed my mind to try to beat anybody out of his end, or see somebody beat me out of mine. I don't believe I had ever been beaten. There was no sweat when he took the suitcase and he and Daly drove off with it."

There was a minor annoyance on the occasion of the transfer of the money. A quick count of the contents of the suitcases showed that both Specs and Gus has been short-changed $2,000. The suitcases contained $98,000 each, not the $100,000 each that had been in the trunk of Specs' car. But there was no time to do more than mention this gyp. Specs, after counting his money, put $5,000 of it in his pocket before placing the loot in Maffie's care.

He was never to see the remaining $93,000 again.

On February 4, 1950, less than three weeks after the robbery, a group of boys playing on a sandbar at the edge

of the Mystic River in Somerville, Massachusetts, found two
rusty revolvers. One of them was tossed in a trash barrel,
taken to the city dump and never seen again. The other fell
into the hands of the police. An alert Somerville officer
identified it as one of the guns the Brink's robbers had taken
away with them on the night of the great heist.

Exactly one month later, bits and parts of a 1949 green
Ford stake-body truck were found at a dump near Stoughton.
An acetylene torch had been used to cut up the truck, and
it appeared that a sledge hammer had been utilized to smash
its heavier parts, such as the motor block. The pieces then
had been put in fiber bags and an effort obviously had been
made to bury the bags. But the ground was frozen.

An FBI progress report at the time read:

> The bags in which the truck parts were recovered have
> been identified as being bags used by Armour and Company,
> LaPlata, Argentina, for shipment of bones to Eastman Gela-
> tine Corporation, Peabody, Massachusetts. This shipment
> arrived at Peabody in July, 1947. In attempting to trace these
> bags it was ascertained that the Eastman Gelatine Corpora-
> tion sold the majority of the bags to junk dealers and that
> probably some of the bags were given away. Investigation
> to date regarding the possible outlet where those bags were
> obtained by the individuals who dumped the 1949 Ford
> truck at the Stoughton dump has been negative.
>
> Continuing investigation as to the bags in which the truck
> parts were recovered has failed to produce any pertinent in-
> formation of value. The Eastman Gelatine Corporation dis-
> poses of its surplus bags either by selling them to Simon
> Myers and Son, junk dealers, Salem, Massachusetts, or by
> giving them to the John Gorvers Company, Lynn, Massa-
> chusetts. No record is maintained as to the disposition of the
> bags, but in the usual course of business the surplus bags are
> forwarded by the Eastman Gelatine Corporation to either of
> the above organizations within a month of their receipt. The
> bags are not sorted in any way and are merely sold on a
> weight basis.

At the Smith Rowland Company, Lynn, Massachusetts, which is a customer of the John Gorvers Company, a group of similar bags was located which had been in the possession of the Smith Rowland Company since August, 1949. The Smith Rowland Company purchases animal products which they ship by barge to their main plant in New Jersey, where the by-products are converted into fertilizer. They use the Armour sisal bags for shipping their products but keep no records of the bags and the supply of bags is available to numerous individuals.

The project of tracing these bags is continuing, but in view of the fact that no records are maintained and the loose manner of handling the bags, it does not appear that the source of the bags found on the dump can be definitely identified.

With regard to the truck parts, it is noted that the following parts of the cut-up truck were not found:

1. Steering wheel and shaft
2. Five wheels, tires and tubes (Goodyear size 700 x 17, tubes size 700-750)
3. Radiator
4. Headlights and taillights
5. Horn
6. Floor mat
7. Battery
8. Seat assembly and cab trim, which was probably brown in color

The FBI had now sent men as far away at LaPlata, Argentina, searching for the answer to the riddle.

And O'Keefe and Gusciora asked themselves why the truck parts had been dumped so close to their houses, and why the guns had not only not been broken up but had been dumped in shallow water not too far from Geagan's home. Both finds put new pressures on Specs, Geagan and Gus from the police.

Geagan was incensed and brought his beef to Specs. "Don't bother me about it," Specs told him. "Go see the Pig and the guy who was supposed to take care of things." Geagan went to see McGinnis and reported to Specs that McGinnis seemed evasive about the whole thing and tried to put the blame on Banfield. "We showed our weakness then by not eliminating him—according to the bargain," Specs says in retrospect.

One day in April, 1950, after Specs had indicated to Pino and McGinnis that there should be more money coming to him, his car happened to pass Pino's. Pino, recognizing him, gave Specs a signal to turn right at the next block. Specs turned right on Walnut Street and parked. Pino parked about a block away and singly they walked into the park.

Once in the park, and out of earshot of anyone, Pino surprised Specs by telling him that he had been overpaid. He said that Specs, Gus and Maffie must give back $10,000 each out of their shares. Specs made no comment or promise. He sought out Gus and Maffie later that day and the three held an indignation meeting. But they took no action, nor did they give up the aggregate $30,000 Pino had demanded.

In June, 1950, Gus decided to go through with his visit to his brother's grave in Jefferson City. He asked Specs to drive there with him. It was decided not to take the mother and father along. They went to the cemetery, took some snapshots for the mother, and pressed a $10 bill on a gravedigger to fill a box with dirt from near the grave of the intertwined Ploesti fliers. Gus said his mother would like to spread the dirt around in the little garden she had planted at the foot of the flagpole from which she daily flew the American flag.

There was another reason for going West, and for not taking the old folks. Specs and Gus wanted to pick up some new guns, clean guns and not easily traceable. They took their time, realizing that a mistake and an arrest at this precise time would be, as Specs puts it, "unfortunate." They did some relaxing pub-crawling in St. Louis and then tooled on to Chicago to visit a semi-retired hoodlum Specs had known many years before. They ran out of ready cash while staying at the Stevens, but Specs arranged for a Boston bookmaker friend to wire him $500. They then continued their leisurely drive homeward.

All FBI field offices located between Boston and St. Louis had been advised that O'Keefe and Gusciora were "in travel status." The offices were instructed to report to the Boston office any information about the two men that might be gathered from confidential informants and police. The offices were specifically instructed not to conduct a surveillance of the pair.

What neither man knew, as they headed homeward, was that they had been recognized by an underworld source during their brief stay in Towanda, Pennsylvania, on their way west. Learning of this, the FBI contacted Towanda's police chief, Dean Meredith, and showed him pictures of the two. He had not seen them during their stay in the city, Meredith told the Federal agents. He was surprised to learn that Towanda had played host, as it were, to two men suspected of having participated in the great Brink's robbery.

Specs and Gus found just what they were looking for in the town of Kane, Pennsylvania. The back door of Moore's Hardware Store at 16 Greeves Street yielded readily to Specs' fingernail file. They entered the darkened store, went directly to the firearms display and selected three German Lugers, a Colt .38 automatic, an H. & R. .22 pistol, and 150 rounds of ammunition. On the way out they picked up some sportsmen's shirts and gloves, from sheer force of habit.

That same night at little Coudersport, Pennsylvania, they entered a clothing store named Rosenblum's, 209 Main Street, and chose several suits that struck their fancy. Then they drove on to Towanda to spend the night.

Resuming their trip on the morning of June 12, 1950, they became confused as to the best way out of town.

"There's a guy who ought to know," Specs said, spotting a police officer on the other side of the street. He swung the Buick into a U-turn and eased it to the curb near the officer. Specs asked him the best way to Waverly, N.Y., a junction

92

that was their immediate target. The policeman gave them direction and routes, said, "Don't mention it," when they thanked him, and waved them on.

Then he walked quickly to the nearest telephone.

About 5,000 persons live in Towanda. With that many to choose from, to ask directions of, Specs had selected Chief Meredith. Meredith recognized them from the pictures the FBI had shown him. He phoned the police of Athens, Pennsylvania, the next town, and asked them to stop the car and arrest the men. The FBI had made no such request.

A detachment of state police, car sirens howling, crowded the Buick to the side of the highway minutes later near Ulster, Pennsylvania. O'Keefe and Gusciora were astonished to see themselves being advanced upon by rifle-carrying cops. They were ordered into police cars at gun-point, while an officer slipped behind the wheel of the Buick. They were taken back to Towanda.

News of their arrest was teletyped through the country with an inquiry as to whether they were wanted anywhere. Boston replied that both men had criminal records but neither was currently wanted. There were no other responses to the inquiry.

But Pennsylvania wanted them quickly enough. A routine search of the Buick revealed the stolen guns and clothing. Specs still whistles over the disposition of their case:

"They rushed us to the can so fast it made your head swim. We sent for a Boston bondsman we had done a lot of business with. He started immediately for Towanda but before he got close they brought us into court before a justice of the peace and he imposed a summary sentence on us . . . ninety days for being 'common and notorious thieves.' This was before they even had a copy of our records. It was a gimmick to prevent us from getting bail in Pennsylvania. We were arraigned for violation of the Uniform Firearms Act and for possession of stolen goods.

"So we laid in the jail from June 12 until early September, when our case came into Superior Court. Our lawyers were losing interest in us. As a matter of fact we didn't see any of them for a month before we went into court. They wanted to dump us, I guess.

"It was a kind of kangaroo thing. When our names were called on the first day of the trial I asked the judge if he would grant us a little time to talk to our counsel because we hadn't seen those guys for so long. His Honor graciously gave us five minutes. We went into the library and figured out something in a hurry. There wasn't any sense in both of us going to the can, so I suggested that I would plead guilty to violation of the Uniform Firearms Act and that Gus should plead not guilty and stand trial.

"I pleaded guilty. Gus was a thousand-to-one shot in that old courthouse, but the jury found him not guilty. The fuzz was furious. They wouldn't let him go. They took him to McKean County, Pennsylvania, where the guns were stolen, and there he was found guilty of burglary—though nobody in the town had seen us, knew us, knew we had been there. It was the kind of case where normally a fellow could walk out of the courtroom laughing. But Gus was found guilty and given from five to twenty years in the Western Pennsylvania Penitentiary at Pittsburgh, a terrible place.

"On my guilty plea I was sentenced to three years in the Bradford County Jail at Towanda and fined $3,000 for violation of the Act. That was the maximum. In Philadelphia or some other big place it would have been a six-month term, with nothing else involved. Or I could have beaten it.

"I wound up doing three years and nine months in that county jail. It was an old joint designed just to hold people temporarily . . . small bits, like a month, six months. I went three years and nine months, probably a record. I seldom saw daylight during that whole time. The windows were bastion-type, wide on the outside and narrowed in to four or five inches wide on the inside of the wall. Like a fortress. Sometimes you wouldn't know whether it was night or day. I never saw the sky.

"There was no work, and that was cruel. The capacity was twenty-five people and the average population while I was there would be ten or twelve. I tried to occupy myself by reading. I studied typewriting, too. My sister sent me a stenotype machine, but I couldn't dig it. The jail itself had no reading matter. What I read I had to buy. I went away to Chicago for my books. I chose mostly textbooks. It wasn't disciplined education. It was haphazard. I don't have any education, and I'm sorry for that.

"Not many would come near me, on account of the heat in Boston. But one exception was a great kid named Johnny Carlson. I had known him for a couple of years but had never worked with him. He was a young knock-around guy who wasn't afraid of anybody. Anybody. He took what messages I wanted delivered back to Boston. He didn't have a nerve in his body. So-called tough guys he just laughed at, to their faces."

Among the toughs Carlson delivered messages to from Specs, were Pino, McGinnis, Maffie and Baker. In due time the Boston underworld buzzed with reports that O'Keefe was pressuring them to contribute money for legal fees he and Gusciora needed. The reports were correct. Yet Specs never discussed the Brink's case with Carlson nor with anyone else at that time. After each account of his pressure tactics was reported to the authorities by Boston informers, O'Keefe would again be questioned in prison about the Brink's case. He always confined his replies to the simple response of giving his name.

Specs' irritation at being forced to waste his life away in a country jail, with nearly $100,000 waiting for him in Boston, was matched by the plight of Gusciora at the Pittsburgh pen. Gus found himself involved in a prison riot. The only role he played was to typewrite the demands the riot leaders made of the warden. This Gus did with the warden's telephoned consent. So Gus attended to the secretarial chore with assurances from both sides that he had nothing to do with the rebellion itself.

But when the rioters were quelled, Gus was quarantined with them. He pleaded innocent when called before the prison board and explained his role. The board gave him fourteen months in solitary, with no cigarettes, no reading material and a minimal food ration. During that whole crushing time he refused to change his plea of innocence or implicate others in exchange for release from his close confinement.

Specs heard about his friend's grueling ordeal, via prison grapevine, and was able (through the messenger service of Carlson) to interest a famed Philadelphia attorney, Frank Truscott, later Lieutenant Governor of Pennsylvania, in Gus's case. Gus was taken "off the shelf," but the experience had cost him his health.

8

LATE IN 1952 THE FBI STARTLED THE GENERALLY HAPPY AND prospering Brink's robbers. The Government men believed they now had enough evidence in their hands to secure indictments. Subpoenas were served on eight of the eleven participants in the holdup, requiring them to appear before a grand jury whose hearings would begin in Boston on November 25, 1952.

It was a gamble on the part of the Justice Department, but one which had to be taken. The Federal Government's statute of limitations on most of the crimes committed in this case would expire the following January 17.

In all, sixty-five witnesses were heard, including all of the gang except Faherty. It proved a harrowing time for O'Keefe, his sister Mary, his brother Donald, and Mary's husband, Paul Hooley. The experience remains vivid in Specs' mind:

"They brought me back to Boston from the lockup in Towanda on a writ of ad testificandum, which my lawyer finally broke down and explained was something that had to be honored. If I balked, they'd drag me back to face that grand jury, the fellow told me.

"The Federal people had a terrific line on this case almost from the beginning. It was driving them daffy, not to be able to nail down some indictments.

"Carlson was called, among other characters. 'Did he know O'Keefe in prison?'—questions like that. He wouldn't answer on the grounds of the Fifth Amendment and whatever other amendments were available. That's the stand I took, too, and so did Gus, when they brought him in from Pittsburgh. The other guys—McGinnis, Pino, Costa, Banfield, Baker, Geagan, Richardson and Maffie—all told some kind of story. But every word they spoke in the grand jury room was an added nail in their coffins. They just didn't have the balls to say that they refused to testify."

In the midst of the two-month hearing, in the course of which Specs, the Hooleys, brother Donald and seven others were cited for contempt, the FBI publicly identified Specs as a participant in the unsolved robbery. Four affidavits sworn to in 1950 by Special Agent John B. Greene of the Boston office of the Bureau, for the purpose of obtaining a search warrant, appeared in the Boston newspapers. Affidavits Nos. 2, 3 and 4 were paraphrases of No. 1, which read:

> The undersigned, being duly sworn deposes and says:
> That he has reason to believe that on the premises known as the O'Keefe house, Lots 152 and 153 Glen Echo Rd., Mountvale Pk., Stoughton, Mass., being the first white cottage on the left side of Glen Echo Rd. going from Pleasant St. to Glen Echo Lake, with a one-car garage, adjacent to the house of Elmer Vaughan or Vaughn, 149 Glen Echo Rd. Stoughton, in the District of Massachusetts, there is now being concealed certain property, namely, a substantial sum of money, to wit, in the approximate amount of $60,000 in denominations 1, 5, 10, 20, 50 and 100 dollar bills, respectively; was on July 19, 1950, and still is unlawfully held and possessed by Joseph J. O'Keefe and Mary O'Keefe or either of them, having been stolen in violation of the laws of the United States in an armed robbery at the establishment of Brink's, Inc., 165 Prince St. Boston, on the night of Jan. 17, 1950.
> And that the facts tending to establish the foregoing grounds for issuance of a search warrant are as follows:
> The said affiant says that he has reason to believe that Joseph J. O'Keefe was one of the participants in the robbery

at Brink's, Inc., 165 Prince St. Boston on the night of Jan. 17, 1950; that about 11:30 that night he escaped arrest by the Boston police department, who were searching for him in connection with the said robbery; that on or about April 27, 1950, the affiant had reason to believe that the above-described money was in the unlawful possession of said Joseph J. O'Keefe and was hidden on the premises at 771 Veterans of Foreign Wars Pkwy., Boston, which premises were occupied among others by Mary Hooley, a sister of the said Joseph J. O'Keefe; that the occupant of the above-described premises on Glen Echo Rd. Stoughton, is Mary O'Keefe, the wife of the said Joseph J. O'Keefe, that said Joseph J. O'Keefe is at present confined in the Bradford county jail at Pennsylvania, serving a sentence of ninety (90) days; that on or about July 12, 1950, in a telephone conversation from Stoughton to said Bradford county jail, between the said Joseph J. O'Keefe and Mary O'Keefe, his wife, he asked his said wife whether or not she had been interviewed by Federal enforcement officials and she said she had, he asked whether or not anything was found and she answered no, and later he told her, "Just take good care of the baby. You know what I mean."

From all the circumstances, I, John Greene, have reason to believe that the above-mentioned money is concealed on the premises hereinbefore enumerated, because of information which I have received that the said money was removed from 771 Veterans of Foreign Wars Pkwy., Boston, and brought to the O'Keefe premises on Glen Echo Rd. in accordance with the said telephone conversation, and that from all the surrounding circumstances of this case herein set out, I, as a cautious person, have reason to believe that the money above-described is concealed somewhere on the O'Keefe premises, so-called, on Glen Echo Rd. Stoughton, Mass.

JOHN B. GREENE
Special Agent, FBI

(Sworn to before me, and subscribed in my presence, William B. Rogers, United States Commissioner)

A swarm of reporters descended on O'Keefe's home. It proved a deflating experience, apparently. The Boston *Post* of December 19, 1952, described the scene:

"LOOT HOME" BARRED TO REPORTERS

Mrs. O'Keefe Won't Open Door in Stoughton

Stoughton, Dec. 18.—"The premises on Glen Echo Rd., Stoughton . . ." described in an affidavit filed in Federal Court in connection with the Brink's case had no $60,000 look about it tonight.

When a reporter knocked on the door of the five-room bungalow at No. 153—the house described in the affidavit —a radio was playing inside. Through the door a woman's voice called, "Who's there?" The reporter shouted, "I want to talk to Mrs. Mary O'Keefe." The voice said, "I don't want to talk to you." Another woman's voice said, "She doesn't want to talk to anyone."

The house is old. It looks like many others you find along the winding roads in the town and nearby. The O'Keefes, neighbors say, moved into it four years ago.

In an adjoining column of the *Post*, neighbor Vaughn was tapped:

Joseph (Specs) O'Keefe, 44, of 153 Glen Echo Rd. was described tonight as a model citizen and neighbor by a man who lived next door to his home.

"He helped me dig a well when it dried up. And his wife was always helping my wife when she was sick or needed assistance in putting up wallpaper," said Elmer Vaughn.

Vaughn registered surprise last night when he learned that his quiet-spoken neighbor was allegedly involved in the huge robbery almost three years ago.

"I moved here three years ago, about a week before the Brink's holdup was staged," he said. "The first I knew about any Brink's investigation was when an FBI agent visited me while I was at work. I'm a foundation contractor. I don't want to be specific on the number of times or when the

FBI agents began to visit me at work—and always at work —never at my home. They asked me not to tell. But I will say their visits were pretty regular. Each time they would ask me what I thought of the O'Keefes. What kind of people are they? Do you like them? How does Joe behave? What kind of man is he?

"I told them. And I was very honest about it. He was quiet-spoken. There were never any wild parties or goings-on over there. I always thought of them as decent people and will continue to do so.

"I don't think Joe had anything to do with that holdup. Why, his home doesn't even have modern plumbing facilities. If he had money, I'd bet he would do something about that old house of his.

"They're struggling people. They've had a hard time of it.

"I used to meet Joe fairly often. He was a bartender, as I understand it. Worked all kinds of hours, but he would be around during the daytime or in the early evening. . . . All I can say is that Mr. O'Keefe certainly never showed he had any money. No man as helpful and quiet as Joe could have had a part in that robbery," said Vaughn.

That ringing vote of confidence proved to be of little help to Specs in the grand jury room and, later, during his month-long contempt trial. Specs later griped:

"The assistant U.S. attorney who questioned me the most had a peculiar name: Hassan. Like the old cigarette. When I first saw the name I figured he was a Turk. But the guy turned out to be an Irishman, and what an Irishman! What a rough guy. Sometimes he'd try to inject a little humor in his questions, but at the base they were always grim. For instance, one day he got so fed up with me for refusing to answer that he stood in front of me, pointed to the window and said, 'Do you think it will clear up today?' I said, 'Maybe you'd better call the airport and ask for the meteorologist; he'd know more about that than I would.' Then he says to me, 'Has your Aunt Minnie been down to see you?' Now who the hell's got an Aunt Minnie? I don't. I said I refused to answer. One of the grand jurors—a nice-looking old lady—spoke up and asked me if I would answer a question from a member of the panel. I told her it all depended on the question and asked her if she had one. 'Yes,' she said. '*Was* your Aunt Minnie down to see you?' I told her I refused to answer on the grounds that it might incriminate me. Or Aunt Minnie.

"Hassan hit the ceiling, he was so sore at me."

In time, a record number of eleven suspects were cited for contempt: Specs, his brother, the Hooleys, Banfield, Maffie, Richardson, Costa, Carlson, Dee Daly and Edward A. Bennett. Banfield and Costa purged themselves of the citation by returning to the grand jury and answering questions, none of which implicated them or their co-conspirators. Gusciora, who had been as uncommunicative as O'Keefe, was not cited.

None had any difficulty getting up his bail, a fact that was to move Federal Judge William T. McCarthy to heights of purple fulmination. The elderly jurist and Specs got along unswimmingly:

"He was an old crotch. He should have known that nothing could come of a case like mine. I was a suspect in robbery, had been named as such by the FBI. There are hard and fast cases, precedents, in a matter of this kind. A suspect does not have to testify against himself, in effect. I believe *U.S.* vs. *Hoffman,* or *Hoffman* vs. *U.S.* is the precedent usually referred to. They had to find me not guilty as soon as I appealed.

"The judge was quite a guy in his own right, I guess. Take the matter of a lawyer to defend me. The rest of the guys who had the same problem hired the best Federal lawyers in Boston. Most of them had served as assistant U.S. district attorneys under Judge McCarthy, who had been the district attorney. They were his protégés. When he wasn't around, they called him Uncle Willie.

"When he finally got around to me I could see that he was

going to be very hostile. He said, 'Stand up,' and when I did he told me to be ready to go to trial the next morning. He sounded as if he was going to burn me. I interrupted him. 'May I speak to the court?' I asked.

" 'What do you want?'

"I asked him if he would be kind enough to appoint counsel for me. Now here were the others laying out big money for expensive counsel, and here I was, the only guy so far named as part of the million-dollar robbery, asking for free legal aid.

"I thought he was going to blow a fuse. 'You mean to tell me you don't have access to money, that you don't have enough to retain a lawyer?' I said, 'Well, your Honor, I have five dollars and if I can find a five-dollar lawyer I'd be very happy.' He looked like he might come down off the bench after me. But he did something a lot better. He appointed as my lawyer a young fellow who had been the class of his assistants, W. Arthur Garrity.

"I don't know what made me say it—maybe it was just a desire to needle the old boy—but as I was being led out of the courtroom to the cell where they were holding me incommunicado I said to the marshal next to me, 'How about that? He gives me Garrity, his fair-haired boy. What a nice little trap that is.' I knew the marshal would tell the judge. Well, the next morning when the judge took the bench I could see that he had a big speech he was going to deliver. In court I noticed Joseph Schneider, a great lawyer. In fact, they call him a 'lawyer's lawyer.'

"The judge went into his big speech. He said he had been troubled all night about this case, that he had given it a lot of thought. 'So I've decided to appoint to you another counsel,' he went on. 'I'm appointing to you a man who will become the first man of his faith ever to become the president of the Massachusetts Bar Association.' He went on like he was delivering a eulogy over his grave.

"Now I've got two lawyers, and I didn't even need one

with such an open and shut case. I've got the two best, and for nothing. Those other guys steamed.

"They took me upstairs to an office, closed the door, and Schneider said, 'Now listen, fellow, I'm here to defend you against the charge of contempt. I don't want you to mention one word about the Brink's case.'

"'How could I mention anything about the Brink's case?' I said to him. 'Why should I? As far as I'm concerned I don't even know how to spell that word. What's the connotation? You're here on my contempt case. I know it should be washed out of court automatically. The precedents are so solid I've got to be found not guilty.'

"'I just wanted to warn you in advance,' he said, and I told him he didn't have to worry about it.

"They did a capable job of defending me, but it took them a month, and every day I was getting banged in the papers. You'd have thought war had been declared and I was the only guy in it. I was the only guy they felt it safe to name, and they abused the privilege. They printed my whole police record, going back to an item that read: '10-14-16, Boston. Breaking, entering and larceny. Probation.' I was eight years old. They kept belting away at my sister and brother and brother-in-law, decent people who were being hounded and persecuted for not talking about something they didn't know anything about.

"A week before Christmas of '52 Judge McCarthy called my sister into his chambers. He was sitting there behind his big desk, in his robes. He knew, of course, that she had been refusing to answer questions before the grand jury.

"'Do you know what day this is?' he asked Mary.

"'Yes, I do,' she said. My sister is a very fine person.

"'Well, what day is it?' Then she realized that he meant what feast day was it, what saint's day. She rattled it off— some saint only Mary would have heard of. Then the judge said, 'In honor of this day, you go down to that grand jury room and answer every question they put to you.'

"Mary was shocked to think that a man in McCarthy's position would put her in such a box, she being a devout person. So she wanted to make things plainer than they were. She went back to the grand jury and when they finally got around to her she refused to answer the very first question they threw at her. Hassan took her back to the judge, who was now in his court. The judge made a big thing of it.

"He looked at my sister as Hassan brought her up and said, 'This is the same woman that I gave some advice to this morning in my lobby?'

"The guy I thought was a Turk said, 'Yes, your Honor. We have advised her that she is not considered in any way as a prospective defendant in the matter before the grand jury. She is a sister of a suspect in this case. We have definite evidence that she is in possession of information that she refuses to divulge. We have, for example, asked her if she ever saw $70,000 in cash. She refuses to answer on the grounds that it might tend to incriminate her. We have asked her many other questions and she has refused to give us the answers. Her whole attitude is one of obstruction. We feel that her evidence would sustain an indictment for perjury. This woman is trying to obstruct justice.'

"The judge took over. He said, 'This woman appears to be in the position of an ordinary citizen who has valuable information that the Government desires. She is obligated like every good citizen to stand up for law and order and give it. Didn't I tell you that this morning?'

"Mary said yes, he had.

" 'I gave you a chance this morning which you didn't accept,' Uncle Willie went on. 'Therefore, I'm going to impose a sentence of one year, to stand until I'm satisfied that you have purged yourself in full.'

"The man was sentencing an innocent person, the mother of three children, who wasn't even represented by counsel. I don't think there's ever been a scene like it in a Federal court. And he wasn't through with her, either.

"He asked her if she was afraid to answer the grand jury's questions. Mary said no. He asked her if she had been advised not to answer questions. She said no again.

" 'Well,' he said, 'after you've served that year I just imposed, if I'm still alive and you haven't purged yourself, I'll give you another year.'

"They were leading her out of the courtroom when a marshal said to her, 'You're entitled to be represented by counsel, you know.' Mary stopped and got the attention of the bench.

" 'What do you want?' McCarthy said to her.

" 'Your Honor, aren't I entitled to have counsel?' she asked.

"After a bit, McCarthy told her to come back to the bench. 'I vacate the sentence I just imposed upon you. Return in the morning with counsel.'

"Later, he still gave her a year, and nine months for my kid brother, who never did a dishonest thing in his life, and nine months to my brother-in-law.

"None of them served a bloody minute. The Court of Appeals saw to that.

"He was a pip, McCarthy. You know how tired you get, sitting on a hard bench for hours. Well, one day as my trial droned on and on, I got cramped and moved around on my bench, changed my position. I crossed my legs. Well, I thought McCarthy would blow his top. He half jumped up and simply castigated me. 'You, sitting there with a look of utter contempt on your face,' he shouted at me. I hadn't even been paying any attention to him or anybody else. I was just sitting there waiting for time to go by. The thing had to run its distance. I knew the outcome of it.

"This burned me. I leaned over to Garrity and said, 'Listen, he may be your Uncle Willie but he isn't my Uncle Willie. If he keeps this up I'll give him cause to jump off that bench.' Garrity, a nice guy, said, 'Pipe down, will you? I'm trying to defend you.' I knew, I told him, but if the judge kept grinding at me something was going to happen.

106

"If I had only known at the time, as I learned later, that he was an old pal of Bernard Goldfine!

"He looked like he was going to send me to jail now for crossing my legs. I would have been the first guy in history ever to get the can for that.

"Another time he directed a question at me and I wouldn't answer. Schneider got up and said, 'Your Honor, I'm here to defend this man because he wouldn't answer questions before the grand jury. I'm not going to allow him to answer yours.'

"Uncle Willie exploded. He took off on a terrible harangue about insults to a Federal judge. But in the end, after a month, he came around and recognized there just wasn't any case against me, and acquitted me. He wasn't very happy about it."

Nor was the United States Government happy when on January 16, 1953, after taking 2,709 pages of testimony over fifty-one days, the grand jury handed up to Federal Judge Francis J. W. Ford a finding which read in part:

> The jury feels that it does not now possess complete positive information as to the identity of the participants in the Brink's robbery. This is due mainly to three conditions:
> 1. The participants were effectively disguised;
> 2. The lack of eyewitnesses to the crime itself;
> 3. The refusal of certain witnesses to give testimony, and the inability of the grand jury to compel them to do so.
>
> The grand jury further feels that certain witnesses who claimed rights under the Fifth Amendment to the United States Constitution did so not to protect themselves but to protect others. We believe that if we could have obtained information which they possess, such information would have shortened our proceedings and may have enabled the grand jury to ascertain all of the facts in this case.
>
> We therefore respectfully report that due to evidence, in our opinion insufficient to warrant trial, the grand jury is compelled to return no indictments as a result of this investigation.

There were recriminations.

The Boston *American* of January 17, 1953, carried this story:

KELLY BLAMES FBI STAND
FOR FAILURE OF BRINK JURY

The failure of the FBI to secure indictments in the $1,219,-000 Brink's robbery evoked words of bitterness and determination today, as charges were made that the case might now be solved if the government had deigned to offer immunity to those whose information might have unmasked the bandits.

As the G-men, refusing to be discouraged in their search for the Brink's robbers, declared they would stay with the case until it is solved, their actions over the past three years drew the criticism of Atty-Gen. Kelly.

Kelly, who leaves office next week, declared his belief that the failure of the FBI to offer immunity to accessories in the crime "closed the door to avenues of information that might have resulted in the solution of the crime." Kelly, who made such an offer on behalf of the state, added:

"I base my opinion on the fact that certain persons who phoned me after the publication of my offer indicated an ability and a willingness to provide vital information conditioned, however, on their also receiving Federal immunity."

The offer came to nothing when no pledge could be secured from the G-men that accessories in the robbery would escape a jail term in exchange for their information.*

Although the Federal statute of limitations, which takes effect at midnight, removed the bandits from the possibility of prosecution in a Federal court, government men said any new information they get will be turned over to aid state authorities if the robbers are brought to trial in Massachusetts courts.

In addition, anyone found with any of the money taken from the company's North End rooms can be prosecuted at

* The FBI does not have the authority to offer immunity.

any time in Federal Court on charges of receiving stolen property.

Joseph "Specs" O'Keefe, 44, named in an FBI affidavit as a suspect in the case, showed no emotion when his keepers at Bradford County Jail in Towanda, Pa., notified him of the failure of the grand jury to return indictments.

Sheriff Fowler Tuton said that Specs, who is due for release next month, will be turned over to authorities in McKean County, Pa., for prosecution on a larceny charge which could bring him as much as an additional ten years in jail.

Boston police and state detectives expressed their willingness to carry on the investigation, and asked for copies of the testimony presented to the jury in its long probe of the case. Supt. Edward W. Fallon of the Boston force declared:

"The case will always be open as far as Boston police are concerned until it has been solved. We will continue our investigation."

Similar determination was voiced by Donald S. Hostetter, agent in charge of the FBI office in Boston, who commented:

"The FBI is continuing its investigation, and we will continue it until the case is solved."

In Washington, the same day, J. Edgar Hoover told John Kelso, of the Boston *Post:* "The Federal Bureau of Investigation will never quit this Brink's case. If the FBI cracks this case within the next three years we will turn the evidence over to Massachusetts for prosecution, where the statute of limitations is six years instead of three as it is under Federal law."

And that same Boston paper was critical editorially of the grand jury:

The first temptation in commenting upon the Federal grand jury report in the Brink's case is to recall the birth of the mouse from the labor of the mountain.

We succumb to it. Six weeks of hearings, 65 witnesses, 2,709 pages of testimony, and the result: a report covering

ten short paragraphs without even a single John Doe indictment and no presentment to enlighten the public as to general conditions which have a bearing on the crime itself and
the failure to solve it.

That a diligent inquiry was ably pressed and all the evidence duly weighed is not to be questioned. Nevertheless the
report is a great disappointment.

And one sentence in it is a puzzler:

"The grand jury feels that it does not now possess positive
information as to the identity of the participants in the
Brink's robbery."

Complete and positive information is never necessary for
an indictment. One reason it did not receive "complete and
positive information," the jury believes, is because certain
witnesses refused to testify, not to protect themselves but
to protect others.

"We believe that if we could have obtained information
which they possess, such information would have shortened
our proceedings and may have enabled the grand jury to
ascertain all the facts in this case."

This is a rather oblique expression of suspicion that some
of the witnesses who clammed up know who did the Brink's
job, though they didn't do it themselves.

We pass along to the hope that some day within the next
three years we will all share the knowledge. Because prosecution of the criminals, if they are ever caught, passes today
out of Federal jurisdiction and in three more years prosecution under state law will not be possible because of the state
statute of limitations.

Judge McCarthy had made many a speech from his bench.
In the immediate wake of the grand jury's deflating refusal
to see the Government's side of the matter, the old judge
blamed "the wall of silence" and the "fear of witnesses" as
the source of the setback.

"The Brink's case must and will be solved," he told reporters, "and I reaffirm everything I said in connection with
this probe, and more."

9

O'KEEFE WAS RELEASED FROM TOWANDA'S COUNTY JAIL A
year after the bog-down of the grand jury investigation.
But Pennsylvania had formed an attachment for him. Mc-
Kean County authorities now wanted him, for "burglary,
larceny and receiving stolen goods." For good measure,
Massachusetts threw in a detainer involving O'Keefe's violation of probation in connection with a conviction in 1945 for
carrying concealed weapons.

His attorneys won him a measure of freedom on a $17,000
bond before the beginning of his McKean trial. Specs
then headed for Boston. On January 23, 1954, he appeared in
Boston Municipal Court on the probation violation charge.
His case was continued until April 1 of that year, and he was
released on $1,500 bond.

With that much out of the way, and more and greater
legal costs looming ahead, Specs sought out Jazz Maffie. It
was time to collect his Brink's money.

Maffie did not have it. He had spent it. All of it.

He had spent it, he explained, on lawyers for O'Keefe, on
the horses, on dice games and whatever else came along to
snare the attention of a hopeless gambling addict. He had
blown his own $100,000 the same way, he tearfully told
Specs.

For O'Keefe the pressures he had undergone since the
night of January 17, 1950, had remained bearable, if scarcely

so, by the knowledge that one day he would be able to claim his share of the historic haul.

Now there was nothing, except the sight of the penitent thief. And his sobs.

Specs thought briefly about killing him on the spot.

But then a change of heart:

"I figured that if Jazz lived he might get lucky again and eventually pay me what was coming to me. I figured, too, that through him I could present my case to the others better. They sure wouldn't stand for that kind of breaking of that pledge we had all taken.

"I told him to stop blubbering and give me a breakdown on what he had spent on legal fees. He made some figures on the back of an envelope and finally said that it came to about $41,000. I gave him the benefit of the doubt. It still meant that I had better than $50,000 due me."

O'Keefe returned to Pennsylvania, was tried and found guilty in McKean County on March 4, 1954, and promptly appealed. He was released on $15,000 bond.

He immediately returned to Boston to devote his time to the most dangerous task of his life—that of getting his bit.

It was not to be easy, he learned quickly enough.

Specs concluded early that the others—with the exception of Gus, who was still in prison—had secretly agreed to make him the scapegoat of the robbery and deprive him of his share. He was constantly griped by the fact that the getaway truck had been dumped near his house and that the guns they had taken from Brink's had all not been destroyed and lost.

He was impatient, too, with their pleas, in some cases, that they had their own costly problems to worry about. Maffie was fighting an income-tax evasion rap (and began serving a nine-month sentence in the Federal penitentiary at Danbury, Connecticut, in June, 1954). Pino was engaged in a costly fight against deportation, a battle that was then in its fifteenth year.

Pino was born in Sicily in 1907. Brought to the United States by his parents as a young child, and raised in a rough neighborhood, he was a seasoned hoodlum before he was ten. Neither he nor his parents apparently ever gave any thought to becoming naturalized citizens.

In 1941, while serving sentences in the state prison at Charlestown, Massachusetts for breaking and entering with intent to commit a felony and for having burglar tools in his possession, Pino was notified by the Naturalization Service that it had instituted proceedings to send him back to Italy. The Naturalization Service cited, as the basis for the deportation action, Pino's then current term and a March, 1928, conviction for carnal abuse of a girl.

He was released from Charlestown in 1944 and taken into custody by Immigration authorities. Through one legal roadblock after another he warded off the Government's efforts to rid the land of him. In September, 1949, he succeeded in removing from his record one of the two criminal convictions cited by Naturalization Service. The Acting Governor of Massachusetts granted Pino a full pardon.

At the height of the grand jury investigation in Boston early in 1953, Pino was taken into custody again as a deportable alien. New items from his lurid past were mentioned in the deportation papers. The authorities had a considerable range from which to choose.

He cried persecution at the hands of the FBI.

The Boston *Globe,* in a copyrighted article signed by Pino, presented this glowing self-portrait on January 12:

> I went wrong in my life and went to jail for it. When I came out a free man I said I'd work hard and never go back. I was a safecracker. The police know it. The FBI knows it. It's on my record.
>
> Since I got out of jail, I've kept clear of crime. I wanted to forget the past, but the FBI won't let me. Every time there's a safebreak or a robbery they haul me in, just on

113

suspicion. I guess it makes them look good. I was a safe-cracker, but I never held a gun.

The FBI seems to think I know somethig about the Brink's robbery. I don't. I told the grand jury that. I told the FBI that. I told everybody that. But the FBI refuses to believe me. I've done wrong in my life, but I'm not a liar. And what I've told the FBI is the truth.

My status in this country is no different from that of hundreds of thousands of others. Why did they single me out for arrest?

The FBI thinks that by persecuting me I'll tell them something. But what they want is something I haven't got.

I came here as a baby in 1908, but they treat me like I was a foreigner. Are they doing this to me because I was brought by my parents from a Mediterranean country?

They are trying to use an old charge against me and it's an old story—persecution for something I had nothing to do with and know nothing about.

The FBI has had men following me for three years, ever since the Brink's robbery. People I talk with are later grilled by the FBI. Then the people stop talking to me.

The FBI walks into my house day or night, anytime. They knocked me out of every job I've ever had, even one paying sixty cents an hour.

Now all my relatives and in-laws, nephews and nieces have been affected. Only last Friday a nineteen-year-old niece of mine lost her job [*Ed. Note:* in a Boston bank] because of the FBI. They don't care what methods they use.

The FBI has made a joke of the freedom I was denied in prison and prayed to have again. An agent told me nearly three years ago that he'd see that I was put on a boat and sent back to Europe. I laughed. I didn't think they could do that in America, to an innocent man. But that's what they're trying to do.

Pino fought the case all the way to the Supreme Court, and won. On April 11, 1955, the highest bench in the land ruled one of the two new cases cited by Immigration authori-

114

ties—a $100 larceny in 1948 for which Pino served no time—"had not attained such finality as to support an order of deportation."

In his early face-to-face meetings with individual members of the Brink's mob Specs attempted to reason with each to "have the courage or the *caution*" to provide for him his proper share. Memories of those days still beset him:

"Take McGinnis for example. He was, and is, a wealthy man. The others who couldn't afford to contribute to my share could have gone to him and borrowed it, to be paid back from some later job. But they didn't have the courage to do that because McGinnis was such a formidable character. Cheap bastard, too.

"I got hotter and hotter and I finally grabbed Jazz. I was convinced that individually they were lying to me, so I figured I'd get two of them together and confront one with the other.

"I grabbed him and took him to McGinnis's store, that beautiful liquor store. It was a Saturday morning. In ten or fifteen years, McGinnis had never missed being there on a Saturday, if he wasn't in the can, so he had to be there this day.

"He wasn't there when we walked in. There was just this fellow Sullivan, the one who had gone to Washington to look up the patents of the bug that worried us at Brink's. Sullivan and a woman, a bookkeeper or something. I asked for McGinnis. Sullivan said he didn't know where he was or when he'd return. Then he asked me if he could do anything for me.

"I said, 'I don't think you can, but I want to tell you what *I'm* going to do if you don't get in touch with the owner, and soon. I'm going to send you and the lady outside and then I'm going to break every damn bottle in this store.' Well, he got on the phone and made a lot of calls, but no McGinnis.

"What we didn't know was that McGinnis had gotten

pinched. He was driving a top-heavy truck of empty five-gallon tins to his farm in New Hampshire, where he had a still, and the thing tipped over. The cops came along, spotted the cans, put two and two together, and pretty soon the Feds were on him like a swarm of locusts. They took his joint apart, broke up the still, and kept looking. They were looking for Brink's money, too. They always were.

"As the time went by, back at McGinnis's store, Jazz started crying again. He was running a small book out of his hotel room and kept bellyaching about all the phoned-in bets he was missing. Finally I told him that the only way he could get away from me that day was to get one of the other guys as a substitute. I told him it didn't matter which one he conned into it. 'I'm going to have one of you bastards with me when McGinnis comes in,' I told him. So he called Henry Baker, who had been ducking me, and told him he wanted to see him. Didn't tell him why. So we go downtown and I grabbed Baker and let Maffie go on to his book. I brought Baker back to the store and we waited there all that day for that skinhead McGinnis.

"A couple of times Baker said, 'I'm not going to wait around here any longer. I'm going to go.' I looked at him, said, 'How *can* you go?' I hadn't shown him what I had on me that day, but Baker knew I probably had one. He didn't make a move for that door. But I let him go, of course, when the word came why McGinnis wasn't there.

"What bugged me was the fear those guys had of Skinhead McGinnis and the Pig. They didn't have the courage to go against them. It was a terrible weakness in those guys. They're still weak toward them, to this day. How the hell can the eight of them live in peace together?

"In one instance there was a guy named Mountain who became partners with Tony in numbers, Treasury tickets, things like that. A good guy. Well, he died suddenly of a heart attack. So Pino goes to Faherty and says, 'Jeez, Jim, you got a bad break. Nitty just died and he was holding $25,000 of your money.'

"Now what kind of a story was that? How could he get away with a thing like that? If he came to me I'd have to say, 'I don't know that stiff. *You're* the guy I'm looking to for my money.'

"Things like that."

O'Keefe was by now of the opinion that he had to do something radical to shake the rest of the group. He kidnapped Vincent Costa.

It was May 18, 1954, and Specs had a new partner, his easygoing fan John Carlson. Specs had been impressed by the way Carlson clammed up and took a contempt citation during the grand jury hearings of the year before. It was an unusual snatch:

"I trailed Costa this day. He was picking up numbers slips or delivering Treasury tickets. It didn't matter. Anyway, I finally spotted him getting into a brand-new Oldsmobile. I sneaked up fast and jumped in after him. So did Carlson, who was with me. I told Costa to drive to a spot I had arranged for, a real crummy tenement you wouldn't want to be caught dead in. You wouldn't put a dog in there. He didn't put up an argument.

"Once I had him there I told him that the only way he could redeem himself, get home, he'd have to come up with some money. He wanted to know how much, and I told him. Twenty-five thousand.

Money that size doesn't come through in a hurry. So after guarding him for eight or ten hours I told Carlson that I was pooped; that I had to lie down. 'You watch him awhile,' I said to Johnny, who didn't know Costa good. 'Now don't even talk to this guy. If he asks you a question, don't answer. Don't become involved in any kind of conversation.'

"A few hours later I woke up and realized I'd better relieve John. So I go in the next room and there they are sitting

117

around, smoking and talking. I said, 'What the hell are you doing, talking to this guy?' Johnny said, 'Gee, Specs, he was telling me a sad story about his five kids.' I told him to cut it out; that I didn't want to hear about how many kids he had because I didn't know exactly what was going to happen to him.

"I held him that night and got in touch with his wife the next day. Strangely enough, her brother, Pino, was released by the Immigration people that same afternoon and he sent word to me that he wanted to see me.

"I went over to his house, after moving Costa to a hotel. I told Pino what the story was. I told him I was tired of waiting for him and the others to do something about my share, or live up to the pledge, and that I was ready to do something about it. I wanted the $25,000 for starters, I told him, and would take the balance later.

"He gave me $2,500 as a down payment then and there and I agreed to let Costa go. That might have been a mistake on my part. I might have indicated weakness of some sort. But I did it. And then the forces of violence moved in, directed against me."

Which is something of an understatement.

Shortly after his confrontation with Pino and the release of Costa, Specs was driving home alone one midnight to a flat he had rented in Dorchester. He was driving Carlson's green and white ninety-eight Olds convertible, and at his customarily brisk clip. As was also his custom, O'Keefe kept a sharp eye on the rear-vision mirror. As he passed Edward Everett Square he noticed the lights of another car pull in behind him. Specs stepped down hard enough on the gas to exceed the speed limit. The car behind him kept pace.

At the next right he turned and stepped down all the way on the gas. He saw the car behind him swerve into the same street and begin gaining on him. He noted also that for a change the street he had chosen, a narrow street, was

118

stripped of parked cars this night, which meant that the car pursuing him had a better chance of pulling up abreast.

As the car behind him, a Plymouth, prepared to overtake the Oldsmobile, Specs pulled over to the left, beyond the middle of the street. The Plymouth's hood was now even with Specs' left door.

With an instinct born of the jungle in which he had been raised, Specs flung himself across the empty seat to his right. Simultaneously, a shattering burst of submachine gunfire entered the car, shot past the point where Specs' head had been the barest instant before, and crashed out through the windshield, carrying with it the rear-vision mirror.

Lying across the front seat of the car, unable to see where he was going at this semi-crazed speed, O'Keefe coolly edged the Oldsmobile a bit farther to the left until he felt it touch the side of the now passing Plymouth. It served as a guide and direction finder.

The Plymouth scraped itself free and roared on.

Specs groped with one of his feet, found his brake and brought the Olds to a halt without colliding with anything on either side of the street. He sat up behind the wheel again and a wave of hatred and a fierce lust for revenge swept over him. In his great anger he tried to give chase, though he had no gun. He hoped to get close enough to the Plymouth to ram it into a curb, a pole or a building, not with a view to bringing about the arrest of whoever had tried to murder him but mainly to identify them for his own satisfaction. But he lost them.

O'Keefe returned to Boston proper, instead of proceeding on to his flat, and sought out Carlson in the latter's favorite delicatessen. He needed a gun:

"Johnny was a funny kind of a kid. Nothing bothered him. If the building fell down, he'd sit there still eating his sandwich. He looked at me—while he ate—and asked me what was the matter. 'They just tried for me,' I said. He kept eat-

119

ing. 'So what happened?' he said. I said, 'For Christ sake, let's get out of here. They might come back here.' I didn't have anything and I wanted and needed something. In a hurry. But he kept chewing. 'Take it easy,' he said. I pulled him up and away from the sandwich and got him outside. Only then did he show any interest, this kid. He said, 'Hey, what did you do to my car? Look at the holes in the windshield.'

"So we went to his place and I got a pistol."

They checked into a hotel that night. Specs left a call for 6:30 A.M., got up, dressed, and headed for Pino's big beachfront house in Wollaston, Massachusetts. Specs took his gun:

"He had a big German police dog guarding the yard. The dog started for me as I started for the door. I didn't want to 'hit' the dog but I would have had to if he jumped me. He didn't.

"I went in. Pino was having his breakfast. I confronted him with what had happened.

" 'I don't know what you're talking about,' he said.

"I told him I thought he did know exactly what I was talking about. His wife broke in and said something like 'I don't know what you're trying to say about Tony. He hasn't been out of the house for days.'

" 'Who could have done a thing like that to you?' Tony said to me.

"I was so upset. I said, 'You know who could have done something like that, you greasy bastard.'

"Well, he denied it up and down. There wasn't much I could do, except be brutal. And I didn't want to be that way at that time."

O'Keefe left Pino's aware that whoever had tried to kill him the night before in all probability would try again. If a paid killer had been employed, and that seemed most likely to Specs, then another attack was a foregone conclusion. A paid killer could not stop with a miss. He would lose face.

He turned his attention next to Baker. An earlier call on

Baker had wrung from the man a sorrowful disclaimer that he had any money. Then O'Keefe learned that Baker had a fairly thriving cigarette machine business, serviced it with a truck he owned and had just bought a home and a new Dodge. To boot, Baker and his wife took a trip to California at a time when it appeared he might be called to testify before a grand jury investigating a stick-up of an armored truck in Danvers, Massachusetts.

O'Keefe gave Baker a call. Answering Service replied and asked if he wished to leave a message.

"Yeah," Specs said. "Tell him . . . ah . . . tell him Mr. Burke called." He did not know why he chose that particular name—which soon would shout from headlines.

He had left his own number. When Baker did not call, Specs and Johnny Carlson advanced on the Baker company. Specs went in:

"Baker's brother and nephew were in the place. I looked around and could see what a phony bum Baker was, crying poor mouth to me. He was crying with two loaves of bread under his arms.

"I told the kids I wasn't there to ruin their business, but I was determined to get some money to help pay a lawyer. I gave the brother a choice: either I'd take all the stock, the loose change, the truck—which might have come to, say, five thousand—or he could sit down and write me a check for three thousand, three hundred. What I needed.

"The kid didn't seem able to choose. So I told him that if he didn't like either idea, he could call the police . . . call them up and tell them the truth, that this was an invasion. But if he did that, I went on, I wouldn't run. I'd stay and face them.

"You see, I felt I had a right to do anything to Baker, or any other participant in the Brink's robbery, because of their failure to live up to our original agreement. After all, this wasn't child's play.

"I guess I knew he wouldn't call the police. He had to

121

know what would have been at stake if the real reason why I was there ever came out. So he said he'd write the check but he'd have to deposit the six or seven hundred dollars in collections that were on the desk, first, so the check would be good.

"It wasn't enough. I went back early the next day. Carlson stayed in our car, parked halfway down the street. Baker's father and brother were there, just about ready to pull away in the truck with supplies for their machines.

"I had just started talking to them when Baker pulled up to the curb. I told the kid at the wheel of the truck to drive on. I didn't want him or the father involved in what might happen. They blew.

"It was a strange place to meet Baker for anything serious. There were a lot of people on the streets, going to work. About a block away a police officer—fatherly type—was directing traffic, protecting schoolkids crossing the street.

"Baker got out of his car and faced me. His face was dead-white. It wasn't a pallor. It was like dead. He had his hand in his right pants pocket. He drew halfway out of his pocket a nickel-plated gun of some kind. That was to impress me. He cursed me—something bad—and then said that this was going to be either his life or mine.

"I said, 'I think it's going to be yours.' I came out with mine, fast. He couldn't do anything now, so he said he was going to get back in his car and go to see Pino right away.

"I told him, 'You're right. You are going to see Pino, but I'm going to take you.' He jumped between parked cars and I banged away at him a few times. I missed him. I'm a lousy shot.

"Well, by now the cop down the block is coming and people are standing around stupefied. Johnny came up fast in the car and we got out of there."

"They tried again a week or so after the miss. It was the sixteenth of June, I remember, two days after my trouble

122

with Baker. Each night when I went to my place in Dorchester I parked in a different spot. I had given up on driving Johnny's car; it was too conspicuous. This night I had a little gray car that belonged to a kid I knew, a little Italian numbers writer. I picked the darkest street I could find near my joint, and sure enough I found a nice parking space. I backed in, locked the car and started up the dark street.

"You know how you instinctively look back at your car after parking it, to see if you left the lights on or something. Well, as I did I saw the nose of a car parked four or five cars back of mine start out from the curb, without lights. I knew that was it.

"About ten or fifteen feet ahead of me and to the right there was the entrance of a housing development's parking space, with cars parked head-on against a low concrete wall.

"I got three cars between me and them before they opened up. Something told me that the best shield I could have would be the hood of the car: the engine block would stop what they would throw at me. But the bursts were so terrific that the bullets seemed to be flying all around me. If I have to go through anything like that again I'll try not to get so close to a concrete wall. Bullets ricochet off them.

"They kept pumping away and I felt that I was going to go. You never want to go without throwing something back. I had the .45 I had picked up from Johnny. I got it out, reached over the hood of this car and took a couple of shots at them. Then I slipped down the side of the car, hoping to get a better shot at them.

"That's when I was hit. Momentarily, you don't know you've been hit. I still don't know whether what hit me came through the body of the car or glanced off the concrete wall. All I know is that I was hit.

"I don't know whether my being alive can be called miraculous, for I may have to suffer all my life from this kind of threat, this kind of attempt. But miraculous has to be the word for what happened to me that night. I got the benefit of two deflections. The bullet that got me on my left wrist first hit my wristwatch. It tore it off my wrist and cut a crease in my flesh, but the watch blunted the force of the slug and the artery wasn't severed.

"I usually carried my little leather-bound memorandum book, address book, in my inside coat pocket. But it had been a warm night and for some reason—maybe because I had my coat off earlier—I put it in my shirt pocket. More accessible.

"That leather was as soft as could be, but in some manner it deflected a bullet that had to be headed for my heart. The bullet went in my chest and came out two or three inches away.

"I reached over the top of the car and emptied the rest of my gun at them. They flew."

Specs got out of there, too, in a hurry, on foot, leaving behind him the .45 and the remnants of his watch. He realized for the first time that he had been hit on the wrist and that his watch was gone. The wound was bleeding down over his hand. But of greater importance to him just then was a mad desire to get close enough to the departing car to read its license. He found himself running aimlessly down streets, only vaguely aware of the commotion back at the scene of the shooting. A number of machine-gun bullets had ricocheted into a neighboring house, narrowly missing a young girl asleep in her bed.

As he ran recklessly into the next block, Specs felt the warmth of blood leaking from his chest and discovered that wound, too. He came to his senses now and fashioned a crude tourniquet for his wrist. The prospect that the bullet was still in his chest was sobering enough to cause him a dizzy spell. But the approach of a speeding car impelled him to leap behind a hedge. He watched it go by, its lights doused and its plates thus indecipherable, and was convinced that it was the same car that had now twice attempted to kill him.

Now, to his surprise, he saw an empty taxicab approaching. He wiped the blood from his hand, pulled his coat closer around himself, dusted his suit, and hailed the cab. The driver paid no attention to his condition. Specs gave him the address of a bar on Northampton Street in Boston. By the time the cab had progressed several blocks it had to pull over to the side of the street to make way for speeding, shrieking police cars headed for the scene of the shooting. When they passed, the cab moved on with its bleeding passenger.

Specs passed City Hospital, among others, on the way to the bar. It never crossed his mind to enter one for treatment, though he had little notion of just how badly he might be wounded.

At the bar he had two fast drinks of brandy, then called Carlson from an outside phone booth near the place:

"He came on the phone after a bit and I told him I had been hit.

" 'How bad?' he asked.

"I told him I didn't really know, so he said, 'I'll be down.' "Took that bum twenty minutes to get there, and he only lived two blocks away. He was the kind of guy who'd have to get burned to death if a fire started in his house. Maybe he had a sandwich before he came. But he got there, looked me over and agreed that I'd better start looking for a croaker.

"Johnny picked up a legit fellow's car—his was too noticeable—and drove me to the house of a friend who might know the kind of doctor I wanted; one that could keep his mouth shut. The guy knew one right off, but I refused to go see him. I knew that particular croaker had been friendly in the past with the opposition.

"I told Johnny to take me some place, any place, where I could examine the wounds. He drove me to a friend's place in Roxbury, and I went to work on myself. The wrist wound was an ugly, jagged-looking thing, but it had stopped bleeding and didn't start again when I bathed it. I poked around the wound in my chest and determined that the bullet had gone clean through. So I said to hell with it; I'd wait until the morning to see a doctor. I went into a bedroom and went to sleep.

"Johnny woke me up after an hour, just when I was sleeping good. I cursed him but he wasn't paying any attention. 'Come on, Joe, I'll take you to the croaker now. I found a good one.' He had become worried about tetanus. So I got up and we went to a doctor whose name I have never mentioned and never will and he gave me the proper shots, including a massive dose of penicillin.

"It helps a guy in my business to have blood that coagulates easy."

10

Bandaged now, and aware that he would surely be rounded up in the inevitable police net that would be thrown over Boston's underworld in the wake of the gunfire, Specs went from the doctor's home to his sister Mary's house, where he borrowed her car. He drove to the house where a girl friend lived, and in the small dark hours of the morning they drove to a New Hampshire hideaway.

At 3 A.M., June 18, Specs called Johnny Carlson at a pre-arranged public phone booth in Boston. From Johnny he learned that Baker and he, Carlson, had been picked up, among others questioned and released. He learned, too, that he, O'Keefe, had been named "most wanted" by the Boston police. But Specs heard even more interesting news over the phone:

"Johnny told me the cops had picked up the fellow who had done the shooting at me. I said that that was crazy: how could a guy be arrested for shooting at me? He'd have to admit it to the cops himself. 'That's what he did,' Johnny told me. 'They got the machine gun too.'

" 'Well, I'll be damned,' I said. 'Who the hell is he?'

" 'Some guy named Elmer Burke,' Johnny said, real casual-like. I cursed him for trying to rib me at a time like that. 'If I could reach you right now I'd golf you,' I said. But then I realized he was telling the truth. Elmer, I knew by reputation, of course. He was the cold, crazy New York assassin the newspapers called Trigger. We don't use names like that, generally. His name was Elmer. Elmer Burke. Burke! Then I suddenly realized why Baker had looked so white and strange that day in the street. He had gotten the message from Answering Service that a Mr. Burke had called, and checked somehow and found that it was my phone number—and he figured that I knew they had hired this murderer to kill me.

"Johnny urged me to come back to Boston. He told me he had talked to one of the assistant DA's and had been told that if I came in and gave myself up he'd see that I'd get a small sentence—three to five years they call a small sentence —for having possession of a gun.

"I asked him what was eating him, with talk like that. I said, 'Why should I come back? Who the hell knows I was in Dorchester except me and this other bum, Burke? How could anyone ever prove I had a gun. It's ridiculous.' But the more I talked the more Johnny talked, and after a while I said okay."

Specs drove his girl home, where she was arrested shortly thereafter on a charge of "lewd and lascivious cohabitation." Specs went on to the apartment where Carlson was waiting for him, and hid out. He was as "hot" as he had ever been in his life. When on the previous April 1 he had appeared in Boston Municipal Court before Judge Adlow and obtained another continuation in the matter of the old 1947 rap, O'Keefe had been given some assurance that when he returned on July 1, 1954, the old case probably would then be thrown out of court.

However, the shootings in June, and the inability of the Boston police to locate him, so outraged Judge Adlow that he declared he would be as stern with O'Keefe as the law permitted.

Specs needed advice, and he took a long chance to get it. He left his shelter and called on the senior of the attorneys who had represented him in the grand jury investigation of the previous year, Joseph Schneider. He was not a client of that respected attorney but knew that Schneider was a friend of Judge Adlow, and he hoped he would intercede in his behalf. Schneider could make him no such promise, so O'Keefe —taking a further chance on being picked up in the streets —called on another lawyer he knew. This one recommended that the best thing to do would be for Specs to appear in court, as scheduled, on July 1.

Specs did not take the advice and as a consequence the police swore out a warrant for his arrest. In retrospect he feels he might have beaten that case on legal technicalities if he had appeared that day. But he burned those flimsy bridges behind him by not appearing, and later had the burden of no excuse for failing to show up.

He borrowed his sister's car again and drove off to Worcester, where his girl now was. She had been questioned and cleared of the vice charge—which Specs, too, was exonerated of later. But en route to Worcester, near Leicester, Massachusetts, Specs saw that he was being followed by a squad car. This came as no great surprise to him:

"The plate numbers of my sister's car had been put out on the air two months before, and now here was a guy with the memory of an elephant following me. He had me pegged pretty good. He'd drop back every once in a while to try to make me think he had lost interest. But then I'd see him again, shortly enough. If I had been in Worcester I could have doubled around a couple of corners, gone up an alley, dumped the car and made a run for it. But this was country-like.

"Well, I lost sight of him in my rear-vision glass, so I decided to make a U-turn and start back in his direction, figuring I might be able to fly by him. I pulled into a road on the right, to start the turn, and swung back across the road, making the turn.

"He was right there—right out of the blue—and I had to hit the brakes to keep from hitting his car head-on. I was blocked. He got out and came over to me with his pistol in his hand. I asked him what was going on here. You know, indignant.

" 'It's a routine thing,' he said.

" 'Routine! What've you got that thing for?'

"So he busted me. He felt he had the right to stop that automobile because its numbers had been broadcast. They took me back to Boston, locked me up and the next day Suffolk County District Attorney Garrett Byrne came to see me. That was unusual, I thought.

"Byrne's a smart fellow. He came right to the point. He wanted to know if I would care to expand on what I knew about the Brink's robbery; that the FBI and his office by now had every reason to believe I was in it, and probably had had some kind of trouble collecting my bit.

"I told him I didn't even want to talk to him. Well, he got hot. He said he was going to send me to jail for the 1947 beef. And he did. The next morning, a Monday, he did an unprecedented thing for a fellow of his stature. He came into that low court, gave me a bitter tongue-lashing—which I suppose I deserved—and he was instrumental in sending me up. Judge Adlow wanted to take no chance of some legal technicality that might come up, in view of his earlier indication that the case was old and should be dismissed. He stepped aside and I had to face a new one, Judge Fox."

Judge Fox gave O'Keefe twenty-seven months, August 5, 1954. Specs served the first few days of his term at the familiar haunt of Deer Island, whence he had escaped years before. Then, under very heavy guard, he was moved to Hampden County Jail at Springfield, apparently to protect him from friends and enemies: friends who might in some way contrive to reduce his sentence, enemies now clearly out to kill him.

One friend who would not be coming, ever, was Johnny Carlson. Johnny was never seen again after August 3. The common understanding in the Boston underworld is that he was killed for his connection with O'Keefe. His green and white Olds was found near his home. District Attorney Byrne suspects that Carlson's body was disposed of in deep water, either in a barrel of cement or weighted and chained.

One enemy who would not be visiting Specs again was Trigger Burke.

On the afternoon of August 28, Burke effected an escape from Suffolk County Jail, Boston, which is still regarded in police and criminal circles as one of the slickest of them all.

As he strolled about the prison yard during an exercise period Burke dashed out of the line of march and bolted toward the heavy steel door that led to solitary confinement quarters. A yard guard gave chase. As Burke approached the imposing barrier it swung open. A man with a stocking over his head—probably a bribed guard—let Burke by and then confronted the pursuing guard with drawn gun. "Back up or I'll blow your brains out," the man said. The guard backed up. Burke fled to freedom through two gates for which keys were provided and a cagelike barrier whose bars had been sawed. One can only hazard a guess at the number of persons who had to be fixed. Heads rolled in a subsequent grand jury hearing into the seamy case.

The getaway car was in place. It departed with a roar. One of the dozens of bystanders later told police that the driver "wore a woman's wig, dress, hat, a black mask and had beefy jowls."

The following day an intern at a Boston hospital called police to report that a Buick that appeared to have no owner —in the hospital, at least—had been parked in the hospital's lot since a short time after Burke's escape. It was Burke's getaway car. Instead of hauling it in, police concealed themselves in the area to look for any detailed interest in it.

One car, it was noticed, circled the area five times. Its license was noted and traced through motor vehicle records.

131

It was Pino's car.

He was taken into custody the following day and freely admitted having been in the vicinity. He was looking for a parking place so he could visit a relative in the same hospital, he explained. He denied any knowledge of how Burke escaped, and was released.

It was not the last Pino heard of the Burke case. In the course of a subsequent hearing on his continuing deportation action, Pino was flatly accused of having brought Burke to Boston from New York to kill O'Keefe and Carlson. The charge was made by Gilbert Zimmerman, investigator from the Washington headquarters of the Immigration and Naturalization Service. It was heatedly denied by Pino's lawyer, Paul Smith. The underground buzzed with the story that Burke was to have been paid $24,000 if he got both O'Keefe and Carlson. Instead, the money was poured into his escape, the story went, because if he had come to trial on the charge of possessing a machine gun he could have been given life under Massachusetts law. That could have prompted him to bargain for less by naming his employers and the reasons why they wanted O'Keefe, especially, killed.

Specs on Trigger:

"He had come up to Boston because the heat was too much for him in New York. He had killed a friend of his named Poochie Walsh in a bar on the West Side of New York. They had come into the joint, palsy walsy, but during the course of the evening got into an argument. Burke excused himself, went around the corner to the place where he was living—I think it was his mother's—picked up a gun, came back to the ginmill and shot Poochie dead. Burke was like that. He killed a number of his friends. He was funny that way. Sadistic, I guess you'd say. Brutal.

"After he was picked up and the pictures were printed I realized that he had been close to me, in different places, from time to time. He was a little guy with a hard face. I think he made himself look that way to frighten people.

Maybe so, maybe not. His brother was killed during a time he was in Sing Sing or Elmira, someplace in New York, and he announced in the can that the fellow who killed his brother was as good as dead; that he'd kill him when he got out, no matter. Well, he got out and it took him months, maybe a couple years, to find the guy, but he did and he killed him.

"He was credited with being some sort of a hero in the war, highly trained as a combat soldier. A Ranger. I don't know about that. I've never seen his record. For all I know he might have been in the Ranger motor pool. There are a lot of so-called 'trained killers' who never saw a gun before they started to kill. But he was generally considered a bad guy, somebody to be feared.

"Gabby kind of guy. After his second try at me, and the story came out that a little girl was nearly killed by the bullets that missed me, he called up the police and gave them some crazy third-person message like 'If Burke ever did anything like that, he'd be willing to come in.' He was a peculiar character who seemed to want police to know that he, an infamous killer, was around and willing to talk to them but had nothing much to say. I don't know why he never seemed to realize that whatever he said—whatever—could be used against him.

"When a detective named Crawford grabbed him the night after the big exchange of shots in Dorchester, and pinned him against a wall, he did so in such a way that Burke couldn't get at the gun he was carrying. I don't know how the cop spotted him; maybe on information. Anyway, Crawford took his gun away from him and Burke said, in effect, that the cop was a pretty lucky guy not to be shot.

"Then he either told the cop where he lived, or somebody had told the cops, and they went there and found several guns, including the burp gun, the grease gun, he used against me.

"He was indicted for possession of a machine gun, not for trying to hit me. That shows where I stood, I guess."

"The escape was smooth . . .

"Burke was away for one day short of a year. The FBI picked him up in Folly Beach, South Carolina, in August of 1955, and lugged him to New York to face trial for killing Poochie Walsh. He had been living in some kind of a seaside cottage, quietly. About the only friends he seemed to have had were a man and his wife named Connelly. Duke Connelly had been raised with Burke. He was on the lam for a robbery, something like $300,000, in New York.

"They were close friends, Burke and the Connellys. That could be dangerous, with Burke concerned. They had two small children, the Connellys. One day one of the children was picked up on the streets of Baltimore. The other kid was found wandering around Wilmington, Delaware. There's a good chance Burke killed the Connellys, drove the kids up there from South Carolina and dumped them.

"Anyway, Burke got the chair at Sing Sing for another guy he hit, his friend Poochie. Screw him."

11

Joe o'keefe sat in his cell at springfield.

The other Brink's robbers were free, except for his friend Gus, who was still serving time in Pennsylvania.

Only he, O'Keefe, had failed to collect his share.

Jazz Maffie, who blew Specs' money, was a successful bookie.

Only he, O'Keefe, who had contributed so much to the success of the venture, was unable to pay his lawyers and underwrite appeals when caught and convicted.

There had been three attempts on his life, counting Baker's abortive try.

His good pal Johnny Carlson had been murdered.

His sister and brother-in-law had gone broke trying to help pay his lawyers' bills.

McGinnis and Pino were winning all cases, living in luxury.

His brother Donald and other members of the family were occasionally questioned by the FBI.

Though the FBI and the police must have had a good line on the identity of the robbers by now, only he had been publicly named as a suspect.

He was serving a twenty-seven-month term on an eight-year-old-rap which a judge virtually promised to set aside.

When his current time was served, Pennsylvania would want him for perhaps "three to twelve" for the burglary, larceny and receiving stolen goods conviction of the previous year, 1954.

And by now there was one less fellow-robber to appeal to for justice and relief. Banfield had died, apparently from natural causes—if the consumption of vast amounts of whiskey can be called natural. What was more, Banfield "took it with him." He died without revealing where he had planted his $100,000 or what was left of it. It lay somewhere, rotting, when Specs so sorely needed money—anybody's money.

All these things stirred in Specs as days moved excruciatingly into weeks and weeks became months with the leisure of the sea eroding the shore. He had few visitors. His sister Mary made the ninety-mile trip from Boston regularly to offer what consolation she could. Occasionally a pair of FBI agents would drop in, and he would either fence with their questions or refuse to speak to them. He saw little or nothing of his wife or the foster son whom he deeply missed.

The Bureau's determination to crack the Brink's case had increased rather than waned since the setback in the grand jury investigation of 1953. Each special agent placed in charge of the Boston office provided fresh thinking and imaginative exploration. The search for the missing money continued on countless fronts throughout the country and abroad. Incredibly, though it was known that suspected members of the conspiracy were spending large sums to hire the best available legal talent, not a traceable dollar had been uncovered.

The Federal statute of limitations on most aspects of the robbery had expired January 17, 1953. The State's statute would be up January 17, 1956.

It was now the fall of 1955. O'Keefe had been in Springfield for more than a year. His accumulated troubles and gripes had built up a tremendous head of steam:

"I decided that I should do something to get straightened out with these guys, money-wise, once and for all. I felt that

I deserved it; perhaps, morally, I didn't deserve it and don't now. But I felt it strong in prison.

"So I wrote letters to McGinnis and to Pino. I worded them very carefully. I had a feeling the FBI had a look at all my letters before they left the prison. I had to be careful not to say too much, not to come right out and threaten to tell the works. But I also had to make McGinnis and Pino realize that I was dead serious and fed up.

"When I didn't hear from them, I made the next two letters a little stronger. And the third set even more bitter—but still avoiding putting anything really incriminating down on paper. The letter to McGinnis was toughest. I concentrated on him because he had the most to lose.

"McGinnis came to see me. They wouldn't let him in because he had once been an inmate there. Then, after a while, Eddie Bennett called on me. Wimpy, we called him. I had been pretty close to him over the years but I hadn't heard a word from him since I was committed, fifteen months before.

"Wimpy came in big. 'How are you, Joe?' he said. 'How's tricks?' I told him to lay off the amenities and tell me who sent him and why. He looked around to see that nobody was listening, then he told me that they—the group—would give my wife $5,000 '. . . and they'll take care of you later, Joe.' It wasn't hard to get the implication.

"I said, 'Look, you go back and tell them that they're not dictating to me any longer; I'm dictating to them. Tell them they've got to come up with my money, all of it, not a goddam pittance. Tell them that if I don't get my end they're all going to be in trouble.'

"I could tell by Wimpy's face that he couldn't believe it, just as the others wouldn't be able to believe it. Wimpy and they couldn't conceive of anybody putting himself in the can by confessing to a crime that nobody could pin on him. What they seemed to forget was that I was already in the can, and that when I got out of this one I'd have to go into

137

another one in Pennsylvania. Still, if they had come through at that time or even later I never would have done what I finally felt I had to do. That isn't saying that the FBI would never have cracked it, but I sure wouldn't have been the key.

"Wimpy came back with the answer the following week.

"He said, 'Joe, it don't look like you're going to get any money. They're not too much interested. They don't fear anything is going to happen.'

"I said he must be crazy, they would be in plenty of trouble if I opened my mouth.

"Wimpy looked unhappy. 'Joe,' he said, 'please don't ever say I told you so, but they're going to have you bugged. They're lining up the doctors, the brains kind, to have you committed. Please don't say I told you.'

"It knocked the wind out of me for a minute, for I knew they maybe had enough money and pull to get away with it, have me declared batty, and knock out any accusation I might make after that. But I said, 'Well, now they're really in trouble. Tell them that. Tell them they've not only got to come up with my bit but also the $40,000 Jazz said he spent fighting the Pennsylvania convictions.'

"Wimpy was finally convinced that I meant business. 'I think I understand now that you really will do this thing if they don't come through.' I said, 'Exactly. Now go back and tell them.' "

A day or two after this scene, Specs' keeper told him that two FBI agents, Jack Kehoe and John Larkin of the Boston Field Office, wished to see him. He refused, as he had done several times before. They returned on December 27 of that year (1955). Specs had spent Christmas alone, further embittered by a menacing silence from his fellow Brink's robbers, the threat of having to go through a rigged insanity hearing and duns from Pennsylvania lawyers.

Now the last barrier was crumbling. The last restraining force that had been largely instrumental in making him hold his silence so long was his respect for Gusciora and his desire

138

not to hurt his friend. Perhaps there was some way he could condemn the others, along with himself, and absolve Gus.

"I'll see them," Specs said.

It was a strained meeting, but for the FBI it was an encouraging meeting. An official Bureau account reads:

> At 1:55 P.M., on December 27, 1955, Special Agents John P. Larkin and John F. Kehoe, Jr., of the FBI's Boston Field Office, interviewed Joseph O'Keefe at the Hampden County Jail in Springfield, Massachusetts. In view of O'Keefe's obvious reluctance to discuss his criminal activities at the outset of the interview, no notes were taken.
>
> When the interview began, O'Keefe agreed only to talk to the two FBI agents through a prison door. He was told that the agents' purpose in being there was to discuss the Brink's robbery with him; and he promptly adopted a negative attitude—inferring that the FBI was responsible, at least in part, for the troubles with which he was then confronted. The FBI agents pointed out to O'Keefe that he himself was responsible for the difficulties in which he found himself, as well as for the embarrassment which his activities had brought upon members of his family. As he sat pondering what the agents said, O'Keefe reluctantly agreed with them.
>
> The agents returned the conversation to the Brink's case by telling O'Keefe that Tony Pino had built a new ranch house; that Vincent Costa was now in the automobile business; and that Joseph McGinnis was also "living high." They also brought Elmer "Trigger" Burke's name into the conversation, and O'Keefe promptly volunteered that Burke was the hired killer who had shot at him in 1954. The two FBI agents then pointed out to O'Keefe that he obviously had received shabby treatment from his underworld associates—even to the point that they attempted to kill him. These sympathetic words appeared to make an impression upon O'Keefe. He looked at the two FBI agents and said, "What can I do? I'm in a box. I'm in a trap and I can't see any way out."
>
> O'Keefe then told the FBI agents that if they wanted the "information" badly enough, they could make some kind

of arrangement which would be beneficial to him. The agents told him that they could make no promises; that they were not in a position to offer him a "deal." O'Keefe replied, "I know that well."

O'Keefe next asked the agents, "If you think I was involved in this Brink's robbery, what part do you believe I had in it?" The two FBI agents advised him that they considered him to be one of the actual robbers. O'Keefe replied, "Well, then don't you think I could give the story? What kind of prosecution is still possible? Give me a straight answer or I won't be able to place any trust whatsoever in the FBI." The FBI agents cited to him several Federal statutes under which prosecution of the Brink's gang members might be successfully instituted. O'Keefe then said, "This is very complex." He then paused, looked at the floor, and after shaking his head for several moments, he continued, "There are just too many involved. I don't see any possible way it can be worked out. I'll have to think it over."

The interview was terminated at approximately 4:55 P.M. on December 27. As they left, the agents reminded O'Keefe that no promises could be made to him. They asked him to give further thought to the matter and told him that they would return. O'Keefe's sole comment to these statements was, "Okay."

Throughout the three-hour interview with him on December 27, 1955, O'Keefe was hesitant and cautious in the statements which he made. He repeated himself several times. Although clearly inferring that he possessed "inside" information concerning the Brink's robbery, he did not make any admissions of guilt.

The following afternoon, Agent Larkin returned to Hampden County Jail accompanied by the Boston Field Office's special agent in charge, Edward J. Powers. Specs agreed to see them immediately. Powers wasted no time. He told O'Keefe that Agents Larkin and Kehoe had informed him on the details of the previous day's meeting. And he added that

140

it was high time Specs placed his trust in someone. He impressed Specs:

"Powers is a peculiar guy, peculiar in my life at least. The best description of him is that he's one of those All-American guys. Larkin is also. In spite of all my difficulty with those people I had respect for them. I particularly had respect right off, for this fellow Powers. He was so earnest, so honest, you might say. And so eager to have me come around to his side. But I wouldn't, just then. I figured I'd give those other people a little more time to come up with that money."

Of this particular meeting, the FBI report states:

> O'Keefe stated that he was under a great strain; that a number of complex problems were involved; and that he "knew" he should not even be talking at all to law enforcement officers. O'Keefe then rambled momentarily concerning his financial difficulties. He then stated, "I just can't bring myself to tell the story to law enforcement officers at this time. I can't guarantee that I'll tell the story, but I'm presently thinking in that direction."
>
> O'Keefe continued that innocent people undoubtedly would be dragged into the investigation and the trial if he "talked." SAC Powers told him that it was impossible to discuss the problem of innocent persons who might be involved in the case—or any of the other problems which were bothering O'Keefe—if he refused to confide in the FBI but, instead, continued to keep the story to himself.
>
> This interview was terminated at 3:50 P.M. on December 28, 1955, when O'Keefe said he wanted "more time to think it over." He asked SAC Powers to "stop by again within the next couple of weeks." SAC Powers stressed to O'Keefe that time was "running out" and that if O'Keefe intended to do anything, he should not delay any longer. O'Keefe nodded to signify that he fully understood.

Specs waited and brooded until January 6, 1956, before he reached his personal point of no return. Of that climactic day, an FBI record reads:

At 2:15 P.M., on January 6, 1956, SAC Powers and SA Larkin again visited O'Keefe at the Hampden County Jail. O'Keefe agreed to be interviewed by them without hesitation and displayed to them a copy of the June, 1955, issue of *Coronet* magazine containing an article by J. Edgar Hoover entitled "What Makes an FBI Agent?" O'Keefe specifically referred to a statement in Mr. Hoover's article to the effect that the FBI makes no recommendations as to prosecution, but, instead, is strictly an impartial fact-gathering and fact-reporting investigative agency. It was obvious that he had given a great deal of thought to the fair and courteous attitude which previously had been exhibited toward him by Special Agents Larkin and Kehoe and by SAC Powers.

O'Keefe still displayed a reluctance to "talk." He was concerned about the publicity which would result and the repercussions which this publicity might have upon his family and friends. O'Keefe revealed that it was entirely foreign to his way of life to discuss his criminal activities with law enforcement officers. At the same time, he appeared to be developing an increasingly strong attitude of trust and confidence toward SAC Powers and Special Agent Larkin.

At 4:20 P.M., on January 6, 1956 [two hours and five minutes after the third interview with him began], O'Keefe made the final decision.

"All right," he said. "What do you want to know?"

From 4:20 P.M. until the interview ended at 4:55 P.M. O'Keefe recounted the details of the Brink's robbery. He named the other participants and explained the role which each had played in the crime.

It was a long story Specs told:

"Eddie Powers and John Larkin stayed in town for four days, hearing it. Each day they'd come over to the jail and I'd go with them into a kind of stall, an old isolation cell, and either continue or go over some special aspect. They were so intimate with the case they could ask me the most pertinent questions. But if I asked them any question, to fix a date in my mind, let's say, they wouldn't even answer me.

They weren't there to tell the story. I had to do it. They'd give me no help.

"They moved a whole FBI group into town, not to question me at the jail—the two of them did that alone—but to check facts at the end of each session. What I told them had to be checked against the known or half-known or unknown facts. What I said had to be transcribed and, I suppose, sent to Boston and Washington for further checking and instructions."

Specs would have to tell his story several times after that, and in the most exhaustive detail.

Under a great cloak of secrecy he was spirited out of the Springfield jail on January 12 and rushed to District Attorney Byrne's office in Suffolk County Courthouse, Boston. When agents informed Byrne that O'Keefe had made a full confession, Byrne said, "Fine, but that doesn't do me one bit of good. Specs, to get this thing going you'll now have to tell *me* the whole story, and when you finish telling it to me I'm going to take you into the grand jury, which is sitting now, and you're going to tell it to them."

Byrne's office and Boston police checked Specs' story as he told it; and when he was led before the grand jury the district attorney knew that the indictments would be forthcoming. They were.

On the same January 12, 1956, FBI Headquarters, Washington, released an announcement, which each of the robbers eventually convicted has cited in his appeal for a reversal—on the ground that it precluded the possibility of a fair trial:

UNITED STATES DEPARTMENT OF JUSTICE
Federal Bureau of Investigation
Washington 25, D.C.
January 12, 1956
FOR IMMEDIATE RELEASE

The Department of Justice announced that intensive investigation by the FBI for the past six years has resulted in the solution of the million-dollar Brink's robbery in Boston, Massachusetts, on January 17, 1950. The FBI today arrested six members of the gang responsible for the robbery. Two of the robbers are in prison on other charges, and one of them is dead.

J. Edgar Hoover, Director of the FBI, identified the six arrested persons as Vincent James Costa, Michael Vincent Geagan, Adolph Maffie, Joseph F. McGinnis, Anthony Pino and Henry Baker, all of whom reside in the Boston area. The two gang members now in prison are Stanley Albert Gusciora and Joseph James O'Keefe. The deceased criminal is Joseph Sylvester Banfield. James Ignatius Faherty and Thomas Francis Richardson are presently being sought by the FBI for arrest.

The arrests were made on complaints authorized by United States Attorney Anthony Julian of Boston and filed before United States Commissioner Francis H. Farrell, Boston. The complaints charged conspiracy to violate Federal laws; bank robbery and theft of Government property.

According to Mr. Hoover, the FBI's jurisdiction in the Brink's robbery is based upon the fact that cash, checks, postal notes and United States money orders of the Federal Reserve Bank and the Veterans Administration district office in Boston were included in the loot. The total amount reported lost in this robbery was $1,218,211.29 in cash and $1,557,183.83 in checks, money orders and other securities.

All of the persons named except Faherty were among the many witnesses who appeared before the Federal grand jury which held hearings in Boston between November 25, 1952 and January 9, 1953, in regard to the Brink's robbery.

The FBI's continuous investigation since the armed robbery occurred on the evening of January 17, 1950, has revealed the following:

The Brink's robbery was a product of the combined thought and criminal experience of men who had known each other for many years. The gang spent more than a year in planning the robbery and they started a systematic study of the Brink's organization after it moved to its present location on Prince Street in Boston.

Before the robbery was carried out, all the participants were well acquainted with the Brink's premises. Each of them had surreptitiously entered the building on several occasions after the Brink's employees had left for the day, and they made a study of Brink's schedules and shipments.

The planning for the robbery included several "trial runs" in which the gang members practiced their approach to the building in a truck and their flight over the "getaway" route. The gang abandoned plans to carry out the robbery several times when conditions were not favorable. During these occasions, one gang member was stationed on the roof of a building on Prince Street overlooking Brink's. He signaled the others with a flashlight. The last of these "false" approaches took place on the evening before the robbery.

During the early evening of January 17, 1950, members of the gang met in the Roxbury section of Boston and entered the rear of the Ford stake-body truck which had been stolen in Boston in November, 1949, to be used in the robbery. Including the driver, this truck carried nine members of the gang to the scene of the robbery. During the trip from Roxbury, seven of the men donned Navy-type pea coats and chauffeur's caps which were in the truck. Each of the seven also was given a pistol and a Halloween-type mask; each had gloves and wore either crepe-sole shoes or rubbers so that their footsteps would be muffled.

As the men approached the Brink's building, they looked for a signal from the "lookout" on the roof of a Prince Street building. The "lookout" previously had arrived in a stolen Ford sedan.

After receiving the "go ahead" signal, seven members of the gang left the truck and walked through a playground which led to the Prince Street entrance to Brink's. Using the outside door key they had previously obtained, the men quickly entered and donned the masks.

Other keys in their possession enabled them to proceed to the second floor where they took five Brink's employees by surprise. The seven robbers ordered the employees to lie face-down on the floor, tied their hands behind them and placed adhesive tape over their mouths.

145

Before fleeing with the loot, the seven armed men attempted to open a metal box containing the payroll of the General Electric Company; but they had brought no tools and were unsuccessful.

Immediately upon leaving, the gang loaded the loot into the stolen truck. As the truck sped away with nine members of the gang, the "lookout" departed in the stolen Ford sedan. The truck was unloaded at the home of one of the participants in Roxbury that same evening. Some members of the gang made a preliminary effort to count the loot, but they quickly dispersed to establish alibis for themselves.

On the night of the robbery, approximately $380,000 of the loot was removed from the house in Roxbury for security reasons. Additionally, the equipment used in the robbery was taken by a gang member for disposal. On January 18, 1950, another gang member took the remainder of the loot from the house; and several weeks later it was divided among the eleven men.

In addition to the cash and securities, the robbers took four pistols from Brink's. One of these was recovered by a Somerville, Massachusetts, police officer on February 5, 1950. It had been found by a group of boys near the Mystic River in Somerville.

Descriptions of the truck used in the robbery were obtained from persons in the vicinity of the crime scene. Pieces of an identical truck were found at a dump in Stoughton, Massachusetts, on March 4, 1950. This truck had been cut up with an acetylene torch.

During the FBI's six-year investigation, thousands of possible suspects were eliminated. Thousands of other persons, possible witnesses and individuals who could furnish background information concerning matters arising in various phases of the investigation, were interviewed. Circulars concerning a $100,000 reward offered by Brink's were distributed to all parts of the country, and no "tip" was overlooked.

Results of the investigation and all facts in the FBI's possession have been presented to District Attorney Garrett Byrne, Suffolk County, Boston, and the question of ultimate prosecution is a matter to be worked out between United

States Attorney Julian and District Attorney Byrne. The FBI will continue to make its investigative facilities available to assist to the fullest extent the prosecutive officials.

Those arrested will be arraigned before the United States Commissioner Francis H. Farrell while detainers are being filed against the two already in custody.

Background data on those arrested is attached:

Vincent James Costa, aged 41, who resides at 100 Pond Colony Road, Pembroke, Massachusetts, was arrested at the residence of Anthony Pino.

Adolph Maffie, aged 44, a resident at 118 Billings Street, North Quincy, Massachusetts, was arrested at his residence.

Anthony Pino, aged 48, who resides at 26 Kennebec Street, Dorchester, Massachusetts, was arrested at his residence.

Stanley Albert Gusciora, aged 36, is presently confined in the Western State Penitentiary at Pittsburgh, Pennsylvania. A Federal detainer is being filed.

Joseph James O'Keefe, aged 47, is now confined in the Hampden County Jail at Springfield, Massachusetts. A Federal detainer is being filed.

Michael Vincent Geagan, aged 47, who resides at 8 Gerald Road, Milton, Massachusetts, was arrested at Pier 17, Castle Island, South Boston, Massachusetts, where he was employed as a stevedore.

Joseph F. McGinnis, aged 52, who resides at 1662 Commonwealth Avenue, Brighton, Massachusetts, was arrested at 3077 Washington Street, Egleston Square, Jamaica Plain, Massachusetts.

Henry Baker, aged 49, who resides at 7 Lenox Street, Natick, Massachusetts, was arrested at 288 Talbot Avenue, Dorchester, Massachusetts.

12

Shortly after he told his story to the grand jury, Specs was brought before Judge O'Brien and pleaded guilty to the crime of armed robbery involving a mask. It was a staggering admission in Massachusetts. Stung by the robbers' escape from the Federal grand jury of 1952-53, and contemplating the day in 1956 when the state's own statute would expire, the Massachusetts Legislature had expanded the statute to ten years, rather than six, on crimes of this specific nature, and increased the maximum sentence to life imprisonment.

Specs was remanded to the Middlesex County House of Correction, East Cambridge, Massachusetts. Sentence was deferred and he was held without bail. He was placed under twenty-four-hour armed guard and his movements were restricted to such a degree that it amounted to solitary confinement. He saw nothing of his fellow inmates for ten months. His cell area was reinforced with bullet-proof steel. He didn't like it much:

"They weren't so much worried about somebody hitting me from inside the prison; they were afraid that somebody from the outside might somehow get in and do it. There were bomb scares during that time, leading up to my testimony in court. Somebody once tried to send me thirty roses, a symbol of death. The papers regularly carried reports that I had been sniped at, or might even be dead.

"The stories I read about plots to kill me before I could testify against those guys didn't hurt me, really. Once you've had the experience of being as close to death as I had been you don't fear it any more."

Richardson, according to Specs, was standing within several feet of Geagan, unloading a ship, when the FBI descended on Pier 17, South Boston, on the day of the big roundup. But he was able to slip away while the agents pounced on Geagan. He hid on the pier for a time, then fled.

As for Faherty, who also avoided the net, in Specs's words "he must have had a premonition of arrest that day and stayed away from his natural habitats."

The FBI put the two names on its list of "Ten Most Wanted Fugitives" and an extensive hunt began. It was to last until May 16, 1956. Specs made a study of that:

"Their hideout was a tenement apartment right nearby in Dorchester during all those months. The place had been procured for them by Tommy Ballou, helped by a fellow named Bill Cameron. Ballou's an associate of a lot of big-time racketeers, a thief himself. Lot of prison terms. Eventually he did a stretch for a wicked, sadistic, rotten mess of a cutting. He cut a man to pieces. The fellow will never be the same. His face is stitched like a baseball. He's a young guy, too, but ruined by that attack.

"Ballou supplied Faherty and Richardson with their needs: food from the supermarket and things like that. Cameron was a good enough guy. He was mixed up with hoodlums but still friendly with Assistant District Attorney Sullivan. Like a lot of others who had a way of sending word into the underworld, Sullivan suggested to Cameron that if he ever ran across the two missing Brink's robbers, or could get word to them, he should urge them to give themselves up; they were going to be caught anyway.

"It made common sense. You can't stay away from the Bureau for any great length of time. Everybody gets nailed, or dies. But in their desperation they decided to stay away.

149

And one night somebody killed Cameron, maybe just for suggesting what he did. I think I know who did it: a small, lame-brained little bastard who can't think about tomorrow.

"Well, when the agents finally came in to get them, there they were, the big dopes. Faherty and Richardson jumped up and tried to make a run for what turned out to be three guns they had left on a chair in the bathroom. The agents were quicker. There were signs all around of a fresh robbery, more than $5,000 in coins—mostly quarters—from the robbery of a cigarette-vending machine agency.

"The agents picked up Ballou, too, and he was indicted as an accessory after the fact."

The story that Specs hoped he would never have to read hit the Boston afternoon papers on May 3, 1956.

Gus was back in Boston. In chains.

The Boston *Traveler*, like the other afternoon papers, gave the story a smashing play:

Weeps, Claims Perfect Alibi
"NOT IN BRINK'S JOB" SAYS GUSCIORA
Brought Here in Chains—

Stanley A. Gusciora bluntly denied today he had anything to do with the fabulous Brink's million-dollar-plus robbery. The 36-year-old convict, former Stoughton resident, said he had a perfect alibi for the night of the record-breaking crime.

He made his statement shortly after arriving in chains in Boston, "loaned" by Pennsylvania to Massachusetts for the forthcoming Brink's robbery trial.

Authorities said the prisoner had made "certain admissions" bolstering the prosecution's case against the suspects under arrest. But there was no direct admission he had anything to do with the fantastic 1950 holdup.

Gusciora said his alibi would place him in Boston on the night of the robbery. He expressed the opinion Joseph J. (Specs) O'Keefe, indicted star witness for the prosecution, had "cracked up."

"He's gone," said Gusciora, adding: "He once told me if he ever did anything like that—like being a stool pigeon—he would positively be crazy—bugs."

Gusciora said three witnesses would place him at a lounge and bar on the night of the robbery. Two are women, he said. He named them as Jean Merrick, a show girl, and Helen Poskus, a former girl friend of O'Keefe's. The third was Adolph (Jazz) Maffie, one of the men indicted for the robbery. Maffie is in custody. He was with them an hour or two after the robbery, he said. He would not give the details of his alibi for the first hour of the holdup.

During the all-night train trip from Pittsburgh, Gusciora spoke bitterly to a *Traveler* reporter concerning Joseph F. McGinnis. McGinnis is one of the men in custody under indictment. Gusciora blamed McGinnis for a recent nervous breakdown he suffered in the Pittsburgh prison.

"This is only my second day out of the hospital," he said. "I've been in there for three months with a nervous breakdown—courtesy of Joe McGinnis."

Gusciora also said Massachusetts authorities have been trying for six years to get him to talk. "They've been trying to make a deal with me for the past six years. They 'married' me the day I went into the can."

Gusciora also said another prisoner at Pittsburgh had tried to get him to tell where Gusciora's share of the Brink loot was hidden. Gusciora contends he never got any; wasn't in on the job. He said the other convict offered to get the cash—wherever it was hidden—and hold it for safekeeping on a percentage basis.

Gusciora was bitter over the role being played by Joseph J. (Specs) O'Keefe in the case. At times Gusciora was bitter because O'Keefe has talked. But in other moments he appears to hold O'Keefe in high regard.

"He showed me how to live," Cusciora said. "Nothing but the best hotels, food and entertainment. We had four wonderful years."

The *Traveler* reporter who made the Pittsburgh–Boston trip with the prisoner asked if Gusciora had considered doing something to cut down his prison time.

151

"I've got nothing but time ahead of me," the shackled prisoner replied. "What have I got to gain by burying a lot of guys?"

Gusciora wept briefly when he was leaving the train at Back Bay station, where a big police detail had been assigned as a precautionary measure. Then he seemed to get a grip on himself as he was taken to police headquarters to be booked on the indictment warrants pending against him.

For the trip from Pittsburgh, he was the prisoner of Capt. Frank Wilson and Sgt. John Howland. One of them remarked afterward: "He's almost in a daze. It's like bringing him into another world. It will take him a couple of days to get his bearings. You've got to realize he's been in stir."

Another officer who has worked on the case for years said: "He's a far cry from the man we questioned five years ago. He's a broken man now."

Details of the remarkable return trip of Gusciora were contained in a front-page feature:

GUSCIORA IN MANACLES HAS "GENTLEMAN'S" MEAL

By Harry Friedenberg

After finishing his first steak in six years—eaten on a railroad dining car with one hand—Brink's robbery suspect Stanley Gusciora said: "I'd like to top this off like a gentleman—with crackers and blue cheese."

He was served them.

Gusciora was glad to be coming back to Boston. He was tickled pink to see Boston officers. Western State Penitentiary in Pittsburgh is "the toughest can in the country," he told officers.

Gusciora has lost much weight. He formerly weighed over 200 pounds. He's now down to 164. He was in a good mood, however, as he left Pittsburgh. He was amazed by the excitement caused by his presence. Newsmen and photographers met him.

A cameraman wearing a beret caused Gusciora to smile and remark: "Where's he from—*Harper's Bazaar*?"

Gusciora ate with one hand because his other was still manacled to a restraining chain around his waist. At his request, the dining car was opened early so he could eat. He had a large orange juice, "the first one of these in six years," a steak (medium rare), salad, French fried potatoes, dessert and coffee. And, of course, the blue cheese and crackers.

At all times tremendous precautions were taken to prevent Gusciora's escape. His train stayed in the station one hour before leaving Pittsburgh. Police guarded it constantly. Word was flashed to other police departments ahead of the train. At each stop a cordon of police circled it while it was halted.

Gusciora's coming to Boston marked the first time in the history of Pennsylvania that a prisoner serving time was removed to stand trial in another state. After the Brink's trial here, Gusciora will be returned to the Pittsburgh prison.

Richard Lamere, a reporter for the same paper, was given access to Gus that same day after he reached the office of Assistant District Attorney Edward M. Sullivan. Here are excerpts from the *Traveler* article which Specs was shown that night.

Q. Are you going to meet with Specs?
A. I will have to see him. Eventually I'll bump into him.
Q. How do you feel about Specs?
A. Not too good.
Q. Why?
A. He caused me a lot of trouble.
Q. What trouble?
A. Don't you see the trouble I'm in.
Q. Are you innocent of the Brink's robbery?
A. I certainly am.
Q. How will you plead when you are arraigned?
A. I'll plead innocent.

Q. Are you and Specs friends?

A. We were the best of friends before.

Q. Is there any reason why Specs would involve you in the Brink's case?

A. We were the best of friends—he must have a good reason. I can't understand his reasoning.

Q. Did he ever loan you any money?

A. I loaned *him* money.

Q. Does Specs owe you money?

A. He doesn't owe me anything.

Q. What are your assets?

A. I have about $175. That's it.

Q. How did you get it?

A. I earned it in six years of scraping and saving.

Q. You mean in prison?

A. Yes, I was a printer down there.

Q. How much did you earn?

A. Fifteen cents a day for six years.

Q. Have you heard from Specs?

A. Yes, in letters.

Q. When?

A. In the first year.

Q. About what?

A. General conversation about our troubles.

Q. Did he say anything about the Brink's holdup?

A. Sometimes, indirectly, he said the FBI were down questioning and hounding him.

Q. Who is paying for your lawyers?

A. My folks are taking care of them.

Q. When did Specs tell you that to be a stool pigeon he would have to be "positively crazy, bugs"?

A. Seven years ago.

Q. Where did he tell you that?

A. A case involving a stool pigeon came out in the papers. We were discussing the case and Specs said the only excuse for stooling would be that a guy was crazy.

McGinnis, Pino, Baker, Maffie, Geagan, Costa and, a bit later, Gusciora, Faherty and Richardson pleaded innocent when arraigned. In lieu of bail, all were held. The bail asked for Pino, Baker, Maffie, Geagan and Costa was $200,000. In McGinnis's case it was $300,000. The grand jury had returned eighty-five indictments against McGinnis, eighty against Pino, and the others proportionately fewer—down to the eight indictments against the somewhat extraneous Ballou.

Gus spent his first night in the East Cambridge jail, separated by three empty cells from Specs. Guards said they did not converse.

From the time he confessed, O'Keefe had been under almost constant questioning about the hiding places of the Brink's cash. On this score he could give no aid or comfort to the authorities. Then, early in June, 1956, there came an unexpected break. The FBI progress report handles this laconically but, as usual, thoroughly:

At approximately 7:30 P.M. on June 3, 1956, an officer of the Baltimore, Maryland, police department was approached by the operator of an amusement arcade. "I think a fellow just passed a counterfeit $10 bill on me," he told the officer.

In examining the bill, a Federal Reserve note, the officer observed that it was in musty condition. The amusement arcade operator told the officer that he had followed the man who passed this $10 bill, to a nearby tavern. This man, subsequently identified as a small-time Boston underworld figure, was located and questioned. While the officer and amusement arcade operator were talking to him, the hoodlum reached into his pocket, quickly withdrew his hand again and covered his hand with a raincoat he was carrying. Two other Baltimore officers who were walking along the street nearby noted this maneuver. One of these officers quickly grabbed the criminal's hand, and a large roll of money fell from it.

The hoodlum was taken to police headquarters, where

a search of his person disclosed he was carrying more than $1,000, including $860 in musty, worn bills. A Secret Service agent,* who had been summoned by the Baltimore officers, arrived while the criminal was being questioned at the police headquarters; and after examining the money found in the bill changer's possession, he certified that it was not counterfeit.

This underworld character told the officers that he had found the money. He claimed there was a large roll of bills in his hotel room—and that he had found that money, too. The criminal explained that he was in the contracting business in Boston and that in late March or early April, 1956, he stumbled upon a plastic bag containing this money while he was working on the foundation of a house.

A search of the hoodlum's room in a Baltimore hotel (registered to him under an assumed name) resulted in the location of $3,780, which the officers took to police headquarters. At approximately 9:50 P.M., the details of this incident were furnished to the Baltimore Field Office of the FBI. Much of the money taken from the money changer appeared to have been stored a long time. The serial numbers of several of these bills were furnished to the FBI office in Baltimore.

They were checked against serial numbers of bills known to have been included in the Brink's loot, and it was determined that the Boston criminal possessed part of the money which had been dragged away by the seven masked gunmen on January 17, 1950.

Of the $4,822 found in the small-time criminal's possession, FBI agents identified $4,635 as money taken by the Brink's robbers. Interviews with him on June 3 and 4, 1956, disclosed that this 31-year-old hoodlum had a record of arrests and convictions dating back to his teens and that he had been conditionally released from a Federal prison camp less than a year before—having served slightly more than two years of a three-year sentence for transporting a falsely made security interstate. At the time of his arrest, there was

* The Secret Service has jurisdiction over counterfeiting.

a charge of armed robbery outstanding against him in Massachusetts.

During questioning by the FBI, the money changer stated that he was in business as a mason contractor with another man on Tremont Street in Boston. He advised that he and his associate shared office space with an individual known to him only as "Fat John." According to the Boston hoodlum, on the night of June 1, 1956, "Fat John" asked him to rip a panel from a section of the wall in the office; and when the panel was removed, "Fat John" reached into the opening and removed the cover from a metal container. Inside this container were packages of bills which had been wrapped in plastic and newspapers. "Fat John" announced that each of the packages contained $5,000. "This is good money," he said, "but you can't pass it around here in Boston."

According to the criminal who was arrested in Baltimore, "Fat John" subsequently told him that the money was part of the Brink's loot and offered him $5,000 if he would "pass" $30,000 of the bills.

The Boston hoodlum told FBI agents in Baltimore that he accepted six of the packages of money from "Fat John." The following day (June 2, 1956) he left Massachusetts with $4,750 of these bills and began passing them. He arrived in Baltimore on the morning of June 3 and was picked up by the Baltimore police department that evening.

The full details of this important development were immediately furnished to the FBI office in Boston. "Fat John" and the business associate of the man arrested in Baltimore were located and interviewed on the morning of June 4, 1956. Both denied knowledge of the loot which had been recovered. That same afternoon (following the admission that "Fat John" had produced the money and had described it as proceeds from the Brink's robbery), a search warrant was executed in Boston covering the Tremont Street offices occupied by the three men. The wall partition described by the Boston criminal was located in "Fat John's" office, and when the partition was removed, a picnic-type cooler was found. This cooler contained more than $57,700, including $51,906 which was identifiable as part of the Brink's loot.

157

The discovery of this money in the Tremont Street offices resulted in the arrests of both "Fat John" and the business associate of the criminal who had been arrested in Baltimore. Both men remained mute following their arrests. On June 5 and June 7, the Suffolk County grand jury returned indictments against the three men—charging them with several state offenses involving their possessing money obtained in the Brink's robbery.

. . . The money inside the cooler was wrapped in plastic and newspaper. Three of the newspapers used to wrap the bills were identified. All had been published in Boston between December 4, 1955, and February 21, 1956. The FBI also succeeded in locating the carpenter who had remodeled the offices where the loot was hidden. His records showed that he had worked on the offices early in April, 1956, under instructions of "Fat John." The loot could not have been hidden behind the wall panel prior to that time.

Because the money in the cooler was in various stages of decomposition, an accurate count proved most difficult to make. Some of the bills were in pieces. Others fell apart as they were handled. Examination by the FBI laboratory subsequently disclosed that the decomposition, discoloration and matting together of the bills were due, at least in part, to the fact that all of the bills had been wet. It was positively concluded that the packages of currency had been damaged prior to the time they were wrapped in the pieces of newspaper; and there were indications that the bills previously had been in a canvas container which was buried in ground consisting of sand and ashes. In addition to mold, insect remains also were found on the loot.

Even with the recovery of this money in Baltimore and Boston, more than $1,150,000 of the currency taken in the Brink's robbery remains unaccounted for.

The wholly unexpected seizure of some of the hot money after all those years was an unparalleled break for the prosecution. Its star witness-to-be, Specs, got a break, too. But it wasn't the kind he would have chosen:

"Reading those stories about how Gus looked when they brought him back from Pennsylvania, things like 'he's almost in a daze,' didn't surprise me too much. Before we went to the can in 1950 I used to worry about it. He'd black out now and then and when he came to a minute later he'd have no memory of having been out like a light.

"In July, 1956, a little over two months after they brought him back to Boston, Gus began getting a series of dizzy spells and vomited a lot. They put him in sick bay. On July 9 he asked for a priest. The fellow showed up and they talked a while. Then Gus suddenly got out of bed. He stood in front of the priest, apparently trying to say something, then fell over, unconscious. Gave his head a bad wallop. Two hours later Gus was dead."

An autopsy revealed a brain tumor and acute cerebral edema.

In a sense, it was almost as much of a bad break for the remaining eight defendants as the unveiling of the stolen money. If Gus had lived, Specs would have become a reluctant witness against him in court and, without really intending to, given others in the conspiracy a possible legal advantage. Instead, with the death of his friend, estranged or not, O'Keefe was more determined than ever to see the others condemned.

13

AFTER REPEATED EFFORTS TO DELAY OR PREVENT THE TRIAL, the impaneling of the jury commenced on August 7, 1956. It can be said with complete safety that seldom in the history of Anglo-Saxon jurisprudence have so many been called and so few chosen. In the next two weeks nearly 1,200 prospective jurors were eliminated. In the following week about 500 more were screened.

Judge Felix Forte, who was somehow to weather the next two months on his bench, heard some all but unprecedented excuses given to avoid service in his jury box.

"I would like to see no man convicted; I don't want to give punishment," cried panelman Patrick F. McGrath of Brackett Street, Allston.

A panelman named Richard H. Burton, a welder in a Cambridge plant, proclaimed that he was such an admirer of the FBI that he could never bring himself to render a verdict against its findings.

An antagonism toward one of the defense lawyers was singled out by John Brook, a Back Bay photographer. He said, "I've noticed that lawyer is frequently the lawyer in criminal cases. That's guilt by association." He was promptly excused.

One who seemed eager to be a member of the jury, a man named Anthony DiGuillio, swore solemnly that he had never taken part in any conversation with anyone concerning the Brink's robbery. He swore he had never discussed the case, which by that time had all but replaced relations between the sexes and all their ramifications as a topic of conversation not only in Boston but throughout the nation. He was excused.

Hundreds were dismissed for assuring Judge Forte that they had formed unshakable opinions in the case. One man who was being questioned by Paul Smith, in over-all charge of the battery of defense lawyers, blurted, "I think they're all guilty." Another said, "I don't think I'm smart enough to serve on a jury." Another avowed, "I've been expressing opinions on this case ever since it came up. Nothing that happens here could change my mind."

In the end, fourteen men were accepted, the customary twelve good men and true and their two alternates. But it was not until August 31, the twentieth day of the court case, that District Attorney Byrne was able to rise and make his opening statement in behalf of the commonwealth. The handsome, gray-thatched attorney had his case well in hand, but he had waited too long to fling it at the jury box like a handful of beans. He rolled it on his tongue, savoring it like a fine brandy.

His opening praised judge and jury, described the place of an opening in a trial, made a scholarly perusal of the jury system dating back to the sixteenth century, and went into the most microscopic details of the huge fabric of the crime. To wit:

". . . It was agreed among themselves that the distribution would be made at a later date. It was agreed that if there was any trouble money—by trouble money they meant any that might get them in trouble—that it should be destroyed. . . . When they reached the house of Maffie and dished it out of the containers, they found they had approximately $100,000 of new money, trouble money. They determined that it was the duty and responsibility of McGinnis to destroy it, even though he expressed the idea at the time that he

161

had some scheme whereby he would run it through a coffee mill and make it look old.

"And it was also agreed, Mr. Foreman and Gentlemen of the Jury, that if any one member did anything that would endanger the liberty or the life of another, that he was to be exterminated.

" . . . We will show you that on one particular day the Federal Bureau of Investigation swooped down and got them all, with the exception of two, the defendant Richardson and the defendant Faherty.

"The learned Justice of this court will explain to you whatever law there is to be explained. From him you take the law, the law of flight, consciousness of guilty. We will show you that Richardson and Faherty absconded, that a nationwide search was made for their apprehension—television, radio, newspapers, [agents] watching their homes, watching their associates, going down to where they worked. They could not be found.

"But three months later, through the diligent search of Mr. Powers of the FBI and his associates, they found them in Coleman Street, out in Dorchester. And when they broke in there, Mr. Powers, followed by Mr. Larkin, Mr. Kehoe and Mr. Schwortzer, there was Richardson and Faherty. Richardson and Faherty could have run into the bedroom, which provided an exit. But they dashed for the washroom, where there was no exit.

"Kehoe, out of the side of his eye, saw three guns in the washroom. He swung Richardson around into the arms of Schwortzer and he and Larkin dived at Faherty and tackled him just as Faherty's hands were within inches of the guns. You will have those guns— two .38's, fully loaded, one .32, fully loaded, which Richardson and Faherty were dashing to and would have reached, except that the agents knocked them down. . . ."

The district attorney had made the most of his time with

162

Specs and the FBI. But he still needed Specs O'Keefe to paint the picture he promised the jury. Specs obliged with a mammoth mural.

O'Keefe's approach to the witness chair was heralded in Boston newspapers as something of an event hardly a degree below that of the Boston Tea Party. There were all kinds of stories dissecting probably illusory plots to do him in before he could blow his memorable whistle.

People literally fought for seats in Judge Forte's courtroom, which could take only sixty-five spectators. A woman courtroom buff, an otherwise placid housewife, literally gave battle with a policeman guarding the approaches to the courtroom—and was arrested while kicking and yelling.

O'Keefe took the stand midway through the session of Friday, September 14, 1956.

> All eyes in the courtroom were on him. [wrote the *Post's* Grace Davidson] The spectators saw a lean man smoothly dressed in a slate-blue worsted suit, a white shirt with the new-fashion English collar with wide points, a red tie meticulously knotted. If he had been sitting in the jury box, he might have looked like a haberdashery salesman doing a citizen's duty.
>
> Specs, with his balding, egg-shaped head seemed a far cry from the commando-type bandit often associated with a sensational and frightening robbery. There on the witness stand he appeared so mild that it was difficult to imagine him capable of the hatred and venom he may now feel for his old friends sitting before him in the defendants' box.
>
> Defendants McGinnis, Pino and Costa sat together in the back row of the dock. Not a muscle moved in their fleshy, scarred necks. Reporters sitting directly behind them have ample apportunity to study the back of their heads.
>
> Only "Jazz" Maffie also in the same row turned his head for a better view of Specs. His dark face with its rugged profile wore an imperturbable mask. There was no indication he was once Specs' chum.

Specs was on the stand during most of the seven days, a performance that was part purge, part persecution of his enemies in the combine, and part penitence. Objections by the staff of defense lawyers, flew like flakes in a Boston blizzard.

The direct examination was conducted by Assistant District Attorney Frederick T. Doyle, a mammoth man who dramatically called on Specs to point out the robbers, one by one, and then led him quickly to the genesis of the historic heist:

Q. Did you have a conversation with the defendant Pino?

A. Yes.

Q. Will you be kind enough, Mr. O'Keefe, to tell us substantially, the best as you can recall, the conversation you had with him, doing it in this form, what he said to you and what you said to him?

A. Well, he called me specifically to discuss a particular thing. He asked me would I be interested in a score, a robbery, and I asked him what kind, what type of a thing it would be; and he said he couldn't tell me, couldn't enlighten me then, but if I agreed to go along he would give me further details. So I told him it was pretty thin, that I'd have to know something about it in order to tell him whether or not I'd go along. So he said it was a big robbery, a big score, and he said it was bigger than Sturtevant's. And I said, "How much bigger could it be?" He said, "It probably would be thirty or forty payrolls at one time." So I told him I'd have to know more about it, you know—who was going to be there, who the participants would be . . . So he said, "We'll talk about it later."

Q. Is that all was said at that time?

A. That's the important part of the conversation.

Q. Well, now, sometime later in the early part of '48

or thereabouts, did you hear from the defendant Pino?

A. Yes. I had a specific meeting with him.

MR. SMITH. Pardon me, may we have a time, some-time better than "the early part of '48"?

MR. DOYLE. That is as near as he can fix it.

THE COURT. You may bring that out in cross-examination.

MR. DOYLE. These gentlemen don't carry diaries.

In the course of his first day on the stand Specs heard himself referred to politely by a judge for the first time in his life.

The defense had lodged Exceptions No. 565, 566 and 567 in close succession in an attempt to block O'Keefe from relating what was said in a pre-robbery meeting involving himself, Pino, Costa and Gusciora:

MR. SMITH. I don't know what is going to be brought out, I don't know what is coming up here, from this point on.

THE COURT. I think we must proceed in an orderly manner, not interrupted at every question. There are not only the rights of the defendants involved here. This man, the witness, is a guest of the Court and as a witness he has the right to tell his story, to answer the questions without constant interruption.

Specs nodded contentedly.

These words must have been pleasing to the witness whose life has been twice threatened. [wrote Grace Davidson. The star reporter was struck, too, by the very presence of O'Keefe in this monumental role:]

All his life, whenever he felt the lure of crime, he had been involved in petty jobs. The Brink's robbery—the Big Score—summed up a dream-come-true in his world. This was his chance, his big chance. He talked about the plans as if he were a small-time businessman getting ready for an unexpected windfall.

Specs was returned to his isolation cell in the East Cambridge jail under heavy guard and spent a weekend that did not come under the heading of restful.

He returned the following Monday and put in a day of soul-baring that elicited sixty-six more objections from the defense. Some of his testimony concerned the machinery of the complicated holdup. In telling of one planning session, involving himself, Gus, McGinnis and Pino, at Pino's house, Specs testified:

A. Pino said we could do either one or two things. We could either surprise them, surprise the [Brink's] people, remain in the building, hide in there and surprise them when they came in early in the morning, or perhaps we could even grab the head guy, whoever he would be, we'd find out who he was, and make him open the vault. But McGinnis said that plan wasn't practicable because perhaps two people had to open the vault, or maybe they had to give the word to the ADT that the vault would be opened, and they may have had some kind of signal back and forth between ADT and themselves; and also, McGinnis said that the neighborhood, that particular neighborhood, would then be coming to life with truck into the market, and we might encounter difficulties in traffic, leaving the place, if we did it that way.

The witness testified, too, that Pino had called a meeting of ten of the conspirators before Boston went on daylight saving time in the spring of 1949 and had announced bitterly that the job would have to be put off until the following winter. By the time the group next met, it numbered eleven. Baker had been released from the Norfolk, Massachusetts prison colony on August 22, 1949, where he had been held since 1944 for "breaking and entering and larceny" and for "possession of burglar tools." Pino was on hand at the colony's gate to drive him back to Boston—and declare him in on the Big Score.

As the summer of '49 waned, Specs testified, the matter of procuring certain of the tools needed for the robbery was taken up at what might have been called a meeting of the subcommittee:

A. Gusciora and I occasionally would run into McGinnis and Banfield and Costa at Pino's house, and talk about what we would do in the fall. At one conversation Pino said we would have to have some tape and rope, to tie the men up, as we would have to go at least that far. So he told us, Gusciora and myself, to get it if we could.

Q. Who said this?

A. Pino. McGinnis told us not to purchase the material —to get it, sneak it, steal it, rather than purchase it, so that there would be no traces of it at some later date, so that it couldn't be traced. That early fall Gusciora and I did get the tape and rope . . . from Sears Roebuck's.

Q. What did you do with it?

A. We cut it into lengths. Maybe thirty lengths or so, thirty or forty lengths. We tied knots in every end, not to keep it from fraying but to make it easier to tie off, if and when it came time to use it.

Q. Where did you keep the rope?

A. In Pino's house. We cut it and tied it in Pino's place.

According to Specs, one of the sharpest points of dissension within the fold, during the planning days, was the opposition to Pino's heavy dependence on impressive fire-

arms. He testified that he and Gus were the first to veto
Pino's suggestion that machine guns be used. They found a
willing ally in Maffie.

A. I told Maffie that Tony wanted us to use machine
guns. He said, "Oh, to hell with him, he ain't going into
the joint. We ain't going to use no machine guns down
there."

Costuming called for special conferences, of course:

Q. Now, would you be kind enough, Mr. Witness, to
tell his Honor and the jury what was said at that meet-
ing in reference to the clothing that was to be worn
on the night of the venture.
MR. SMITH. I object.
THE COURT. Objection overruled.
MR. SMITH. Exception. [No. 624]
THE WITNESS. That was a discussion—
Q. What was said?
A. There was a talk about shoes that would be worn
that night.
Q. What was said about them?
A. Tony told—
MR. SMITH. Pardon me. If that is the answer, I move
to strike it.
THE COURT. Was that part of the conversation?
THE WITNESS. Yes, sir.
THE COURT. Then it may stand.
MR. SMITH. Exception. [No. 625]
THE WITNESS. And Tony told us that we should all get
crepe-soled shoes to prevent any noise when we did go
in the building.
Q. What else was said about the clothing?
A. He said that our clothing on the night would have
to be more or less uniform. We couldn't go in there with

nondescript clothing, ragged clothing, or anything like that, dirty clothing; that we would have to go in with a uniform appearance similar to the appearance of the Brink's guards.

Q. And was there a conversation at the same time in reference to masks?

MR. SMITH. I object.

THE COURT. Objection overruled and exception noted.

Q. Give that conversation to his Honor and to the jury.

A. Tony told us that he had already procured the masks that we were to use, and he brought them out in a box. There were maybe twelve of them, maybe more. They were a full type of mask, a hoodlike, and he said that we would all have to wear those because of a previous incident where something happened, where a man was identified by his mask having slipped and that this type of mask couldn't possibly slip. We tried them on.

Q. Was there any conversation as to where Pino procured the masks?

A. Yes. He said he got them in Chicago and there was little likelihood that they would be traced, the purchase of them would be traced.

Smith took his 651st exception while Specs was testifying about the role of Pino, Costa, Gusciora, Baker and himself in the split-second business of getting keys made while those who remained behind in Brink's held their collective breaths. The objection annoyed the judge:

THE COURT. On what ground did you object here, Mr. Smith? Here is a man that testifies that some of the defendants and the witness went out and changed locks and got keys. Now, you objected to that testimony. On what ground? If you are going to object, you have to state a rule of law here.

169

MR. SMITH. I am prepared to state a rule of law; but I am not prepared to argue this in front of the jury.

THE COURT. Well, you can state the rule of law. I will ask you now, because you objected in front of the jury. I am going to ask you to state the rule of law upon which you base your objection.

MR. SMITH. My rule of law is that in any case where a witness testified involving several defendants, he should be required to limit his testimony to which defendant he is referring. He should also be required to testify as to who did what acts, so that on cross-examination, counsel for the defendant or several defendants may have an opportunity to learn what he is to cross-examine about, instead of having him repeat the whole story.

THE COURT. Very well. You may bring those things out in cross-examination. I am glad to have on record the basis of your objection. Mr. Doyle, you may now proceed.

MR. SMITH. Now, may I take an exception to your Honor's statement of law in front of the jury?

THE COURT. I did not state any law; you did. I asked you to state the law, so that we would know on what you are basing your objection. Proceed, Mr. Doyle.

O'Keefe listed the allotted chores of the robbers on the night of the robbery, but only over repeated objections by the defense:

A. [McGinnis] was supposed to take care of all monies. If there was any money that needed to be changed from one type to another, he would do it. If there were any monies to be cleaned of any notations on them, or anything such as that, he would do it. He was to destroy all evidence, all equipment, all evidence of the crime.

Pino would be in the truck. He would take a position

170

in the truck and remain inside the truck all the time that the robbery was in progress.

Costa would be on the roof and give us the signal whether or not the vault was open.

Banfield was to drive the truck.

Maffie was to take his position in the line of us going into Brink's . . . so was Faherty. Gusciora was told his position as I was told mine.

Tony told me that I would be the man who would open the doors, lead them in.

Baker was told to carry. Tony told him that he and Richardson were to carry in the bags that we were to use.

Q. Did you see any bags in Pino's house?

A. Yes . . . of two types. One was such as is used in wastepaper shipment or the shipment of wool. The other was a smaller bag of heavier construction. I don't know just what—it was a heavy bag.

Q. Do you recall any name that appeared on the heavy bag?

A. The only name that I recall on the smaller bags was the word "LaPlata."

Q. I show you Exhibit 21, Mr. O'Keefe, and ask you to to examine it.

A. Well, if that wasn't one of the bags we took there, it's a brother to it.

MR. SMITH. I move that that be stricken, your Honor.

THE COURT. It may stand.

MR. SMITH. Exception. [No. 667]

Specs then told of Pino's decision not to strike during the Christmas season and of his warning to Gus and himself not to undertake "any other business that would interrupt our being available for whatever night he told us to be ready." Mr. Doyle then attempted to narrow the focus on the robbery night itself, but his first question directed at O'Keefe in the witness chair, at this juncture, produced another courtroom tempest. A bizarre one, to boot.

Q. Well now, you testified here Friday that on January 17, 1950, you were a participant in the Brink's robbery?

A. Yes.

MR. SMITH. Wait a minute. I object.

THE COURT. In what sense are you using the word "robbery," Mr. District Attorney?

MR. DOYLE. That they went down with guns and grabbed a couple of million dollars in cash and change.

THE COURT. All right.

MR. SMITH. I ask that the jury be forcefully instructed to disregard that statement.

THE COURT. No, the jury shall not disregard the statement. We have got to call this episode by some name and not use silk gloves.

MR. SMITH. And I object—

THE COURT. The word "robbery" is an English word and every person understands it. Later on, the court will instruct the jury as to the technical requirements of a robbery and, in fact, perhaps we may do it right now to save further objection.

MR. SMITH.—May I have my exceptions recorded for the record?

THE COURT. To what?

MR. SMITH. I except to your Honor's statement and I except to your Honor's refusal to instruct the jury the statement made by the district attorney is prejudicial, and I except to your Honor's refusal to instruct the jury. [Exception No. 674-A]

THE COURT. I am going to read the definition of the word robbery from an English dictionary, Mr. Foreman and Gentlemen, and then I am going to give you, very briefly, the technical, legal definition of the word robbery so that we will have no further discussion whenever the word robbery is used.

The defendants here are charged with the commission of the crime of robbery, and for that reason the word robbery is to be used in this trial. This is not a trial of some other crime . . . but of robbery.

Now, I will give you the definition of robbery in the English dictionary—and I have here Webster's New Collegiate Dictionary—so that all parties can use the word robbery whenever they intend to express the general meaning of robbery.

"Robbery. An act or practice of robbing. Larceny of property from the person or immediate presence of another in possession thereof, accomplished by violence or putting him in fear." That is the definition of the word robbery in ordinary English.

When the time comes that I shall charge you, Mr. Foreman and Gentlemen, I shall charge you that the legal definition of robbery is the taking of personal property from a person by the exercise of violence or putting in fear, taking that property from that person with intent to deprive him of that property permanently.

Now, there isn't too much difference between the two, so I now instruct all lawyers that they can use the word robbery because I have explained to the jury both the dictionary definition and the legal definition. And the rights of all defendants are duly saved. [Exception No. 675]

MR. SMITH. Well, let's get the rights of the defendants—

THE COURT. That is enough. I have saved your rights and you are entitled to nothing more.

173

The prosecutor moved O'Keefe along to an especially sensitive area of the trial:

Q. If I may revert to the meeting a week before Christmas, you testified that the defendant Baker was there?

A. Yes.

Q. Did Baker say something about how the participants should act with the loot?

A. Yes. Baker spoke at that meeting and he said that we should take some precautions against any individual connected with the robbery if the individual did something to endanger the others—such as buying a Cadillac or a house or something of that nature, or making his position known. He said we should have some method planned so that we would do away with that person, whoever that person would be.

Q. And what was said by the others, if anything?

A. The others agreed to that.

Q. You can't say "agreed." What did they say, sir?

A. They spoke along the same lines.

MR. SMITH. I move to strike.

THE COURT. The answer may stand. And may I ask you, Mr. Witness, did anybody object to that statement at that meeting?

THE WITNESS. No, sir.

THE COURT. The objection is overruled and exception noted.

MR. SMITH. An exception.

THE COURT. Yes. [Exception No. 676]

MR. SMITH. And objection to your Honor's question and exception to the ruling which I assume your Honor is now going to make.

THE COURT. Very well. [Exception No. 677]

Judge Forte and the chief defense attorney again tangled as Specs attempted to explain the meaning of Costa's various signals from the roof adjacent to Brink's. In the confusion Smith asked, "Is there a question before the witness now?"

The judge tartly replied, "I think if you do less objecting and more listening, you will probably get the question."

O'Keefe's third day on the stand was devoted largely to his account, under direct examination, of the big night and the division of the spoils. The flow of his testimony was again interrupted by repeated objections, however, including a resumption of the semantics struggle between the judge and Smith. The springboard this time was Specs' testimony about one of the five dry runs on Brink's.

> A. We proceeded down through the playground until we got to the point where we were to receive the signal from Costa, and we received no signal, so we returned to the truck and abandoned the project for the night.
>
> Q. That was on Thursday night?
>
> A. Yes.
>
> Q. Preceding the robbery? The robbery, as I understand it, was on a Tuesday night?
>
> A. Yes.
>
> MR. SMITH. I object.
>
> MR. DOYLE. It has already been testified to about forty-seven times.
>
> MR. SMITH. Well, I don't know about that. I am objecting to the term "robbery" despite your Honor's ruling.
>
> THE COURT. Very well. Then it will be placed on record that you object every time the word "robbery" is mentioned.
>
> MR. SMITH. What's that?
>
> THE COURT. Let it be on record that you object every time the word "robbery" is mentioned. You need not waste an objection to it every time.
>
> MR. SMITH. I am objecting to this question now, if your Honor please, and would like a ruling.

THE COURT. Well, rephrase your question, Mr. Doyle.

Q. I understand, sir, that it was on Tuesday that the robbery took place, January 17; am I correct?

MR. SMITH. I object.

THE COURT. What would you call the incident to which the witness refers as having taken place on January 17, 1950?

MR. SMITH. I didn't understand that he referred to any incident on January 17. But apart from that, I don't think that I can categorize it, and I don't think your Honor can until all the evidence is in and until there is evidence to that effect—until there is evidence that the jury has a right to believe and may believe, and until the jury comes to a conclusion as to certain—

THE COURT. I am going to say now that I shall not entertain any further objection on that ground because there has already been such evidence, if the jury believes it.

MR. SMITH. If they believe it.

THE COURT. Exactly. There is evidence that some persons were held up at the point of a revolver, their hands were tied and their feet were tied, a revolver was pointed at them, that they were frightened and property was taken out. Now, that's enough to constitute robbery.

MR. SMITH. If they believe it.

THE COURT. But there has been evidence of robbery in this case. Both parties can refer to it as a robbery.

MR. SMITH. Well, we don't. We don't want to refer to it as a robbery. I think that is for the jury to decide, your Honor, and I don't think the commonwealth should refer to it as a robbery until there is a final determination.

THE COURT. Very well. Now, I don't want any more objections on that ground. It is understood that if the word is used, your rights will be protected and the rights of all the parties protected, because I am sure that the word may appear time and again and, therefore, I say this merely in the interest of saving time. But your rights and the rights of every defendant will be protected to the same extent as if you deliberately objected every time the word was used and your objection was overruled each time and an exception noted each time.

MR. SMITH. Exception to your Honor's ruling just now. [Exception No. 693]

Q. Now, Mr. O'Keefe, I believe that, for discussion purposes, it was Thursday night that you testified to?

A. Yes.

Q. The Thursday night preceding the robbery?

MR. SMITH. I object, if your Honor please.

THE COURT. I am going to ask the jury to go to their rooms and I am going to confer with counsel. We will suspend for now.

There is no stenographic report of what ensued in Judge Forte's chambers. It must have been interesting. When court was resumed eighteen minutes later, the word "robbery" no longer ignited Mr. Smith.

So it came to pass that Specs was able to get to the point that a straining courtroom had come to hear:

A. So we remained in that position until the first one noticed us—the man who came out of a vault. I am quite certain it was Mr. Lloyd. The other people were working, bending over and working and fooling around with the bags. When Lloyd saw what it was he was taken aback and the others straightened up. The man nearest Lloyd wanted to go for his pistol, but Lloyd told him he didn't want any trouble. Lloyd said, "Don't, don't."

We told them to remain quiet. They froze. We called the guy that was closest to Lloyd over and made him open the door. The man opened the door and I removed

177

his pistol and I went in and told him to lay down on the floor. We all went in then, myself, Gusciora and Maffie, Geagan and Richardson, Baker and Faherty. Gus tied them up. He put a piece of tape across each mouth, and we quickly went to work filling the bags and the hampers.

And during that time, a buzzer sounded, and it was sort of a shock to us, but we didn't stop working. We continued until finally somebody pulled my coat and said—Oh, first, Gusciora came to Lloyd and asked him who that was outside and what was the meaning of that buzzer. So Lloyd told him. He said, "Apparently, somebody wants to come in," or some words to that effect. I don't know exactly what he said.

The buzzer was insistent. Somebody pulled my coat and I turned around—I afterwards learned it was Geagan—and he said, "Let's go around the other way and grab the guy." So he and I went out into the executive offices and we opened two doors there and peeked out into the garage, and the man who had been pressing the buzzer was walking away. He just walked away, so we didn't bother him. We let him walk. He was too far away from us to have caught him at that time, anyway.

Q. Go ahead. Continue. What did you do after you and Geagan went out and made the observation?

A. We went back into the vault room and continued to remove the stuff that was there.

Q. How many vaults were there in the vault room?

A. One vault was open. There were two.

Q. Continue. You kept moving the stuff?

A. Yes. And because of the interruption by the buzzer we had to hasten our work and we were afraid that possibly the man who pressed the buzzer would cause us some trouble, so we prepared to leave.

Q. Well, now, while you were there removing the bags,

the Brink's bags and the contents, did you see anyone try to open a big box?

A. Yes. Gusciora. There was a box on casters and it was painted between gray and white, and he tried to force the lock of that box, but he was unsuccessful. We had no tools with us to open the box.

Q. Was there any particular one of the group of seven that was directing operations?

A. It was a scramble then, at that time.

Q. Go ahead and tell us what happened.

A. So we prepared to leave the building. We all left the vault area, and I met Baker in the hallway between the fourth door and third door and he asked me who was with them people back there. I told him I didn't know, that I didn't think anybody was with them. So he said, "Well, somebody has got to be with them."

So I went back to stay with them until I got word that it was all right to leave.

Q. Well, tell his Honor and the jury what you observed and what you did when you were in the process of leaving the building.

A. In going down the stairs from the second floor to the first floor there was a great mass of bags, you know, great big old bags. The door hadn't been opened to them out on the truck yet. Then it was opened suddenly and we threw all the stuff on the truck and we left.

The entire courtroom moved to the edge of its collective seat as Specs was led into the matter of the split:

Q. What rooms [in Maffie's house] did you move it into?

A. From the yard you go through a little rain shed into the kitchen, take a right off the kitchen, and right into a room, a fairly large room. That's where we put it.

179

Q. Was there any furniture in that room, as you recall?

A. There was a large table in there—no other furniture. Maybe a chair.

Q. Any heat on in that room?

A. I don't believe there was any heat. There was enough heat on us in there.

(Laughter in the courtroom)

THE COURT. That may go out.

Q. Tell us what happened there.

A. We cut the bags open, put it on the table, as much as we could. Whatever change there was we dumped into a hamper. We started counting the money. We stayed there for a couple of hours. During that time McGinnis and Banfield came into the room. Costa came in and took twenty thousand.

A great deal of the money was in block form. It was tied, bound, with the amount on the outside of the wrapper. One particular package of money I remember was very small. It contained ten $1,000 bills, which we put aside. It was obviously new money—bills that had never been separated from each other, new, brand-new. We put it aside.

We separated the money, tried to arrange it as best we could for counting purposes.

Q. Did you count the new money that night?

A. Roughly we counted it . . . ninety-eight or ninety-six thousand.

Q. You said you also found a package with ten $1,000 bills?

A. Yes, a single package in which was ten $1,000 bills.

Q. Did you observe anything about those bills?

A. No.

Q. At some time McGinnis and Banfield came into Maffie's house?

A. They came in while we were working there.

Q. How long after you arrived was it that Banfield and McGinnis came into Maffie's?

A. Maybe an hour or so—an hour and a half or so.

Q. What took place while McGinnis was there, and Banfield?

A. I remember particularly Baker had a bag in which he said was one hundred thirty or one hundred thirty-five thousand. But when it was cut open it contained veterans' checks. I remember McGinnis being there at that time.

Q. Any money taken from the loot that night?

A. Yes. Costa and Richardson. Richardson said he needed some money, and he took $20,000. Costa said he wanted some money for himself and Tony. We said, "Take the same amount Sandy did." So he took two packages of $20,000 for himself and Pino.

Q. Any other money taken out of the house that night?

A. Yes. Baker said that we shouldn't leave all the money in that room—we should separate some of it so that in the event anything happened, it all wouldn't be found. So he took a hamper and filled it up with money in block form. Amounted to $380,000. Somebody helped him out into his car with it, and he left with it. He said he was going to put it in a friend's—some place where it would be safe.

Q. Did you determine roughly the amount you had taken from Brink's?

MR. SMITH. I object.

THE COURT. He may answer that yes or no.

MR. SMITH. Exception. [No. 696]

Q. What was the amount?

A. Roughly . . . I think it was one, one, four, three.

Q. One million?

A. $1,143,000.

Q. Did that include the $98,000 new money?

A. No. We didn't figure to be able to use that money anyway.

Q. How about the ten $1,000 bills?

A. Those were put up on the mantelpiece so that they wouldn't become lost in the confusion. They were to be destroyed.

Q. Were you the last to leave?

A. The last three to leave were myself and Jazz and Gus.

Q. Richard left with $20,000?

A. Yes.

Q. Costa left with $40,000?

A. That's right.

Q. Baker with a hamper—$380,000?

A. Yes.

Q. What did you do before you left?

A. Well, we piled the money as closely as we could in the corner, covered it with a blanket, and also covered the new money that was in the opposite corner with a blanket.

Before the luncheon recess that day in Judge Forte's court, Specs got around to his own short-lived association with the Brink's money.

Q. At some time did you get some of the money?

A. Yes. On the second day when we met back at Maffie's, Gus insisted we take our end, take our end then because we knew from the count that we were going to get at least a hundred apiece.

Q. One hundred what?

A. $100,000. So we selected the monies we wanted to take with us; laid them in packages, five blocks of $40,000, then bound the whole package together with wire, with boards on the ends. That night either Mc-

182

Ginnis or Banfield went out and got a truck and parked it alongside the gate at Maffie's. We moved all the money out onto the truck—a stake-body truck with no cover or anything. McGinnis said it would be better that way. He did have other objects in the truck, though, ashcans or something. When we left the house it was clean—there was nothing there that could connect it with the robbery.

The needle and thread of O'Keefe's testimony, directed by the prosecutor, now stitched McGinnis more closely to the conspiracy—though he had the impressive alibi of having been talking during the time of the actual robbery to the very police officer who was to conduct the Boston end of the investigation. Slowly, surely, Doyle led the witness through the maze of his arrest on suspicion shortly after the robbery, the sending of word to McGinnis to pick up the parked car in whose trunk rested the $200,000 belonging to Specs and Gus, and an eventual meeting between Specs and McGinnis.

The courtroom sighed with disappointment when Smith at this point asked for another whispered conference at the bench. What actually transpired follows:

MR. SMITH. I submit, if your Honor please, that unless there is going to be an admission by McGinnis, unless the commonwealth represents that there will be some admission by McGinnis, the question should be stricken, or the answer, rather, should be stricken.

THE COURT. How is it relevant?

MR. DOYLE. Unfortunately, your Honor, I can't get close enough to the bench to hear.

THE COURT. He said that unless there is an admission by McGinnis, he objects to what McGinnis may have said to the witness. Is there an admission of some kind?

MR. DOYLE. I know what he means, that there should

be a limitation as to McGinnis. Well, this relates to the distribution [of the Brink's money]. That is a part of the plan.

THE COURT. I think I would rule that the distribution of the loot is still part of the general scheme, so I am going to allow it.

MR. SMITH. Exception. [No. 696]

The attorneys and the court stenographer returned to their positions and Doyle pressed his point:

Q. Where did you have the conversation [with Mc-Ginnis]?

A. I met him in the area of the store that he owns.

Q. And what was the conversation?

A. In regards to getting my money.

THE COURT. The question was: What was the conversation?

THE WITNESS. The conversation was that I told him I wanted my money at that time, and he said, "Do you have a place to put it?" I said, "Yes, I do. I've made arrangements with one of the others to take care of it for me." And he said, "In that case, you can have it any time you want. Give me a couple of days and we'll meet some place and I'll give it to you."

O'Keefe, at this point, told how he and Gus met McGinnis at an obscure roadhouse between Stoughton and Brockton, and were handed separate suitcases. His money was $2,000 short, and, he testified, he believed Gusciora's was $3,000 shy. McGinnis blandly promised the two somewhat menacing figures that the shortage was accidental and would be made up.

They had the more serious beef of the gun that had been found in the Mystic River.

184

A. We asked him why the guns were thrown out there and who threw them there. He said that Banfield had thrown them there. We also asked him whether the rubbish might be thrown out there: the checks and the bags and the clothing and so forth. He said, "No, those are all taken care of, but the guns were thrown out there by Banfield."

It was a disturbing turn of events, the witness went on, and described how he and Gusciora then confronted Pino and asked him if he knew why the guns had not been destroyed as planned. Pino swore ignorance of the whole matter. The witness related, also, his pressing need to conceal the somewhat condensed hoard that had come to him.

Q. Did you see Maffie after you had gotten your money?

A. Yes . . . the next day, in Roxbury. I told him I had the suitcase with me and I wanted to transfer it. He had told me he had a safe place to plant it.

Q. What did he say when you told him you had the suitcase with you?

A. He said, "Okay, get it," and I did. And I put it in his car.

Q. I see. And then what took place?

A. I left. We split.

Q. Did you ever get your money back from Maffie?

A. No, sir.

The discovery of the dismembered truck on a Stoughton dump one mile from Gus's home sent Specs and Gus back to McGinnis, the witness testified.

Q. Now, would you give the conversation?

A. I asked him why the truck was found in the town

in which I lived and in which Gusciora lived. He said, "I didn't know you lived there." I said, "Well, it may have been all right that you didn't know I lived there because I haven't lived there long, but surely you knew that Gus lived there. He's lived there fourteen or fifteen years." He said on his word, he didn't know.

McGinnis had other disconcerting news for O'Keefe, Specs brought out during his long third day in court.

A. We had one conversation shortly after the robbery. He told me, "I've got the money that Baker took, the $380,000. But it came back $35,000 short." I told him, I said, "I don't see how it could be thirty-five short because we were exact in the count before putting it in the hamper."

Q. What did McGinnis say?

A. McGinnis said, "Well, that's what he gave me back." He said he threw it on the truck and took it out in the country. He didn't tell me where he stowed the money.

Q. Did you [then] have a conversation with Baker?

A. Yes. I asked him about the shortage. I asked him what happened to the money, and he said he didn't know. He said maybe there was a mistake in the count. I told him that there was no mistake in the count. So he said he couldn't conceive of the person to whom he took it taking a part of it; he just couldn't understand how the money was short.

Before the trying day's end, as Specs gave testimony about a visit he had received from Baker during his stay in Bradford County Jail, he had a chance to unload before his erstwhile friends in the dock a matter close to his heart.

Q. By whom did you send word [to Baker] to come to see you?

186

A. John Carlson.

Q. Do you know where John Carlson is now?

A. I have a very good idea.

Q. Well, where can I reach him?

A. I don't think you or anybody else can reach him.

MR. SMITH. All right, now. I move that that be stricken, and the jury be instructed to disregard the question and answer.

THE COURT. First of all, that is only admissible as against Mr. Baker, and therefore the other defendants have no rights.

MR. SONTAG (for Baker). I will make the same motion.

MR. SMITH. Your Honor, this is prejudicial to all defendants.

THE COURT. Oh, no, it isn't. It is not to be considered against anyone except Baker. Now, I will be glad to strike it out if counsel for Baker will either produce the man or admit he cannot be reached, so you won't argue later and say, "Where is he?—Why didn't the Government produce him?" If you're not going to argue that way, I will strike out the answer.

MR. SONTAG. Your Honor, I think the entire subject matter is—

THE COURT. All right, you don't want to answer the question. Then the question may stand. Your objection is overruled and I note an exception for you.

MR. SONTAG. Your Honor, I am not—

THE COURT. Proceed now. That is the end of it.

MR. SONTAG. Exception.

THE COURT. I have saved an exception for you.

Through the remainder of that day Specs related his attempts to collect, primarily from McGinnis and then individually from the other co-conspirators. With almost every man, he swore, he ran into pleas of poverty or bitter grumblings against McGinnis. Costa claimed to have been shorted $25,000 by McGinnis, Richardson $20,000, Pino $10,000. No one wanted to go with Specs and challenge the richest of the bandits. In fact, Specs told the court, Maffie offered to go out and commit enough burglaries to repay O'Keefe personally. But Specs would not hear of it.

In the end, Specs went after McGinnis alone, before and after his imprisonment in Bradford County Jail. But all he could wrest from the strong man, he testified, was $600 and a series of empty promises and confusing charges against the others.

O'Keefe's direct examination consumed only the first minutes of his fourth day on the stand, and the trial's thirty-first day. In that brief exchange with Doyle a final spear was launched at the portly figure of Pino, but McGinnis was impaled, too.

Q. Well, now, Mr. O'Keefe, a short time after January 17, 1950, did you have a conversation with the defendant McGinnis wherein the name of Lieutenant Crowley was mentioned?

A. Yes. McGinnis told me that at the time we were down to Brink's, Crowley was talking to him in his store and talked for quite a while there. He told me that while Crowley was there he, McGinnis, called Tony—

Q. He what?

A. He called Pino at his house and told him that if he wanted to be seen by Crowley to come right over to the store and make believe he was going to buy a bottle or something, or buy a bottle. He said that Tony did come into the store while Crowley was there. But he also told me that Pino had showed so much emotion. He was sweating and fidgety and nervous to the point that McGinnis thought that he might give away to Crowley the fact that something had happened just prior to that.

Q. And so, in 1954, you went to jail in Springfield.

A. Yes, in August.

Q. Were you visited personally by any of the defendants.

A. No.

Q. Did you correspond with any of the defendants?

A. Yes.

Q. With what defendant did you correspond?

A. With Pino originally, and then I switched my attentions in correspondence to McGinnis.

Q. Did you receive any written answers from either McGinnis or Pino?

A. No.

Q. When did you first tell your story, the story, if I may characterize it, of your connection with Brink's?

A. The first week of January of this year.

Q. To whom did you tell it?

A. To Agent Powers and Agent Larkin and Agent Kehoe.

Doyle turned and gazed for a moment at the eight defendants and then, with a brief bow to Paul Smith, curtly said:

"You may inquire, sir."

14

THE LONG DUEL BETWEEN PAUL SMITH AND SPECS O'KEEFE began on an almost courtly note. But it was a deadly game the two played. Neither could afford to drop his guard. O'Keefe was out to search the innermost recesses of his gift of almost total recall. Smith's determination was to demolish the jury's confidence in the commonwealth's principal witness and, in doing so, fend off the impending life sentences which dangled heavily over the crowded defendants' box.

Like an astute boxer, Smith began with a series of jabbing questions concerning the number of times Specs had prowled in Brink's before the robbery. It was questioning intended to portray O'Keefe as what he was, a common burglar. But it led to a jolting climax.

"Every person in that box was there with me," Specs volunteered, icily surveying the prisoners' dock.

In response to a question as to how he gained admission to that supposed Gibraltar of counting houses, Specs gave Judge Forte's courtroom an elementary course in lock-picking. His tone and manner were academic.

> Q. How did you open those doors [before the keys were made]?
> A. With celluloid . . . a piece about four inches long by two and a half inches wide. You see, sir, between every doorjamb and the lock there is a space to insert

a very thin object. I inserted the celluloid—it was the heavy-duty type—and pushed back the tongue of the lock.

Q. How long did it take?

A. I couldn't say exactly. Maybe a minute. Maybe less.

Q. Why at one time did you substitute an ice pick for the celluloid?

A. Well, Mr. Smith, there is always danger in using celluloid. In the event it snaps off, it remains jammed in the door. Unless the door could be opened, the flakes could not be retrieved—and that might endanger our plan.

Q. What if the ice pick cracked?

A. If a sharpened ice pick snapped, the broken object would drop to the floor and we could retrieve it.

The consensus in the Boston press was that Specs had handled himself well in his first brush with the defense. Other figures in the court scene visibly drooped with fatigue at the end of the first day of cross-examination, notably the prosecuting attorney Doyle, who clashed several times during the day with defense counsel. "I can't stand on my feet another minute," he said at day's end. "I want to get home."

But Specs was jaunty almost, for a self-effacing man, at the end. He had survived a day that he had privately dreaded, as must any witness in his position. He had faced the spokesman of his eight enemies and weathered the inquisition without a bruise.

Emile Dumas, the veteran sheriff who convoyed Specs back to Middlesex jail that evening, said of his charge, "He's an easy man to get along with. I had him thirty years ago in jail. He's no trouble. Real agreeable, neat and mild . . . He's got a lot of things on his mind, a lot of things to get off his chest these days."

That same day, a Massachusetts voter in the state's gubernatorial primary cast a write-in ballot for Specs. This minuscule vote of confidence, if it was that, was quickly nullified. A check showed that another vote for the same high office was cast in behalf of Trigger Burke, then awaiting execution at Sing Sing.

The second day of cross-examination was more barbed. Smith went after O'Keefe on the latter's use of language. He berated the witness's assertions that Pino, "who reads only comic books," had told the others that Costa's car would "impede" police chase and that the show of machine guns would be "more impressive" inside Brink's.

"I am not a grammartarian, whatever you call it," Specs tried to explain. He agreed after much dueling on this point that he may have quoted the substance of conversations rather than a verbatim report.

The day's session broke up in a welter of confusion. The tangle began with a dramatic question:

> Q. Who was the brains of this thing, as you have referred to it?
>
> A (pointing to prisoners' dock). You can pick one of them out. I don't care which one.
>
> Q. Do you know a gentleman by the name of Kimball?
>
> A. Kimball? You would have to give me more than just Kimball. I maybe know two or three people named Kimball.
>
> Q. Did you ever meet a man by the name of Kimball at the Essex Hotel in Boston?

There was an immediate protest from the prosecution, and the legal rivals headed for Judge Forte's bench, to the dismay of the avid followers of the courtroom scene. This was their whispered exchange:

> THE COURT. This is cross-examination and I should give you a wider latitude, Mr. Smith. If you are going

to connect Kimball up, all right, but just mere insinuation would not be enough. Now, I don't want you to disclose your purpose, but leaving it in the air is not enough.

MR. SMITH. All I know is that you have said to me, Judge, when I objected, that you assumed that there was going to be something said by the commonwealth to connect it up.

THE COURT. That was because I heard the district attorney's opening. I haven't heard any opening from you. Now, if you are going to tell me now that you are going to introduce evidence that Kimball had something to do with this, I will take your word for it.

MR. SMITH. The witness asked me—and there was no objection at the time—to name the chief or the boss of this thing, and I am getting ready to do so.

MR. DOYLE. Oh, no, no.

THE COURT. Not unless you have evidence, Mr. Smith.

MR. SMITH. I have an affidavit. What am I supposed to do—introduce it now and let them see it?

THE COURT. No, but you have got to produce it by credible evidence. I will take your word for it. You don't have to produce for me any affidavit.

MR. DOYLE. He comes in here and says, "Do you know a man named Kimball?" Of course, in the case of *Kelly* vs. *Halox*, there are certain limitations on cross-examination and—

THE COURT. I have already ruled that in cross-examination there is a wider latitude than in direct.

MR. DOYLE. If your Honor please, matters of defense do not come out until the defendant opens. You cannot bring out a matter of defense in cross-examination until the defendant has opened, because in that way you can see the materiality of it. But to ask a witness whether he knows a man named Kimball, asking questions like that and going through it that way, well, that's out.

MR. SMITH. I am going to follow it up. I don't intend to stop there.

MR. BYRNE. The witness has said, "You can pick him out of the box." He has limited it to the box.

MR. DOYLE. And Kimball is not in the box.

MR. SMITH. The defendant has a right to prove that somebody else committed the crime.

THE COURT. I am not going to add any more to what I have already said. I have told you my feelings. If you tell me that you are going to produce credible evidence in mentioning that name, I will allow you to do it.

MR. DOYLE. That Kimball committed the crime?

THE COURT. Yes.

MR. SMITH. No, if your Honor please. I don't think I am under any obligation to the court or to the commonwealth to disclose at this point why I am asking that question. All I am asking is, "Do you know a man named Kimball?" Now on direct examination that would be perfectly admissible.

MR. DOYLE. Of course not; not until it can be tied up.

THE COURT. In other words, what I don't want you to do is put in insinuations without evidence.

MR. SMITH. I have no such intention. I am going to follow it up. My next question is going to be something else involving Kimball.

MR. DOYLE. Well, here is the point: he is now trying to put in through cross-examination what he claims is like an affirmative defense, and I submit he is not entitled to do so. He is not entitled to do so until he makes an opening.

THE COURT. Give me the case again.

MR. DOYLE. The case is *Kelly* vs. *Halox*. It's an early case.

MR. SMITH. Let's look it up now.

MR. DOYLE. All right. It's almost four o'clock, Judge.

194

THE COURT. All right.

(End of conference at the bench)

THE COURT. The jury are excused until tomorrow morning at ten o'clock.

The name "Kimball" appeared briefly, but only briefly, the next morning the thirty-third day of the trial. "He" came up in the first question directed at Specs:

Q. Mr. O'Keefe, yesterday afternoon at recess, I asked you whether or not you ever met a man by the name of Kimball over at the Essex Hotel in Boston. Do you recall the question?

MR. DOYLE. I object. I pray your Honor's judgment.

THE COURT. The question is excluded.

Q. Do you know a man by the name of William Kimball, Mr. O'Keefe?

MR. DOYLE. I pray your Honor's judgment.

MR. SMITH. Yes or no to that, Mr. O'Keefe.

MR. DOYLE. I pray your Honor's judgment.

THE COURT. That is excluded.

MR. SMITH. May we come up to the bench?

(Conference at bench, at which the following took place)

MR. SMITH. I thought we were agreed in the lobby that I should ask the question and the witness would be ordered to give the answer yes or no?

MR. DOYLE. I object to that.

THE COURT. Would you allow the district attorney to ask O'Keefe if he knew Archbishop Cushing, Mr. Smith?

MR. SMITH. Sure I would.

THE COURT. Oh, no, you know you wouldn't. I have looked it up, so I am going to exclude the question.

MR. SMITH. That is perfectly all right with me, but I thought we had an agreement in Your Honor's lobby last evening that I should ask him this question.

THE COURT. You people discussed that among your-selves. We left it this way: you were going to ask the question and I was going to rule on it. Do you want to make an offer of proof?

MR. SMITH. Yes.

THE COURT. Make your offer of proof now and we will proceed.

MR. SMITH. I offer to prove that if the witness were allowed to answer, he would answer yes.

THE COURT. All right. I will note your exception. [Exception No. 709]

(End of conference at bench)

Just as, earlier, there had been an objection raised by Smith as to whether it was proper to call the Brink's robbery a robbery, now there came an objection on the part of the prosecution over calling Specs a robber. It evolved out of Smith's cross-examination pertaining to the establishment of alibis in the immediate wake of the stick-up.

Q. Didn't you say on direct examination that it was agreed that everybody would prepare alibis in advance?

A. No, sir, I said it was agreed that those who worked on this thing, the participants, would return to their normal activities. If somebody formed an alibi after-ward, it was all right with me.

Q. So it had been agreed they would return to their normal activities?

A. Yes.

Q. And, of course, your normal activity was going out and robbing people, right?

MR. DOYLE. Don't answer that. I object, your Honor.

MR. SMITH. I will withdraw it.

MR. DOYLE. Oh, no. That's like kicking you and say-ing, "I apologize."

THE COURT. That was highly improper, Mr. Smith.

196

You shouldn't have asked that question. I hope the jury will completely disregard it, because I admonished the jury at the beginning to divorce themselves, their minds, of anything that they read or heard about this case, before the case began. I want to repeat that. You are to decide this case on evidence which is admissible, which is proper for your consideration. The last statement was not proper, and let the matter be closed. Proceed now, Mr. Smith.

MR. SMITH. Mr. O'Keefe, what were your normal activities in January of 1950?

MR. DOYLE. I pray your Honor's judgment.

THE COURT. Well, I will see counsel at the bench on that.

For reasons best known to himself, Smith made much of the fact that the chauffeur's cap the robbers left behind them on the night of the heist was Specs'. Smith pursued this point, and more, after briefly skirmishing with the proposition that O'Keefe may not have been in on the robbery at all—a point he quickly discarded.

Q. Now, at that time that you went back to the vault room, were the other participants leaving the place?

A. Yes.

Q. And you were the last one to go back into the vault room?

A. I believe I was.

Q. Do you recall saying, at any time when you went back to the vault room after the others had left, "I'm going to fix those so-and-sos"?

A. That, of course, never was said, Mr. Smith.

Q. All right. Do you recall going back and saying, "I'm going to fix those . . ." hold that for a minute. I'm not certain of the exact language.

A. Bastards?

Q. Bastards. All right. Do you recall saying that "I'm going back and fix those bastards"?

A. That never was said, sir.

Specs O'Keefe's thirty-one hours of testimony, covering seven days, was ended. The defense promptly announced it would call ninety witnesses to test the credibility of his long and detailed story. But first there were odds and ends for the state to clear up. It produced the locksmith Jake Dana to point Pino out in court and testify that he had made keys for him. It produced 15,576 bits of currency, totally $54,548, the rotting remains of the $98,000 in new and consecutively numbered bills which McGinnis neglected to destroy, as bargained. In all, the commonwealth used sixty witnesses, resting its case with testimony from FBI Agent Kehoe, who told of the rough and tumble capture of Richardson and Faherty and of a remarkable explanation Geagan had given him, in April of 1951, when questioned about a sudden rise in the man's standard of living.

Kehoe said he questioned Geagan about two homes he bought in 1950 after the robbery. He asked Geagan where he got the $5,000 for a down payment on the second of these homes, and the man replied that it was money he had saved from the Merchant Marine during 1943 and 1945 and money he had earned as a longshoreman.

"I told him he had also bought a new car, was paying a hundred dollars a month on it, another hundred dollars a month for the second house and fifteen a month for storm windows he had bought for it," the agent testified with typical thoroughness. "I then asked him how much money he made a year and he said three thousand dollars.

" 'How can you live as you've been living on that kind of money?' I asked him.

"Geagan shrugged and answered, 'I just can.' "

Defense Attorney Smith waived his opening.

"Mr. Foreman and Gentlemen," he said, "the district attorney made a lengthy opening and very ably. You know what an opening is. I will not waste your time or the court's time by making one.

"The defense will produce witnesses and it is up to you jurors to determine if they are credible. It will be for you to determine the defendants' guilt or innocence."

The first witness called by the defense was Arthur J. Ahearn, a retired Boston police officer, who testified that several days after the robbery he had demonstrated to other police officers, including his superior, that the Brink's locks were a "joke." He opened the five doors leading from Prince Street to the vault room with a simple fingernail file, averaging fifteen seconds per entry, he testified. He produced the same file from his pocket in court and Smith—over Doyle's objections—introduced it as evidence that "anybody," not necessarily his clients, could have stolen the money on the night of January 17, 1950.

Smith next attempted to prove that the Boston police had been gagged, so far as its relations with defense counsel were concerned. In the course of this delving it was disclosed that the police had lost a report by Lieutenant Crowley, made shortly after the robbery, in which the police officer stated that he was speaking with McGinnis in the latter's liquor store at the time of the robbery and with Pino "about that time."

Eleanor Maffie, the handsome wife of Jazz and mother of his two children, took the stand to support his alibi that he was dining with her at a tavern named Jimmy O'Keefe's while Brink's was being robbed. It was a determined and courageous attack on Specs' testimony about Jazz's participation in the titanic theft. But not a happy time for the wife or the husband she tried to save.

On direct questioning, Mrs. Maffie testified that when she and her brother arrived at the restaurant at seven o'clock to meet Jazz for dinner, they found him talking to a police officer. She identified the officer first as "Lieutenant Crowley," then as "Lieutenant Cronin," and in hapless confusion concluded, "I am really not sure of anything."

Under the fire of Doyle's cross-examination Mrs. Maffie said it was a "Sergeant Condon" who was talking to her husband at the time Brink's was being robbed.

"You know that Sergeant Condon is dead, don't you?" Doyle asked her, knowingly. Mrs. Maffie replied that she believed she had heard something to that effect within the past month.

"You were in error when you named 'Lieutenant Crowley' and 'Lieutenant Cronin'?" Doyle pounded away.

"Yes," Mrs. Maffie said nervously. "I'm surprised I didn't say his name was Maffie."

Before he excused her, Doyle made the witness say she may have had dinner with her husband before seven o'clock that night, or after seven-thirty, and that he was not even there when she arrived—but appeared "fifteen or twenty minutes later."

Maffie's sister and father were brought to the stand to hack away at O'Keefe's story. The sister, Mrs. Margaret Connolly, testified she was a daily visitor to the home of her parents, surely must have visited them during the period when—as Specs testified—the home served as the drop for the Brink's money and the discarded clothing used by the robbers. She saw no sign of these things, Mrs. Connolly swore, and she challenged O'Keefe's description of the Maffie dining room. It was a fully furnished room, she said. She acknowledged she knew Specs, but, staring coolly at the seven defendants seated around her brother, she said she had never seen them before in her life.

The father, eighty-three-year-old Nicola Maffie, speaking through an interpreter, identified his son in the dock and said of the others, "I have never seen any one of those people before in my life." Jazz wept.

The wife of Sandy Richardson was briefer and much more to the point than other defense witnesses. She testified that when she arrived at her home at 6:45 P.M. on the night of the robbery, there was Sandy, snoring in a living-room chair. She couldn't rouse him, she said, because "he had been drinking." Richardson's twenty-one-year-old son, Thomas, Jr., corroborated that testimony and added a touch of his own. The father was so drunk, he said, that he had dropped a lighted cigarette on the sweatshirt he was wearing. The cigarette had burned through the shirt and into Richardson's chest without awakening him, the son swore.

To Faherty's defense came a retired police officer, Patrick J. Ryan, and an ex-waitress, Dorothy Lipfin, mother of four. They testified stoutly that they were with Faherty in a bar named Gustie's throughout the period of the robbery. Their stories could not be shaken by the prosecution.

Geagan's alibi, supplied by his wife and substantiated by a neighbor, was that he was busy—during the period of the robbery—washing the Geagan infant's clothing in their basement.

Before the defense rested its case, alibis were introduced for all except Henry Baker, and O'Keefe's long police record was read to the jury.

None of the defendants took the stand in his own defense.

Speaking in behalf of Baker, Defense Attorney Henry Sontag said briefly:

"Baker's only offense was that he was a good Samaritan who visited Specs O'Keefe in a Pennsylvania jail." He pointed to testimony from a Brink's vault room guard to the effect that the robbers, as he recalled them, were all of the same height. "Baker is six inches shorter than Maffie," he appealed to the jury.

Attorney Robert DeGiacomo spoke feelingly for Maffie. It had been brought out during the trial that Maffie gave FBI agents a tussle when they went to his home to arrest him after an indictment had been handed down. In the course of a scuffle in Maffie's bedroom, ending in his being subdued and handcuffed, either Mrs. Maffie or one of the children—

weeping on the ground floor of the house—called the Boston police department. DeGiacomo touched on that in his plea to the jury:

"This issue in the case is a simple one," he said. "The guilt or innocence of the defendants I shall not enumerate. There is one issue that goes beyond: Did the witness, O'Keefe, lie?

"The truth will out and your obligation now is to weigh these facts and come to what you think is the truth. The commonwealth propounds to you through the testimony of a convicted thief—an admitted thief—that the man Maffie and the others with him should be convicted. It is on his word they call on you gentlemen to say these men are guilty.

"And what does the defense say? It was the defense that brought out that this man's family—he who O'Keefe says is a thief—it was this man's family who called the police.

"Is there such a thing as consciousness of innocence?

"Does a man who took a gun and held it up to a grill and took a million dollars—does that man call the police?"

He begged the jury to believe Mrs. Maffie. "Her story was not fantastic and hard to believe," he said. "She is not a professional witness and a smiling wit like O'Keefe."

Attorney Lawrence O'Donnell, counsel for Geagan, Faherty and Richardson, spoke for an hour and a half in their defense, protesting their innocence and excoriating the FBI and Specs.

"The Federal Bureau of Investigation wanted a conviction in this case at any price," he charged. "Their attitude was: 'Get this monkey off our backs. Get a conviction, no matter who or how.'

"Democracy is in danger," he continued, "when one's liberty is at the mercy of this parasite O'Keefe, diseased, crime-hardened, and of depraved mind.

"Mind you, O'Keefe, as a result of collaboration with the FBI, becomes an adviser to law enforcement after a lifetime outside the law. That's the well-spring of your information.

"How would he know the story? I suggest to you that Mr.

O'Keefe read about it. And now he wants this television plot to go over. How much credibility can you give this man? It cannot be said that the FBI has a case against these defendants, because it bases what it has on a polluted source."

The gist of Chief Defense Attorney Smith's summation was that O'Keefe was a colossal liar and the defendants had been deprived of their right to a fair trial by the publicity the case had been given in advance.

He called Specs' long performance on the witness stand "the greatest dramatic production in the history of trials in this commonwealth." He said O'Keefe was a liar and that the robbery could never have happened in the way he said it did.

"This is the first case where the defense has come in and carried the burden of proof," Smith cried. "This is a shocking display . . . a tremendous build-up, tremendous production." He named the many defense witnesses and asked the jury if it was going to say they all committed perjury ". . . and O'Keefe, the thief, told the truth?"

Smith struck at what he felt were soft spots in the commonwealth's case, particularly the prosecution's failure positively to link Pino to the theft of the truck. Then he returned to his main target:

"What it all comes down to is Mr. O'Keefe. This self-confessed thief, this self-admitted convict, this man who gave his address as 'I have no home.' This poor orphan of the storm, this individual was put on the stand and instead of the 'deses and doses,' after studying his language for seven months, he came in with a pretty steady story.

"We never expected to break O'Keefe in cross-examination. You don't think, after seven months of preparation, that O'Keefe was going to break on the witness stand? All we wanted him to do was to make certain statements that we could later show to be false.

"Of course, we would have liked him to crack on the stand and say, 'Yes, I'm lying,' but he was a student. He had studied his lines well. He said he wasn't a 'grammatarian,' " Smith said, advancing to the rail of the jury box, his voice rising to a shout. "But I'll tell you what he is," he roared, smashing his fist down on the rail. "He is a liar!

"He is a liar because it never happened, the way he said it did. It defies the imagination. It's something out of science fiction.

"He got on the stand prepared to lie and he did lie. He dodged everything he couldn't answer. His story was the greatest thing since the days of Frank Merriwell. In his testimony he said that he and Gusciora and Banfield cased Brink's. He always had someone with him who is now dead.

"In any event, here is a thing that defies science fiction. Imagine these men going into Brink's some twenty-seven times. They went into any room they wanted. Bear in mind from the testimony of witnesses, no one knew when the people in there were going to leave the building, because the hours were so irregular.

"Twenty-seven breaks! Does it need twenty-seven visits in a vault room to see where the safe is? Any thief could get in once and case the joint and then make a set of plans . . . We are dealing with a psychopathic person, a person with a demented mind.

"Now O'Keefe says that Pino said to them, 'Let's use machine guns,' and then he quotes Pino as using a lot of high, flowery phrases—Pino the comic-book reader.

"Well, how are you going into Brink's with machine guns and then carry out all this loot and all the debris, etc. What are you going to do with the machine guns? There couldn't have been any such suggestion. That's gilding the lily.

"Are you going to say that this thief, this convict, is telling the truth and Patrick J. Ryan, a disabled war veteran, is lying?

"To convict these defendants, you have to say that Dorothy Lipfin is lying and that O'Keefe, the thief, is telling the truth." He ran down a list of other defense witnesses and drew the same admonition at the end, including "that wonderful human being Nicola Maffie. He would not lie. He would have taken his son by the ear and thrown him out of the house if anything like that went on.

"Here you have decent married women, respectable people, people without records, coming in here and telling the truth. Are you going to jail all of them for perjury. That is the indictment you are preparing against them if you do not believe them."

15

Dᴵˢᴛʀɪᴄᴛ ᴀᴛᴛᴏʀɴᴇʏ ɢᴀʀʀᴇᴛᴛ ʙʏʀɴᴇ's ᴀʀɢᴜᴍᴇɴᴛ ɪɴ ʙᴇʜᴀʟꜰ of the commonwealth, on the afternoon of October 5, 1956, remains a classic of its kind:

"May it please the court, Mr. Foreman and Gentlemen of the Jury.

"Might I say at the very outset that I have been around the district attorney's office for many years. I have witnessed and participated in the trial of many cases. Never in my experience have I witnessed the patience and ability exemplified by one of the greatest justices of all time, Justice Felix Forte of the Superior Court."

[A conversation which Boston authorities had overheard between McGinnis and Pino had indicated earlier that the two robbers were hopeful of "straightening out" judge, jury, district attorney and every other honest person who stood between them and their liberty. The conversation, mostly unprintable because of Pino's vicious language, was revealing in other details. Here are edited excerpts:

McGinnis: "The guineas down the North End say every guinea in Boston is against us. Brink's spoiled the rackets— too much local law and the FBI now."

Pino: "There must be some way we can get out on bail and really take care of this thing. I hope Richardson don't fold up and dump his guts. That'd be two of them. Oh, this place: sit down, stand, sleep, sit down, stand, sleep. They ask me if I wanted to go to a show. What good? With these glasses I can't see nothing. They said I can have everything I want, but I get nothing."

McGinnis: "All those stories are no good for us. Look at all the baloney about Costa having been pinched for non-support, and about my father, how he killed a man. My father never killed a man. Why, he almost killed my mother once for taking a drink. My mother died in 1914. She didn't die of TB. She died of pneumonia. All that cheap baloney."

Pino: "How the hell can we get a fair trial with all the stories going on? That judge may be one of those noble Italians who gives us life."

McGinnis: "O'Keefe has told what went on, and you know and I know those are the facts."

Pino: "That damn O'Keefe. The only real way to end this is to . . . And Gus. How do we know what he said. They're brainwashing the witnesses. You can't tell what the foolish bastard raved about."

McGinnis: "Look, you can talk all you want, understand? But we've got to get the action, understand? We've got to reach the judge and the jury and bag the DA, understand?"]

The robbers, of course, never came close to corrupting any of those they discussed.

Continuing his discourse as the trial approached its climax, District Attorney Byrne said:

"I perhaps will not be as prolific or as profuse in my thanks to you men who sit here today as my fellow brothers who sit at the bar, but it will not be because my heart does not wish to pour it out. It will probably be because of the fact that I take my responsibilities seriously. And I feel, Mr. Foreman and Gentlemen of the Jury, that when you not too long ago held up your right hands, and keeping in mind that you did not have to sit here, you felt that way too. There were many ways that you could have taken yourselves from jury service, but you assumed the responsibility that I have assumed. You represent the same commonwealth that I represent. You have the same duties and you have the same responsibilities.

"And whatever sacrifices we have made, I know that you feel we have made them in order that we might live in a government of decent people.

"Because of the intemperate remarks that were made by one of the counsel yesterday, it is necessary that I tell you gentlemen a little story. Perhaps this might have been left unsaid, but because of the remarks made I have now to take you to the Department of Justice in Washington. And I want you to view a blue and gold seal, and on it, Mr. Foreman and Gentlemen of the Jury, there are three words: Fidelity, Bravery and Integrity. Underneath that seal, which suspends from a wall, there is a bronze plaque. Engraved on that plaque are the names of young men who gave their lives in the performance of their duties. Underneath those names there is a story of the lives that were lost in their fight against crime. And underneath that, Mr. Foreman and Gentlemen of the Jury, there is a page in history: one name, one boy, one young man. He was shot down in a bank by two robbers. Before he died, he assisted in their apprehension; and as his companions held him in their arms, before he took the last gasp, he said, "Tell Edgar Hoover that I did my best."

"That is the creed of the Federal Bureau of Investigation. Since that time, Mr. Foreman and Gentleman of the Jury, throughout the length and breadth of this land, there has been heaped upon them encomiums through the halls of Congress, and what they have done has been emblazoned across the world. Their fight has been a fight for decent people.

"And when we hear someone, as we heard yesterday, propounding home the question of civil rights and the protection and the preservation of the institutions that have made this country what it is today, always remember that when our forefathers sat down, when they gathered around that table in order to protect and preserve those things that

208

we find so necessary and so essential, it was to protect you and it was to protect your family and it was to protest decent people.

"And in order to protect decent people and in order to protect those institutions that are the very bulwark of our nation, our home, it became necessary to put safeguards around it to protect everyone.

"There is another school of thought that suggests that where we decide, perhaps, to protect our families and ourselves, we should not bend over to destroy the very things that we intended to preserve.

"But if I must choose the Powerses, if I must take the Larkins, if I must take the Friziolis, if I must take the Mc-Namaras, and on down the line, if it is a question of choosing between them and the McGinnises and the Pinos and the Maffies and the rest that sit in that box, then give me—and thank God we have it—the Federal Bureau of Investigation.

"Mr. Foreman and Gentlemen of the Jury, on January 17, 1950, there was a robbery, the biggest robbery in history, perpetrated in our city of culture, a city that had gained the respect of people throughout the nation, a city in which we sent our children to school, the metropolis that bragged about its medical centers, that [principal] part of a nation of culture.

"It was a monumental robbery. It was well planned, planned with meticulous care, with nothing left undone, with no way of discovering the participants.

"Don't you think that the FBI knew that? Don't you think, Mr. Foreman and Gentlemen of the Jury, that the only way that it could have been broken was from within? It had to be done from within. There could be no identification. They were concealed with masks. Their getaway was complete. There was no way that this crime could have probably ever been discovered except from within.

"If they had spent large amounts of monies, if they had started to live in any other way than usual, if they had picked

209

up with the female sex and devoted their time to expensive presents, there would have been detection, yes.

"But if, as Baker propounded at the very beginning, 'Let no man do anything that might have a tendency to jeopardize the life and the liberty of another member,' and if that was done, then there would be no way that the Brink's robbery could possibly be solved except from within.

"The FBI came in here. The likes of you men would welcome them, a ray of sunshine throughout the entire land. You heard one Federal Bureau of Investigation agent, one alone, say that he had interviewed a thousand witnesses. Up and down the land, back and forth, up and down for six long years, Mr. Foreman and Gentleman of the Jury, until one days, six days before the six years elapsed, in the city of Springfield, through persevering, through untiring efforts, through constant going back and forth, asking questions time after time, they finally, at long last, find the answer in Springfield: Specs O'Keefe.

"Specs O'Keefe sent for them and he talked to them, and that was the breaking point of the robbery that happened on January 17, 1950.

"I am not here to defend Specs O'Keefe. He came here as a guest of this court. He came here without any fear or promise. He took that stand, Mr. Foreman and Gentlemen of the Jury. He submitted himself for your perusal and for the examination of defense counsel. They could have kept him on there for two weeks if they had wanted to. They didn't have to stop. But it is for you to determine what kind of witness he made.

"He may be a thief. He may be anything that you might want to call him. But he came here and he didn't have to. He could have gone on another week in Springfield. He could have done whatever time he had there and perhaps then have gone to Pennsylvania and after completing his time there perhaps then become a free man. But he came in here and he said to you, "Here I am."

"They are not only thieves, those men who sit there, but they were thieves within thieves. They not only stole from Brink's but they stole from him, Specs O'Keefe.

"He submitted himself for three long days to a direct examination and then four more days to the rigid scrutiny of defense counsel. I submit that it wasn't Specs that quit. It was they. You saw it all, Mr. Foreman and Gentlemen. You had a chance to observe it.

"Now, let us take Mr. Maffie. Let us take that exponent of night-clubism. Let us take Jimmy O'Keefe, and Maffie, who crawls out of bed at one o'clock in the afternoon and leaves O'Keefe's sometime around one or two in the morning. He doesn't crawl out of bed like you do, Mr. Foreman and Gentlemen, to go to work. He doesn't leave home in the morning at a certain hour like you do to protect and preserve those whom you love and respect, and then return at night.

"Would you call this person [Mrs. Maffie] a liar? Would you say that she fabricated? It is up to you to decide what person is lying or what person might be innocently mistaken. But in order that we might have some understanding of what an alibi stands for, and so that you will not have to judge on the one hand Mr. Smith here or Mr. Byrne there, as to whether they are fabricating, and in order that you may understand more fully, let me acquaint you with what one of the greatest justices of this commonwealth said about an alibi. I am now going to read a statement from Chief Justice Shaw of the Supreme Judicial Court in *Commonwealth* vs. *Webster.*

"Justice Shaw said—not Smith and not Byrne and not De-Giacomo—but Chief Justice Shaw said:

" 'This is a defense often attempted by contrivance, subornation and perjury. The proof, therefore, offered to sustain it is to be subjected to a rigid scrutiny.'

"Now I have here the testimony of the alibi witnesses for the Robin Hood of Jimmy O'Keefe's [Maffie]. Mr. Foreman and Gentlemen, he doesn't care whom he destroys. He even drags his sister in here to say that every day, whether there was a hurricane or a rainstorm or whether it was freezing or warm, whether it was in the valley of heat or in the peak of the snow, that every day she went up to that home. But that is not she. Don't blame her. That is he.

"Even Specs O'Keefe—call him a thief if you want to, call him anything you have a desire to—but even Specs O'Keefe tried to keep Maffie's father out of it. Even he, from that stand, said, 'I don't want to make him an accessory.'

"But not Maffie. He wouldn't care what temples might fall. He wouldn't care what lives might be destroyed so long as he could continue to roll out of bed at one o'clock in the afternoon and get over to Jimmy O'Keefe's and play the same old game day in and day out. That's Maffie . . . the Maffie that dragged in his eighty-three-year-old father. That poor soul took the stand and said he was so tired he goes to bed at seven-thirty each night. If there is any respect left in that dock, Mr. Foreman and Gentlemen of the Jury, it isn't left in Maffie. He'd do anything to save his soul, to save his hide.

"Now take Faherty and Richardson, the homebodies. Well, they were not home on the day they were picked up, nor were they in any of their usual haunts. There had been a nationwide search for them through television, radio and the newspapers. Everyone was looking for those two innocent men, two innocent men being condemned and pilloried by the Federal Bureau of Investigation and by the district attorney's office.

"And where did we finally find these poor souls who should now be sent back home to their wives and their children? You know.

"I have heard so much talk about their poor wives and what their wives think of them. May I ask you, Mr. Foreman and the rest of you gentlemen, when you confine yourselves to the solitude of your little room upstairs in order to decide whether the people of this commonwealth should be protected or not, if you want to give any thought to anyone, would you just give a little thought to your own wives and a little thought to your own families; and if somewhere in between there you can find a little space to give thought to someone else, give a little thought to my wife. Because that is the kind of government we are trying to protect. That is the kind of government we are trying to preserve and that is the kind of nation we want to live in, a nation of decent people.

"They are not gunmen? They are not potential murderers? They are not robbers? Take those guns with you, Mr. Foreman and Gentlemen of the Jury. Those guns were loaded. Then ask yourselves if you want to invite them to your home. Ask yourselves if that is the type of individual you want in society.

"Were they going to use these things? Everybody seems to have forgotten this part of the case. Well, let's see. You saw Kehoe, the FBI agent, a clean, decent young man with no thought on his mind but to protect you. In the FBI, in order to join, the prime qualifications are truth and integrity, and the only method of advancement is merit and achievement and accomplishment. The FBI is a credit to our nation.

"What did Kehoe say? Are you going to call him a liar? Are you going to call Kehoe a liar when he says, 'I walked in and I had to grab Richardson and throw him over there, because if I didn't, I never would have got Faherty.' Faherty had his hand reaching for the gun. What was he going to do with it? Why didn't they surrender?

"And remember, Mr. Foreman and Gentlemen of the Jury, no matter what you might think of Specs O'Keefe, he took that stand. There is no man who could lie for seven days on that stand. I recognize the astuteness of Mr. Smith. I recognize his ability. There is no man who could lie to him for seven days and get away with it. Specs knew more about Brink's than anybody else because he was in there. No man could have that knowledge of a place without having been

213

in there. He never made a mistake. They couldn't do anything to him. After his complete examination, all the Government had to do was ask him two questions, because they had shaken him in nothing.

"How can we read the minds of men? How do we know what is going through Specs O'Keefe's mind? We do know this, Mr. Foreman and Gentlemen. We know they stole his dough; they took his money. We know he gave them every opportunity to do the right thing, as far as he was concerned in the criminal code, and they did not do it. How do we know but that it might be the first and last decent thing he ever did, the only decent thing that he ever conceived of or ever thought of: to take from society potential murderers, robbers.

"Now let's get to McGinnis. McGinnis, the master mind. McGinnis, the leader. McGinnis. Cool, calm, the brains. The manipulator. The operator. McGinnis. Money to work with—the businessman. McGinnis. The Mr. X of the situation. McGinnis, the Mr. X, Mr. Foreman and Gentlemen of the Jury, the man who didn't want to go in. Oh, no. If any slip-up comes, he is not going to get the bullet. He is the man that stays behind the gun. He is the accessory before the fact. He is the one that will get rid of everything. He will get rid of the truck. He will get rid of the gun. He will get rid of the masks. He will get rid of the money, and he will circulate it at a later date.

"McGinnis, who never went in. I will show you, Mr. Foreman and Gentlemen of the Jury, the most damaging evidence against Mr. McGinnis, this exhibit [seized money] and you are going to take this into your jury room. You remember the testimony of Specs O'Keefe when he said, 'We took a hundred thousand dollars and put it aside. It was trouble money that could have been detected. It could have been read because it was new money.' That was the money McGinnis was to destroy. You will have approximately sixty thousand dollars of that money, and also the ten thousand-dollar bills.

"There it is, Mr. Pino, but not you, really, because you and McGinnis are one.

"There it is, Mr. Geagan, Mr. Faherty and Mr. Richardson, and Costa and Maffie and Baker. McGinnis and Pino not only stole from Brink's but they stole from you. They were so cheap they wanted to save it all. But in their desire to save it all, they destroyed themselves.

"That is McGinnis. McGinnis, the cute one, who wants to send to Washington to get the inside records [of the vault alarm system]. McGinnis. Don't get me in danger. My influence. My money. My ability to take care of things. I will establish the alibi. If you get in trouble, I will get you out. But you, Specs, you go in first. You go in there in case there is any gunfire. And you, Faherty, and you, Richardson and Geagan and Maffie and Baker, you follow him.

"Pino? Oh, no, not Pino, nor his brother-in-law, Costa. Oh, no, they don't go in. They stay outside. They stay outside and McGinnis doesn't go near the place.

"McGinnis. The operator, the manipulator. Oh, how he must regret the day, Mr. Foreman and Gentlemen of the Jury, when once again through the diligence and perseverance of that great organization, the Federal Bureau of Investigation, they got those ten thousand-dollar bills.

"That's McGinnis, Mr. Foreman and Gentlemen of the Jury. Don't forget the name.

"And then we come to Pino. Pino is the machine gun. Pino is the one that wants to use the shotgun. Pino will blow up, if necessary, the ADT system in order that there might be no interference in their plans. Pino, who stays in the truck. Pino furnishes the guns. Pino furnishes the masks. He furnishes the pea coats. He furnishes the guns that can't possibly be identified. They must never be used any place else, he says, for fear that if they are found there might be some detection. That's Pino.

215

"Is there any question in your mind, Mr. Foreman and Gentlemen of the Jury, about Jake Dana, the locksmith?

"Jake Dana took that stand. He didn't have to leave it when he did. They could have kept him on there day after day. His testimony is that Pino called him week after week for a matter of five weeks to make keys. There is no evidence that Pino called him at any other time except, I think, the fall or the early winter of 1949 to make five keys for five locks, and that the cylinders were brought over there to him.

"And that is the same Pino, Mr. Foreman and Gentlemen of the Jury, who used to run over and get the key made and then bring it back in order that they might have efficiency. And, believe me, it was efficiency.

"It was the perfect crime. There were no loopholes in it.

"Pino and his five locks. Pino, who used to sit down with McGinnis and figure everything out. Pino, who rode in the truck, who put his brother-in-law up on top of the roof with a flashlight. Pino. The meetings always in his home. 'Where did you meet?' 'In Pino's home.' Was there any evidence offered in this court to show that they never gathered in Pino's home?

"Now, Mr. Baker. Baker, who when he was arrested by the Federal Bureau of Investigation made a statement. They told him about the confession of Specs O'Keefe. What was his answer, Mr. Foreman and Gentlemen of the Jury? He said, 'I have known Specs O'Keefe for twenty years. I am a very good friend of Specs O'Keefe. If Specs O'Keefe said I was in the Brink's holdup, then I am in trouble. If Specs O'Keefe said that I participated in the Brink's holdup, then I am in trouble and I need a lawyer.'

"Are those the expressions of an innocent man?

"Take Costa, the brother-in-law, the fellow who snapped the flashlight on, the one who drove the black sedan.

"How would you men ever know that a black sedan had anything to do with this robbery if Specs O'Keefe didn't tell you about it. He told you that on December 15, 1949, on

216

St. Stephens Street, he stole that automobile and that he broke in the front vent window. And we brought into this court a man who took the stand and said, 'My Ford sedan was stolen on the fifteenth and it was stolen by the breaking of the front vent window.' It is unanswerable, Mr. Foreman and Gentlemen of the Jury.

"And who could procure the necessary bags for the money? Where would you get bags like these with the names of a foreign country on them? Who could get them. Longshoremen. Geagan? Yes. Richardson? Yes. Geagan, who said he was home washing diapers when the robbery was taking place. He remembered January 17, 1950. He was home washing diapers at exactly seven o'clock. There isn't any person in the world who can go back that number of years and give you the exact time and the exact minute.

"I don't know what your wealth may be, Mr. Foreman and Gentlemen of the Jury. I don't even know what your businesses may be. But for a longshoreman who makes approximately $2,500 to $3,000 a year to be paying notes of over $200 a month and buying a $17,500 house down in Quincy, well, it seems to me that there must be some income other than what is visible to the eyes.

"Mr. Foreman and Gentlemen, as we go through this old life of ours and we reach a certain stage, we live not so much for ourselves as we live for our fellowmen. We respect and we love and we honor the institutions that have made our great country the country that it is. We settle down and we get married, and we bring into this world children. We make up our minds then that the opportunities we did not have we will see to it that our children have."

There followed, at some length, a dissertation on family, decency, patriotism, and a strong stress on the accusation that the Brink's robbers were potential murderers.

The district attorney dramatically concluded:

"You have a grave responsibility far beyond what I could describe. There is no screen that could depict it. This has been the largest robbery in history. It could not have been solved if it had not been solved from within, and it took the greatest organization of its kind in the world six long years and thousands upon thousands of witness interrogations.

"You are intelligent men. You are businessmen. You are decent men. You believe in the preservation of family life. You believe in the continuation of government. You represent Massachusetts and, as Webster said, 'There she stands. She needs no explanation. She needs nothing from me.' I say to you, you are Massachusetts, and you tell the world you are Massachusetts.

"We don't want any racketeers. We want to live decent lives. We were a city of culture, of hospitals, of education, a leader in all things until the night of January 17, 1950, when they—these men—made us the butt of every joke and every comedian in the nation. But we have caught up with them.

"And so, men of Massachusetts, you take it and decide whether or not you are the barrier of the onward rush of those thugs. And when you go into your jury room, Mr. Foreman and Gentlemen, just take those guns with you and ask yourselves if those are the garments that decent people should wear. If they are, then I have no conception of the right manner of living. If those are the things we stand for, if you are not the bulwark and barrier of the onward rush, then God help the Commonwealth of Massachusetts."

16

THE WIVES OF MCGINNIS, PINO AND COSTA WERE AMONG THOSE
in the crowded courtroom when Judge Forte charged the
jury. These were the highlights of his scholarly instructions:

"A false verdict against the defendant is as deep an injury
to the community as a false verdict in favor of the defendant. . . .

"Silence, failure to testify, cannot be taken into consideration by you in determining whether a defendant is or is not
guilty. If he remains silent, the law jealously guards and
preserves his rights, cuts off all injurious comments and, as
far as possible, protects him from unfavorable inferences.

"A defendant has the right simply to deny his guilt and to
rely upon the legal presumption of his innocence, and no
presumption or inference against him shall be drawn by the
jury because of his neglect or refusal to testify. . . .

"If you are convinced of a particular fact beyond a reasonable doubt you have the right to draw reasonable inferences
from such a fact. Proof by such an inference is no less sound
proof than by direct testimony.

"What is an inference? Perhaps an inference can be explained by a simple illustration. Suppose you go out into
the kitchen and a kettle is on the stove and steam is coming
out from the spout. You are convinced of such facts. You
don't have to put your finger in the kettle to find out whether

the water in it is hot or not. You infer from the fact that steam comes out of the kettle that the water is hot. . . .

"As for conspiracy, the rule is well established that, when sufficient evidence has been introduced at a trial of an indictment for conspiracy to support a fair inference of the existence of a conspiracy, the acts and declarations of a defendant, which previously had been admitted only against him, become competent against all the defendants if such acts and declarations are shown to have occurred during the pendency of the conspiracy and in furtherance of its object; but that if such acts and declarations are shown to have taken place after the conspiracy came to an end, they are not admissible against the other defendants.

"Limiting the definition of conspiracy to the indictments in this case, a conspiracy is a combination of two or more persons by some concerted action to accomplish some criminal or unlawful purpose. The gist of a conspiracy is the unlawful confederacy to do an unlawful act.

"If you find that these defendants or any of them conspired, entered into an agreement, you are warranted in returning a verdict of guilty.

"A conspiracy once formed may be enlarged. It is not necessarily limited to the terms of an original illegal agreement. A conspiracy may be enlarged and it is enlarged with each new item that enters into the plan while it is still on foot, just as it might be enlarged in the number of its members. That is, after it is formed, new members can come in and it is part of the same conspiracy.

"It is not necessary that all the conspirators join in every part of the unlawful transaction. . . . If the defendants agreed upon a plan for some of them to visit the Brink's establishment in order to survey it and to prepare further plans, the act of each such person visiting the establishment in the furtherance of the plan is the act of each conspirator. . . .

"To constitute breaking and entering, it is not necessary literally to break down a door. Merely the opening of a closed door, though it is not latched, though it is not bolted, though it is not locked, constitutes breaking. It is immaterial whether the door is fastened or unfastened, locked or unlocked, so long as it is closed. In this case it is alleged that a number of doors were locked and that the defendants by the use of keys unlocked the doors. If you find such to be the fact, the defendants are guilty of a breaking. If you find they entered the premises as a result, they are guilty of breaking and entering. . . .

"The essence of robbery was the exercise of force, actual or constructive, against another in order to take personal property of any value whatsoever, with the intention to steal it, from the protection which the person of the other affords. Robbery is the larceny of personal property from a person by the use of force or putting in fear. As applied in this case, it is the stealing of money, any amount more than one hundred dollars, from the person of Lloyd, Allen or Pfaff. . . .

"The evidence shows that neither the defedant Pino nor the defendant Costa entered the Brink's premises on the night of January 17. They were not physically present in the vault room when Lloyd, Allen and Pfaff were allegedly put in fear and deprived of the monies under their control.

"But if you believe that Pino handed to O'Keefe the keys with which to unlock the doors at 165 Prince Street, accompanied in the truck those that did enter the building, and remained in the truck ready to give whatever assistance he could in the entering of the building, in moving the loot into the truck, in protecting the others in any way, in aiding in their escape, he is as guilty as if he had entered the premises and actually held up Lloyd, Allen or Pfaff. In other words, he is a principal.

"As to Costa, if he drove to Prince Street and did go to the roof of 109 Prince Street, gave a signal to enter Brink's and then drove his car to Prince Street sufficiently near to 165 Prince Street to render whatever help he could to the principals in protecting them from being interrupted and in helping them escape, he too is a principal to the same extent as if he had actually entered the premises and held up Lloyd, Allen and Pfaff or any of them.

"A person is a principal if he is present, or consents to the unlawful acts—and in this case the unlawful acts charged are the breaking and entering and the robbery—and in a position where he might render aid and assistance. . . .

"Each of the defendants except Baker has set up a defense usually called an alibi; that is, that the accused was elsewhere at the time that the offense is alleged to have been committed, that is to say, it being impossible that the accused should be in two places at the same time. . . .

"It is very desirable, gentlemen, that you should reach a verdict. The juror who tries to impose his will upon his fellow-jurors is a traitor in the jury panel and is unfit for jury service. His mind is not open.

"While each of you should have your own individual opinions about the evidence and cling to those opinions if you conscientiously believe them to be true, nevertheless each of you should listen to the opinions of your fellow-jurors, and see if, by yielding and conceding, there is not some common group upon which all can agree.

"Your verdict must be unanimous. A disagreement, gentlemen, is always in the nature of a failing of justice."

The all-male jury deliberated just under three and one-half hours before returning guilty verdicts against all eight defendants on all counts.

It was 2 A.M., October 6, 1956, when Foreman Thomas F. Donohue began quietly repeating "Guilty" to the sonorous questions offered by Clerk of the Court William M. Prendible in respect to the seventy-one indictments involved. The eight defendants stood like thick, graven images to hear their fates tolled. In the spectator section of the crowded room their wives and families sobbed. Mrs. Marjorie McGinnis collapsed and was carried to an elevator by police officers, held unconscious but upright in her chair.

Smith asked that the jury be polled but his motion was denied after Prosecutor Doyle objected. The defense chief took his 850th exception.

The district attorney then asked that the eight convicted men be remanded without bail to the Charles Street jail and that sentencing be delayed until the following Tuesday. He won Judge Forte's nod on both requests, and the men were led away, each accompanied by a court officer.

"I want to thank you on behalf of the court for the duty that you have performed on behalf of Suffolk County," the judge, smiling wearily, said to the jury as he dismissed it. "I am sure the county is proud of your courage, the courage of your convictions. You are now discharged and you may return to your homes."

The room cleared slowly. The FBI agents, their work at long last done, seemed reluctant to leave. SAC Powers said:

"The verdict of the jury justifies the six long years of exhaustive work. I have much praise for Garrett Byrne and his entire staff for presenting the case which finally ended successfully for the commonwealth."

"The commonwealth is satisfied," the DA said. "We feel that justice has been done."

Paul Smith retorted: "Of course, we are going to appeal. We have twenty-one days to file that appeal. These have been nine long weeks, and we want a few days to get things straightened out." Other defense lawyers said much the same thing, but Lawrence O'Donnell, who represented Richardson, Faherty and Geagan, added on leaving the court, "My best wishes to all the members of the commonwealth staff and other government agencies that presented the case and met success at the trial level. Along with co-counsel, I will appeal on behalf of the three clients I represent.

"I have just left my three clients and they reacted in a manly fashion to the verdict."

Juror Walter H. Grahame, of Winthrop, a Navy Yard official, disclosed: "We took ballot after ballot on count after count. It was guilty all the way, excepting on the first ballot. That was eleven to one. But it turned out the single vote was cast through a misunderstanding.

"Everybody had the same reaction to the evidence—remarkably so. We got down to business the minute we went into the deliberation. We didn't need the exhibits. We had enough evidence without them.

"We weren't keen on sending anybody away, but it was the only thing that could be done under the circumstances."

In the dimly lighted "cage" section of the East Cambridge jail, Deputy Sheriff Emile A. Dumas banged on the bars of a lonely cell.

The man sleeping on the prison cot within stirred and sat up. "What is it?"

"Specs," Dumas said through the bars, "they just brought in the verdict and found them all guilty."

Specs did not say anything.

"Don't you want to say anything about it?" Dumas asked him.

"No comment," Specs said. He walked back to his bunk, lay down upon it and went back to sleep.

On Sunday, October 7, 1956, seven of the eight defendants attended Mass in the chapel of the Charles Street jail. Henry Baker was visited by a rabbi. Later in the day, the fathers of Pino and Costa called on their sons and were permitted to speak to them through a wire grill that had been added to the prison interior in the wake of Trigger Burke's escape. The elderly men brought along a large container of steaming spaghetti, laced with a fragrant meat sauce that permeated the stale odors of the pen.

Mrs. Pino and Mrs. Costa, who accompanied the fathers

to the prison but were denied admission, were bitterly disappointed.

Mrs. Pino said of Specs, "None of O'Keefe's family, including his wife, ever believed him. So how could that jury take his word against twenty reliable persons who testified and supplied alibis for our husbands?"

Mrs. Costa kept saying, "They didn't do it—they're not guilty."

"I was a waitress before I got married," Mrs. Pino told a reporter. "I guess I'll have to go back to work. There isn't any money and they've attached my home. Tony and I will be fifty this year. We have two grandchildren. If he goes to jail, even for a little while, it's a long time out of our lives."

The old men emerged, shaking their heads. Pino's father spoke for a time in Italian to his daughter-in-law. He took out his wallet and extracted from it its only bill, a $10 note. Mrs. Pino handed it to the prison's gate officer.

"Will you see that Tony gets this?" she asked. "He doesn't have any money. We're flat broke."

17

THE MACHINERY OF THE SENTENCING MOVED WITH WHAT MUST
have been a maddening slowness for the eight convicted robbers. It was Tuesday, October 9, 1956, the forty-fifth and
final day of the trial.

Judge Forte, who seemed hardly in a mood to speed the
proceedings, took his chair shortly after noon.

THE COURT. Are there any other motions besides the
motion made by the district attorney for the imposition
of sentences here in these cases?

MR. SMITH. If your Honor please, there will be a motion filed by the defendant Pino, which will be filed subsequent to any imposition of sentence, if there is an
imposition of sentence.

THE COURT. Very well.

MR. SMITH. If your Honor would prefer to see it now,
I would just as soon file it with you. I have already given
copies to the district attorney and to the Immigration
people.

THE COURT. You may file it now, but I shall take cog-
nizance of it after the imposition of sentence.

MR. SMITH. Surely. I would prefer it that way.

THE COURT. Very well. Before I hear arguments on the
district attorney's motion, I think that I ought to make

226

clear to all parties concerned what my objective is going to be in the imposition of sentences so that counsel for both sides can give me all the help I possibly can get.

I fully realize the responsibility on the shoulders of one person. The only consolation that I can think of is that if sentences are to State's Prison, or the Correctional Institution at Walpole, as it is now called, the particular defendant has a right of appeal before the Appellate Division of this court. Of course, I also know that that Appellate Division has the power to increase as well as decrease a particular sentence.

The time has passed when justice demands an eye for an eye and a tooth for a tooth. Why, there used to be a time in this state, way back in 1641, when the first compilation of statutes in Massachusetts called for the death penalty for at least twelve different offenses. I don't believe any attorneys had anything to do with that compilation, because in 1641 attorneys were not very popular in the colony.

In England at one time there were more than a hundred crimes—probably a hundred and twenty crimes, to be accurate—that called for death as a punishment.

Oh, civilization has made great progress in that field of penology ever since.

Well, in the eighteenth century a man named Cesare Beccaria revolutionized penology. He wrote a little book on "Crimes and Punishment" that in eighteen months ran into six editions and was immediately translated into twenty-two different languages, and revolutionized, as I said, penology. He was against confiscation as a punishment, against capital punishment, against torture. He wrote against the confinement of debtors, against the filth and horror of prison, the cruelty of jailers, and was against equal punishment for the same offense. If two people committed the same crime, both would get the

227

same punishment—the judge had no discretion—when, as a matter of fact, it would be possible for one to deserve less punishment than the other.

But the judges had no discretion until this man Beccaria wrote that book. He wrote:

"If equal punishment be ordained for two crimes for injury to society in different degrees, there is nothing to deter men from committing the greater, and often it is attended with greater advantage. Crimes are to be estimated by the injury done to society. The degree of punishment, and the consequence of a crime, ought to be so contrived as to have the same possible effect on others, with the least possible pain to the delinquent."

And Beccaria was the one who said at the very start of his work: "Crimes are more effectually prevented by certainty than the severity of punishment."

No improvement was made in the administration of criminal justice until another century, the nineteenth century, and of course counsel are well aware of the lifelong research of Cesare Lombroso. He made a distinction between individuals. If both commit the same crime, they should not be punished the same if they are of different degrees of criminal responsibility. After Lombroso's works were published, judges were given a wide latitude of discretion so that it was possible thereafter for two people to have committed the same crime, one to receive a very slight sentence and another to receive a severe sentence.

From about 1860 on there was no great improvement until our own century, when probation was introduced, when for the first time we looked into the question of reformation and rehabilitation. What good is there in a defendant? If there is any good, why can't society experiment with him and help him to change from a social liability to a social asset? Probation has justified its existence. Only one out of ten who are placed on probation come back to court.

As I said, today a justice is given a wide latitude of discretion in fixing sentence, and it is this wide latitude that this court is empowered to exercise that makes him hesitate and ponder to see to it that both the commonwealth and each defendant gets full justice in accordance with the standing and the tradition of the great trial court of this commonwealth. The only times when the court has no discretion in Massachusetts now are in the instances of murder in the first degree when the jury does not recommend leniency, and murder in the second degree; but in all other cases, the court is given discretion.

Personally I do not believe in long sentences. (There were wheezes of relief from the robbers.) In many, many cases, a sentence of one week is as demoralizing to an individual, certain individuals, as a sentence of one year or two years might be to another. Long sentences are justified only when the wrongdoer is incorrigible, when he is hardened, a hardened criminal and vicious. In such a case, a long sentence is meted out for his own benefit, strangely enough, because if he were given freedom, he eventually would land in the electric chair, and for his own good he is kept from committing such possible crimes.

And another justification for long sentences is that the man is such a danger to society, is so anti-social, that society must be protected. In such cases, and in such cases alone, are long sentences justified, in my own humble opinion.

Now, before I hear counsel, I think I should explain what I am interested in in this particular case. So far, I have talked generalities.

What are some of the factors which ought to enter into the determination of a sentence?

First, the nature of the crime, the gravity of the crime, the seriousness of the wrong done to the state.

Secondly, the defendant himself.

The greater, the more serious the crime, the greater, of course, the penalty. The state does not believe in vengeance. As I said, the day of an eye for an eye and a tooth for a tooth has long passed. But the nature of the crime calls for consideration because one of the main purposes of a sentence is that it should serve as a deterrent to others, not necessarily as the punishment to the wrongdoer.

And when we talk about the defendant himself, I would like help from counsel in evaluating the degree of the criminality of each particular defendant here before the court. Was he a leader? Was he responsible for the wrongdoing of other defendants? That is an important factor. Was he the brains of the commission of the crime? Or is he weak-willed and a follower, who never would have been in trouble had he not had the influence of the first that I have described? Is he a victim of human frailty? Is he a big leader or is he a little leader? Is he a first offender or has he had a long criminal record? Has he had opportunity after opportunity to reform and to become a good law-abiding citizen as every other citizen in the community is expected to be?

I am interested in the general character of each defendant, his habits, his status in society. I am well aware that some of these defendants offered no defense at all, as they had a right to do; but others added perjury to the commission of the crime charged. All those characteristics of the personality of the particular defendant are to be weighed in determining sentences.

Yes, the defendants are human beings. We mustn't forget that. They have committed a wrong, a serious wrong, but they are still human beings and should be treated humanely. Therefore, I am interested to know all the good that can be said about each one.

Is there any chance or opportunity of reformation or rehabilitation? Has there been any sign of remorse or repentance? I am interested.

Now, I offer these suggestions, gentlemen, to show that we are not revengeful. We don't intend to be. But he who seeks mercy should show some consideration of goodness. For instance, five thousand dollars in silver was found [in the flat where Faherty and Richardson were captured]. There has been not a word of explanation. Undoubtedly that was not the result of the robbery in January of 1950. No, there is no question about that. But I also feel that that silver was not the result of a church collection either.

Now, if counsel would like to discuss it, there is an opportunity. I would like to know what good there is in every one of these defendants before I can evaluate the character, the degree of criminality of the particular defendant.

Sometimes, of course, the family relations are given consideration, but not because the defendant deserves it. He should have thought of his family, not others, not the district attorney or the defendant's counsel or the court. He should have thought of his family and his children and the effect that his own conduct would have on his own loved ones. But, nevertheless, we do temper justice with mercy and we do not overlook the relationships.

Now, these are some of the considerations that serve as a guide, and I think counsel, as far as this court is concerned, have an opportunity to be of assistance to the court as officers of the court to give me every bit of help that I can get, because, to state my problem in another way, my factors and guides are:

231

First, the protection of society. That comes first. That is the first consideration that I will have to take.

Secondly, the punishment should act as a deterrent to others, not to encourage others to do the same thing. It is the function of the criminal court to so dispose of cases as to discourage further commission of crimes of that nature. Yes, the punishment is to be taken into consideration as a factor, as a discipline, but to me I take that as a secondary factor. I am more interested in the protection of society.

The punishment should serve as a deterrent and to take advantage of every possible opportunity for reformation and rehabilitation.

I know these principles may not have been spoken of before. I made an outline of those propositions which I shall be glad to give counsel, and I think I should give counsel an opportunity to confer with each other and to confer with their respective clients so that they can say that they have been given every possible opportunity and every possible consideration. And I am going to, while the court reads the probation records, call a recess and resume the hearing after recess.

MR. SMITH. Judge, we are ready to go ahead now.

THE COURT. Very well. Then I will be glad to hear from you, although I said I do want to study these records.

MR. SMITH. Would your Honor consider the recess until about two-thirty. I didn't realize that we would be this long this morning.

The afternoon session began with a whispered wrangle at Judge Forte's bench:

MR. SMITH. On behalf of all defendants, we wish to take exception to your Honor's statement that "other defendants added perjury to the crime charged."

THE COURT. I didn't mean to say that the defendants themselves—

MR. SMITH. Your Honor said "some of the defendants put on alibi witnesses . . ."

MR. BYRNE. No, he didn't say that.

MR. SMITH. Well, then, you said "some of the defendants, the defendants didn't take the stand . . ." Now, the way I have it—

THE COURT. Added perjury to the crime, is what I said. And I had in mind, for the sake of the record, Mr. Smith's argument to the jury: "If you find the defendants guilty, that means Mr. Maffie lied," that so and so— I forget the names—"lied"; and Mr. Smith mentioned a number of names of witnesses that lied. Well, if they lied on the witness stand . . .

MR. SMITH. I didn't say they lied.

THE COURT. . . . then that is perjury; that's what I said.

MR. SMITH. I'll tell you what I said. I said that if you find that O'Keefe was telling the truth, you must, of necessity, find that these witnesses committed perjury or lied.

THE COURT. That's right.

MR. SMITH. That's what I said. But I didn't say anything about Maffie; I didn't limit it to Maffie.

THE COURT. I didn't mention Maffie.

MR. SMITH. You just did, your Honor.

THE COURT. In my talk this morning, I did not mention Maffie. It is all in the record.

MR. SMITH. Just this minute—

MR. BYRNE. You mean right here now?

MR. SMITH. Yes. I don't mean in his discussion this morning.

THE COURT. I was talking in general, and I had in mind your argument, which I have here right now as to that

233

particular part that you put to the jury that these witnesses were lying.

MR. SMITH. Wait a minute, Judge. I don't say they were lying. All I said was that if you believe O'Keefe, then you've got to find that these people were lying or committing perjury. That is a vast difference from what your Honor just said. I didn't say that the witnesses were lying.

THE COURT. Oh, no, of course not. You asked the jury to find—that if they found a verdict of guilty, then these people were lying. That is what I had in mind. Now, there is another possibility which you didn't mention; which is possible: namely, that they could have been honestly mistaken.

MR. SMITH. That is what Mr. Byrne argued.

THE COURT. Well, your rights are saved.

[Exception No. 895]
(End of conference at the bench)

THE COURT. The court will hear counsel for the defendants. As for the order, I will leave it to counsel.

MR. SMITH. Well, does your Honor want to hear the recommendation from the commonwealth first?

THE COURT. The court will hear from the defendants, if they have anything to say.

MR. SMITH. Well, may it please the court, it is my general understanding that the purpose for which the court is now sitting is to impose sentence; and that in determining what sentence should be imposed, the court normally takes into consideration three factors: namely, what punishment should be meted out to people who are convicted of a crime; whether or not there is a reasonable opportunity for rehabilitation or what the elements of rehabilitation may be; and the third issue being—what deterrent there is to other potential criminals.

Now, I must be frank to confess to the court, and I would be less than frank if I did not say, that after listening to your Honor before the recess, I could not discuss with my clients what your Honor had reference to because, frankly, although your Honor expounded certain principles of law and certain considerations and certain historical data, I did not know precisely what I should take up with my clients.

It seemed to me that at one point your Honor was suggesting a belated confession. And I must state to the court now that my clients have continuously maintained their innocence and still continue to maintain their innocence.

So that as consequence, there can be no belated confession. And as a consequent, if that is going to be a determining factor as to whether or not you add an X number of years or reduce X number of years, it is an unfortunate situation. But my clients are in no position to state that they were guilty of a crime.

Now, if your Honor please, the court is sitting in a different function than the court was sitting during the trial. During the trial your Honor was simply the judge of the law, and as your Honor instructed the jury, you were the final arbiter of the law. You are now sitting in the capacity—a dual capacity now—as both judge and jury; that is, determining various collateral facts that would affect the degree of sentence, the severity of sentence, or the minimization of sentence. And you are also sitting in a capacity of the judge on the law as to the amount of sentence that you can give the defendants.

Your Honor referred to the question of vengeance in your statement before recess. And, of course, I completely agree with the court; that in an enlightened society, the element of vengeance should no longer exist.

We are not people who are looking for what the Germans call *rache*—revenge, vengeance. We are living in an enlightened society. The element of mercy and justice prevails.

Now, it is awfully difficult to convince your Honor as to what you are to do to any less degree than it was difficult to convince a jury, which we have contended from the very beginning could not come to a fair and impartial decision.

Your Honor has heard talk about guns, people being held up, people being robbed, and potential murderers, etc. And before I go into any further questions, I would like to point this out to the court: within a couple of days after this crime was committed, the president of Brink's, Incorporated, issued a public statement which was carried in the press for two and three days thereafter, that there was a reward for the apprehension and conviction of the people who committed this crime. And he said this, if your Honor please, "We want them dead or alive, but we would prefer them dead."

Now, of course, if this court is going to concede that that is followed out—and by "dead" I mean confining them to an institution to a point where they will never come out alive—why, then, Mr. Plant of Brink's, Incorporated, has accomplished his purpose.

But I don't think that is the purpose of any enlightened court. I think the purpose of a court is not to go in, if your Honor please, and I say this with all due respect, to go into the history of Cesare Lombroso—whose philosophy and theories of distinction of degrees of crime have been exploded by Sheldon Glueck of Harvard—

THE COURT. That part where he says that criminality depends upon the shape of a head, yes, I agree with you absolutely.

MR. SMITH. I don't believe that we can adopt a general theory. I believe that your Honor must confront yourself

236

with a very fundamental and basic fact here. Are you, as the court who is supposedly objective, going to be overwhelmed by the hysteria of this case? This is nothing more than an armed robbery. That is all this case is. The mere fact that it happens to be Brink's, and the mere fact that it happens to be $1,200,000 doesn't make the slightest bit of difference than the Sturtevant case that your Honor sat on in 1948, with which I happen to be somewhat familiar, with which Mr. Doyle happens to be somewhat familiar; and that at that time was the largest armed-robbery case in the history of the commonwealth. And at that time, one Samuel Granito, who I think was about forty-two or forty-three years of age, was convicted of armed robbery, and he was brought up before the court here. That was a robbery involving the use of a gun. That was a robbery involving where people wore masks. That was a robbery in many respects similar to what the commonwealth says took place in this case.

And in that case, if your Honor please, and I noticed particularly your Honor's statement in advance of argument, that the court is not necessarily bound by what took place in the past; and I agree with you: you are not bound by it; but I think there must be some sort of consideration of what has gone on in the past.

Your Honor then sentenced that man to a term of sixteen to twenty years, and at the time you sentenced him—and this crime was in no way as severe as that crime because there was evidence in that crime that people were knocked down—in this case, if your Honor please, there hasn't been the slightest bit of testimony that anyone was pushed around or knocked down or hurt or harmed. And if your Honor will remember, every one of those people who were in there at Brink's were asked by me, "Were you knocked down?" And they said, "No." They were told to lie down.

237

I just want to point out to you in something that may sound in a satirical vein, but I hope it isn't taken that way, the gentility of these people who went into Brink's. They tied these men up so that within one minute after the robbers left they were able to free themselves. The only violence that was committed was that somebody's glasses were taken off. You don't have a case where somebody was hit in the head. You don't have a case where somebody was shot. You don't have a case where somebody was injured. You have a simple armed robbery.

If your Honor is going to be overwhelemed by the publicity and by the immense build-up of this case, and differentiate that from any other armed robbery, then I have no basis on which to argue to your Honor.

I say this is a simple armed-robbery case, and that in simple armed-robbery cases the degree of sentences has been limited. You have had defendants before you in the past with long records. Other judges of this court have had defendants before them with long records on armed-robbery cases. And the sentences have not been such as have been predicted in the press: that you are going to give them forty years, sixty years, eighty years.

This is a simple armed-robbery case, period. And the only one that was hurt by it was an insurance company in London. Nobody in Brink's was harmed. Nobody in Brink's was hurt. Nobody in Brink's was hit. Nobody in Brink's was shot. The crime consists of only one thing, and that is taking by force and violence.

THE COURT. And putting in fear.

MR. SMITH. And putting in fear. Well, if your Honor please, that happens, I'd venture to say, in this court-house once a week, twice a week, maybe. Nobody gets so excited about the thing that you talk about sixty or eighty or forty years, or life, after life, and all that business that has been going on here. This is an ordinary

238

armed-robbery crime and shouldn't be treated any differently, despite all of the play that has been going on from those two or three [press] tables back there.

Your Honor made a statement during the course of your discussion before recess—I'm trying to get the exact language, if I can: "The degree of criminality . . . was he the leader, the brains of the commission of the crime? Or was he weak-willed and a follower . . . a victim of human frailty?" Is he a big-leaguer or a little-leaguer? You said that was a factor that ought to be taken into consideration.

THE COURT. That's right.

MR. SMITH. Well, I asked the Government's chief witness, Mr. O'Keefe, whether he was the brains and he said, "No." And I said, "Who was the brains?" And he said, "Pick any one of them."

Now, other than that, is there any testimony that any one of these people were the so-called brains? Again, you've got the press that has built this up: McGinnis is the brains; Pino is the brains. But in this courtroom, in this room where your Honor has listened to the evidence, has there been any testimony that McGinnis is the brains? Has there been any testimony that Pino was the brains? Has there been any testimony that any of the other defendants are the brains?

Well, I leave it to the court now. Who was the brains? All I know is that if you are going to accept Mr. O'Keefe as being the soul of honesty and as telling the truth, then he is the only one, apparently, who can identify the so-called brains. And he says, "Pick any one of them."

I do know this much: that in every one of the activities that O'Keefe talked about, he was the leader. He went in first. He stole the rope. He stole a car. He did this; he was the fellow who went into the ADT and stole the plans. He was the fellow who apparently was the leader.

Now, I have a very serious question to raise with the court now, and that is the question of perjury. Your Honor said, "Others added perjury to the crime charged."

THE COURT. I put it in the form of a question, or I intended to put it in the form of a question. Did any defendant, in addition to committing this crime, add perjury to that original crime? That was the intent. I repeat that statement because if a person committed a crime and is convicted, it is a different situation if, in addition, he tries to insult the intelligence of a jury by adding perjury to it. That was a general abstract proposition. I am here now to get the facts.

MR. SMITH. Well, if it is an abstract question, may I just point this out? The variance in testimony resolved itself down to O'Keefe on one side and sixteen or seventeen witnesses on the other side. If there is any evidence of perjury, I think your Honor ought to call whoever it is that you suspect and have him indicted or hold him in contempt. And I submit, if your Honor please, that the only one who can possibly be regarded as having committed perjury is O'Keefe.

But the implication from what your Honor said was that some of the defendants' witnesses committed perjury. If that is so, I sincerely entreat the court, entreat the district attorney, I beg any enforcement official to bring any witness that the defendants have had on that stand and charge them with perjury.

To smear them in a general way by implying that they committed perjury, I think, if your Honor please, is most unfair to any witness who was called in here and who, to the same extent as Mr. O'Keefe, was a guest of the court. Bring them in and charge them with perjury. But to implicate them by innuendo, mothers of children, decent, honest working people, that is something else. I pray that somebody will bring them in and not let this shadow be over their heads. If they have committed perjury, let them be convicted. But let them be vindicated if they haven't committed perjury.

Now, the only other thing I want to say to your Honor is with respect to my particular three clients. Your Honor has their probation records before you. To argue as to whether one is or is not a first offender or a second offender would be futile.

I do say to the court that Anthony Pino will be fifty years of age on May 10 of next year; James Costa is forty-two years of age; Joseph McGinnis is fifty-three years of age. I have in mind what your Honor said in the Granito case. I assume that your Honor has the same principle in mind today.

These people are too old to steal, and they will be too old to steal when they are fifty-five or sixty years of age. And I submit to this court, if you are looking for *rache*, if you are looking for vengeance, that is different. You can send them away indefinitely.

But if you are going to adopt the high-minded principles that your Honor spoke about, then I submit, having in mind the serious doubts that must exist in your Honor's mind with respect to the testimony in this case, I submit that if you gave Pino a sentence of ten years, he'd be sixty years of age . . . sixty years of age, married and with grandchildren—

THE COURT. I know, but he would be eligible for parole in three years, isn't that it?

MR. BYRNE. That's right, your Honor.

THE COURT. That is the point. Now, you say let him serve ten years. But to have him serve ten years he has to get a sentence of thirty years. A sentence of ten to twenty years now, under the new parole eligibility, makes a man eligible after serving forty-seven months.

241

MR. SMITH. Well, that is four years, of course. But that only makes him eligible. That doesn't let him out.

THE COURT. No, of course not.

MR. SMITH. All right. And any student of the parole system in Massachusetts would readily recognize the fact that in the past five years it has been only on rare occasions that people have been paroled on the minimum. But be that as it may, I say that if Pino had to do ten years, I mean actually had to do ten years, he would be sixty years of age, and coming out on a crutch or a cane, and I don't see where anybody could expect he would then be going out to rob anyone.

Costa, who has a wife and children, would be fifty-two years of age.

With respect to McGinnis, he is fifty-three today. What is he going to do at sixty-three? He would be in the same position.

With respect to their records, of course you've got before you police records which show arrests. Your Honor has been on the bench and in the practice of law long enough to know that certain people are picked up at the slightest provocation, and notation of that act appears upon a police record.

But I ask your Honor to take this into consideration: as far as Pino's legal record is concerned, his actual record today. All that appears on there is a case that goes way back to sometime in the twenties, where he was sent to Concord on an indeterminate sentence. The other one is the larceny of a dozen golf balls. If your Honor is going to regard any other part of what you have before you concerning Pino, well, that is the same as regarding any gossip that might be spread about any one of us. The fact is, as a legal proposition, he's got the golf ball larceny and he's got the old Concord indeterminate sentence case when he was eighteen or nineteen years of age.

242

As far as Costa is concerned, the only thing he's got, as I understand it, was in 1939—an indeterminate sentence.

As far as McGinnis is concerned, the last conviction he's got is in 1938, where he got fifteen months, and that was a Federal rap on a conspiracy. I say to your Honor, that if you take those things, having in mind that Pino's goes back to 1927, I think that any sentence that involves more than ten years for these men is a cruel and unusual punishment, because I think that then the hysteria of the Brink's case is going to carry everyone away.

THE COURT. May I interrupt you to say something? One of these defendants was sentenced to thirty-eight to fifty years on one occasion.

MR. SMITH. If your Honor please, I am talking now only for Pino, McGinnis and Costa.

THE COURT. All right.

MR. SMITH. I have able and competent co-counsel, with whom it has been one of the most joyous events of my life to have been associated with. They are completely competent to talk about their own defendants, their own clients.

So I submit, if your Honor please, that if the commonwealth is looking for vengeance, because Brink's lost a million dollars instead of losing only a thousand dollars or a hundred thousand dollars, that is one thing.

If the commonwealth is particularly concerned with Lloyd's of London, that is another thing.

But if the commonwealth is interested in looking at this objectively, this is just another armed robbery. No one was hurt. No one was knocked down. And, without being placed in the position of engaging in satire, these Brink's people were able to disengage themselves from these ropes or strings within a matter of a minute. So nobody could have been too cruel to them.

If your Honor will remember, there was a buzzer sounded. There was an old man who walked by. If they were the vicious potential murderers that has been suggested to the court, wouldn't it have been a lot better from the standpoint of safety of the commission of the crime to go out and slug this poor old man over the head?

He was allowed to go about his business. Nobody bothered him. Nobody was hurt. And so I sincerely submit that your Honor should not, and I don't believe your Honor will, regard this in any capacity or any manner other than an ordinary armed-robbery case.

Your Honor should take into consideration the ages of these men. Your Honor should take into consideration their family backgrounds. And I submit then, if your Honor please, that a sentence of ten years will more than enough satisfy society, because I don't think that the society of the Commonwealth of Massachusetts or of the United States is particularly concerned about Lloyd's of London.

THE COURT. Very well. Now, with reference to perjury, I was looking through your argument, Mr. Smith, and I find that you in substance said to the jury that if they believed O'Keefe, then Ryan is lying. And on the same page, "Dorothy Lipfin, the waitress, she is lying; and O'Keefe, the thief, is telling the truth." And on the same page: "Officer McDermitt is lying; Crane is lying; and O'Keefe, the thief, is telling the truth." Then, on page 4202: "Mrs. Maffie is lying—"

MR. SMITH. I didn't say Mrs. Maffie was lying. I said that is the choice, either—

THE COURT (reading). "So you are going to say O'Keefe, the thief, is telling the truth and Mrs. Maffie is lying."

MR. SMITH. That's right.

THE COURT. Now, lying on the witness stand I construe to mean perjury.

MR. SMITH. Exactly.

THE COURT. Here, on page 4203: "Margaret Connolly committed perjury, if O'Keefe, the thief, is telling the truth."

MR. SMITH. Exactly. Precisely.

THE COURT. Well, that is the question I put.

MR. SMITH. If your Honor please, I respectfully submit—

THE COURT. Some of them undoubtedly were mistaken. I don't believe they were all perjurers.

MR. SMITH. Well, now, I didn't ask your Honor to rule on that phase.

THE COURT. There is no ruling to be made.

MR. SMITH. All I suggest to the court is that your Honor said, "Others added perjury to the commission of the crime charged." That was your Honor's statement. I respectfully submit that there is no evidence of it, and if there is any evidence of it you have an obligation and the district attorney has an obligation to bring them in here and charge them with perjury.

MR. BYRNE. I understand my obligation, if your Honor pleases. He doesn't have to remind me of anything.

THE COURT. Very well, Mr. Smith. Anything else you want to add?

MR. SMITH. No.

THE COURT. Next counsel.

MR. DE GIACOMO (for Maffie). There is no mathematical formula, as you have said, for the determination of wise and just sentences. It would be indeed simple, although I submit unfair, if in the imposition of sentence a judge could just add and subtract and deal with human beings in a mathematical manner. But by virtue of the fact that we are dealing with human beings, there is no mathematical formula, and for that we are blessed.

245

Your Honor requested that counsel be of some assistance in this most important function, the imposition of sentence. Whatever assistance I can render to your Honor, as an officer of this court, and in behalf of Maffie, whom I represent, I shall attempt to do.

Now, who is Maffie? We all know him as a defendant in this course. But who is Maffie? Maffie is a man forty-four years old. He is married and has two children. But is there anything good that can be said of Maffie, for, you say, he has been convicted of armed robbery?

We all have learned one lesson in this court: people are just not black and white. Unfortunately, most of us are gray, and so is Maffie.

What is there good in Maffie? Who can answer a question such as that? For most of us to say or answer, "What is good about an individual?" is a most difficult proposition. Perhaps the best way to answer, "What is good in Maffie?" is to define what is bad in Maffie, and subtract it. And that is what I propose to do.

Up to the time that early morning when the foreman of the jury said, "Guilty, guilty, guilty," about Maffie, what was there bad about him? I have in my hand a record, a certified copy of a record from the United States District Court for the District of Massachusetts, which I know is before you.

It shows that Maffie, on a plea of guilty in 1954, was committed to the Federal Institution at Danbury, Connecticut, for a period of nine months, for the failure to make an income tax return.

Prior to that, what was there bad about Maffie? Maffie is a gambler. He has appeared in the past in the District Court, to the best of my knowledge, on one or two petty gambling offenses. Now, as far as the record that I know of, and I have diligently searched to find what is bad about Maffie, there it is. Up to the time that the foreman announced that verdict, there was no conviction

246

against this man for a crime that shocked the conscience of society. That was his record.

And as far as what is good, your Honor, you subtract it and what you have left is what is good in Maffie. Has he done anything constructive for society in the forty-four years in which he has lived? Is there anything that indicates he can be rehabilitated and returned to a normal life?

Has he ever served his country? Maffie served his country for two and a half years. He was honorably discharged. For his service, strange though it may seem in view of these circumstances, a thankful Government awarded him a pension as a disabled veteran.

Now that is something good about Maffie, that is something constructive about Maffie. Millions of others served, also, but at least it is something good and something constructive for Maffie.

At one time in this court, I quoted Mr. Justice Cardoza and I stated that he said that "the law has its record of blunders and blindness and superstition, and even cruelty, but that it has never lacked the impulse of a great hope, the vision of a great ideal."

And I submit that ideal is what must be satisfied by your Honor in this court; that ideal is to return a man to his home and to his family and to society as a useful citizen—if it is at all possible. That is what your Honor should consider in the imposition of sentence on Maffie.

THE COURT. All right. Next, Mr. O'Donnell.

MR. O'DONNELL (for Richardson, Geagan and Faherty). May it please the court, I was delighted to hear the comments of the court recapping the history of theories of punishment and penology. Right along, I have had confidence in his Honor by virtue of your personal long experience on the bench. I think it would be presumptuous of me to attempt to advise this honorable and able court in regard to the clients that I represent.

I did think for a while, before hearing your Honor's comments, that we would be fortunate if the court was not asked that these men be committed to the cages at Franklin Park Zoo for the perusal of a curious public. I am very encouraged that that isn't going to happen.

And in regard to the probation record that you have in your possession regarding my clients, by virtue of your able and long service I know in this instance that like a legal surgeon you will subtract and eliminate fancy from fact. The narratives that are so fixed with coloration will not impress. His Honor, with his long experience, addressing himself to those documents, will look at the meat of the entire matter.

I respectfully urge that as you do go over those documents I hope that included among them will be the outstanding and excellent service rendered by Michael Geagan when he submitted himself to the cause of medical science. During the early years of World War II, medical science was benefited by using him as a subject of their experiments.

So I respectfully suggest, your Honor, because of your wide and long experience, that you who enunciated the doctrine of mercy, the doctrine of the Golden Rule, and of love of neighbor, will agree we can still love them, my clients. We may not like their acts, but it is the act and not the actor. And there will be no recrimination for us as a result of being encouraged by your remarks.

In closing, I look to English literature for the comment of Shakespeare, when he said, "If we all received our just deserts, who would escape the whipping?"

THE COURT. Well, what gives me a problem, Mr. O'Donnell, is that Mr. Richardson had been sentenced to State's Prison for five to seven years, back in 1934, twenty years ago. Mr. Geagan was sentenced to twenty-eight to thirty years for armed robbery, twenty-two years ago. Yes, he was paroled because he risked his life for science. But I wonder if sentence should be reduced each time a man comes to court or whether it should be raised, if he commits the same crime? And I see Mr. Faherty in 1937 received a sentence of twenty to twenty-five years in State's Prison.

All right, Mr. Sontag.

MR. SONTAG (for Baker). May I state simply and directly that Henry Baker is fifty years old and has been engaged for the last six or seven years in business. He has apparently become a good member of the community, spoken well of by his neighbors.

All during this trial Mr. Baker has maintained his innocence. At this time he continues to maintain his innocence. I state that simply because I inferred from the court's remarks before lunch that there was some mention of a post-trial confession.

In that regard, my client maintains his innocence. With respect to the remarks of perjury, I am sure the court did not intend that I be included directly, in view of the fact the defendant Baker presented no witnesses directly in his behalf.

It is unfortunate that a death occurred which caused or rendered a witness for Baker unable to appear here in court. However, I would like to say to all of the counsel here that no perjury was committed in behalf of the defendant Baker or any other defendant here willfully.

I submit further, your Honor, that to sentence him without hope of ever doing his term and getting out would be in the poor interest of the Government. I think that penology today requires that each person be given some hope, some reason for living; and I respectfully request that this court render mercy with justice.

THE COURT. Mr. Byrne.

MR. BYRNE (for the commonwealth). May it please the court, there is no one who agrees more than I with the philosophy propounded by this court as to the certainty of punishment rather than the severity being that for which we should all reach. I have, sir, in behalf of that particular principle, nol-prossed a first-degree murder case since I have been district attorney. I have accepted pleas, many times, where men have been indicted for first-degree murder for that of second-degree murder, because I felt—even though I realized that the crime was a vicious one—that hope should not be abandoned. Even though they committed the ultimate crime, and in order that some day they might be able to prove that reformation and rehabilitation is really the law of the land, I have given them that opportunity, always hoping they would become rehabilitated and returned to the land of decent people.

But if your Honor pleases, certainty of punishment rather than severity is a principle that should be abided by but not where the individual about to be sentenced is a hardened criminal and a potential murderer.

Take the case of Mr. Faherty and Mr. Richardson. They are no strangers to State's Prison. They have been there before. And they were there, if your Honor pleases, because once again they were back in the old profession of wielding guns into the stomachs and the sides of individuals for the purpose of committing armed robbery.

So we catch up with them again in 1956, these men who should be returned to society, and where do we find them? We find them out in Coleman Street, once again with the instruments that they seem to be so familiar with and that are so contrary to the policy of decent people—guns, guns. And it reached a stage that, if we are to believe the evidence presented in this case, it is a lucky thing that John Kehoe can be here today to witness the pleas of counsel in behalf of them for a small sentence.

How ridiculous, if your Honor pleases, to have counsel stand here and say that you should consider this as an ordinary robbery, an ordinary twenty-dollar robbery. If we believe the decision that those twelve men brought in here, these men had in their possession $1,100,000. But counsel stands up and says they are innocent, insofar as he is concerned.

They are guilty insofar as this commonwealth is concerned, because twelve men have come in and said so. Take Geagan. He walks down into the City Hall of Brockton, puts a gun in the side of a police officer and takes his money in an armed holdup, for which he received twenty-eight to thirty years in State's Prison.

Take McGinnis. He is no stranger to guns. He was sentenced in the State of Rhode Island, in the City of Providence, for six years.

Take this disciple of righteousness and common decency—Pino. He was sent to Concord Reformatory for abuse of a female child. He was sent to State's Prison after that for breaking and entering into Rhodes Brothers, where they found every burglarious instrument it was possible for a burglar to have in his possession—not twelve golf balls.

Now come down to Baker. But before we do, let me say I have given it a lot of thought; it is not an easy task, if your Honor pleases, for a public prosecutor under any circumstances to stand here and recommend what I intend to recommend in order to protect the decent people of this commonwealth.

We hear so much bunk about the protection of burglars and rapists and murderers, under the cloak of civil rights, that I am beginning to wonder if we are not slopping over backward. I am beginning to wonder if they should have the right to sit there with long criminal records and contend that we cannot introduce the major portions of those records. I am beginning to wonder if that is the proper way to protect the decent people of this commonwealth.

Now back to Baker. At times I felt sorry for him. No one came forward in his aid, no one seemed to want to help him. He just slouched down there. I looked, I tried to find the loophole that might have helped him.

But you take a look at his record: in and out of State's Prison as though it was his second home. And the last time he came out, Pino was there to meet him, and he became a participant in the Brink's robbery.

I looked at Maffie, and I was hoping that something could be done there. He had done time at a Federal institution, true. But the worst thing he ever did was when he provided the dump for the Brink's robbery, provided the home of his poor old mother and father, on the verge of that precipice from which there is no return.

Take them all down the line. Costa. Costa is no stranger to State's Prison. Costa is mixed up with guns. Their whole life, their whole method of living, the road they want to travel, is absolutely contrary to that of decent people. It is about time we caught up with them and their guns, guns, guns.

McGinnis, of course, was the leader. The court must rely upon and understand that it took nine months, nine solid months, to attain this day. I don't think there is any assistant district attorney in the commonwealth or in the country who could have prepared a better case than my assistant, Mr. Frederick T. Doyle . . . with the help of Mr. McAuliffe, Mr. McGonigle, Mr. Mulhern, practically half of my office staff. I had also the full benefit of every piece of knowledge in the possession of the Federal Bureau of Investigation. I had the full benefit of every bit of knowledge in the possession of the Boston police department.

There are many things that could not be presented

in the course of the trial because they had no direct part in the trial. But you cannot drive out of my head the fact that William Cameron was murdered behind the Fargo Building an hour after he left the home of an assistant district attorney, who had questioned him in this case. You cannot drive out of my head the fact that one of the accomplices and closest friends of Specs O'Keefe disappeared, perhaps for all time, shortly after he left the district attorney's office, and that Specs O'Keefe shows from his left shoulder to his wrist where he was shot one night in Dorchester.

I assure the court, as an officer of this court and as the district attorney of this county, that these men have just reached the end of their rope; that their mode and their method of living has been nothing but by the gun. They have been nothing but thieves and robbers. Their records show it. Their very existence shows it. They have been nothing but a menace to society. I can see no hope for them. If I could see a ray of sunshine that would deliver them back once again into society, I would be the first one to tell this court.

But I am thinking of the decent people of this commonwealth, people who demand the right to let their daughters walk home at night, demand the protection of the institutions that make this country so decent a place to live in.

The whole record of these men shows that there is no opportunity of rehabilitation. Society has not a chance so long as they continue to live amongst decent people.

They have committed a $1,100,000 robbery with guns. How silly can we be to stand up here in court and say, as if in absolution, that men weren't knocked down. Those men had .38's shoved against their stomachs, they were in fear of their lives, they wondered if they would ever get home. But the fact that they were not knocked down is advanced as an argument.

With their records and their method of living, I recommend sincerely that they be deprived of hope, that they be given life sentences from which they cannot be paroled until after the expiration of twenty years.

The sentences fell like blows from a broadax:

"Anthony Pino. The Court in consideration of your offense, as set forth in Indictment No. 1214, sentences you to be imprisoned in the Massachusetts Correctional Institution at Walpole for and during the term of your natural life.

"On Indictment No. 1215, the Court sentences you to be imprisoned in the Massachusetts Correctional Institution at Walpole for the term of not more than ten years and not less than eight years.

"On Indictment No. 1216, the Court sentences you to be imprisoned in the House of Correction in the County of Suffolk, there to be kept at hard labor for the term of two years from and after the sentences imposed upon you to the Massachusetts Correctional Institution.

"You stand committed in pursuance of these sentences. You have three days within which to file a request for leave to appeal to the Appellate Division of this Court."

"John Adolph Maffie. The Court, in consideration of your offense, as set forth in Indictment No. 1214, sentences you to be imprisoned in the Massachusetts Correctional Institution at Walpole for and during the term of your natural life.

"And on Indictment No. 1215, the Court sentences you to be imprisoned in the Massachusetts Correctional Institution at Walpole for not more than ten years and not less than eight years.

"And for your offense on No. 1216, the Court sentences you to be imprisoned in the House of Correction in the County of Suffolk, there to be kept at hard labor for a term of not more than two years, this sentence to take effect from and after the sentence imposed on you to the Massachusetts Correctional Institution.

"You have three days within which to file a request for leave to appeal to the Appellate Division of this Court."

"Michael Vincent Geagan. The Court, in consideration of your offense, as set forth in Indictment No. 1214, sentences you to be imprisoned in the Massachusetts Correctional Institution at Walpole for and during the term of your natural life.

"And on Indictment No. 1215, the Court sentences you to be imprisoned in the Massachusetts Correctional Institution at Walpole for a term of not more than ten years and not less than eight years, this sentence to be served concurrently with the other sentences.

"On No. 1216, the Court sentences you to be imprisoned in the House of Correction in the County of Suffolk for a term of two years, this sentence to take effect from and after the previous sentence to the Massachusetts Correctional Institution.

"You have three days within which to file a request for leave to appeal to the Appellate Division of this Court."

"Vincent James Costa. The Court, in consideration of your offense, as set forth in Indictment No. 1214, sentences you to be imprisoned at the Massachusetts Correctional Institution at Walpole for and during the term of your natural life.

"And on Indictment No. 1215, the Court sentences you to be imprisoned at the Massachusetts Correctional Institution at Walpole for a term of not more than ten years and not less than eight years, this sentence to be served concurrently with the sentence on No. 1214.

"On No. 1216, the Court sentences you, for your offense, to the House of Correction in the County of Suffolk, there to be kept at hard labor for the term of two years from and after the sentences imposed to the Massachusetts Correctional Institution.

"You have three days within which to file a request for leave to appeal to the Appellate Division of this Court."

"James Ignatius Faherty. The Court, in consideration of

your offense, as set forth in Indictment No. 1214, sentences you to be imprisoned in the Massachusetts Correctional Institution at Walpole for and during the term of your natural life.

"And on Indictment 1215, the Court sentences you to the Massachusetts Correctional Institution at Walpole for a term of not more than ten years and not less than eight years, this sentence to be served concurrently with the sentence imposed on No. 1214.

"On No. 1216, the Court sentences you to be imprisoned in the House of Correction in the County of Suffolk, there to be kept at hard labor for the term of two years, this sentence to be served from and after the sentences imposed to the Massachusetts Correctional Institution.

"You have three days within which to file a request for leave to appeal to the Appellate Division of this Court."

"Thomas Francis Richardson. The Court, in consideration of your offense, as set forth in Indictment No. 1214, sentences you to be imprisoned in the Massachusetts Correctional Institution at Walpole for and during the term of your natural life.

"And on Indictment No. 1215, the Court sentences you to be imprisoned in the Massachusetts Correctional Institution at Walpole for not more than ten years and not less than eight years, this sentence to be served concurrently with the sentence on No. 1214.

"On No. 1216, the Court, in consideration of your offense, sentences you to be imprisoned at the House of Correction in the County of Suffolk for the term of not more than two years, this sentence to be served from and after the sentence imposed upon you to the Massachusetts Correctional Institution.

"You have a right within three days to file a request for leave to appeal to the Appellate Division of this Court."

"Henry Baker. The Court, in consideration of your offense, as set forth in Indictment No. 1214, sentences you to be imprisoned in the Massachusetts Correctional Institution at Walpole for and during the term of your natural life.

"And on Indictment No. 1215, the Court sentences you to be imprisoned in the Massachusetts Correctional Institution for a term of not more than ten years and not less than eight years.

"On Indictment 1216, the Court, in consideration of your offense, sentences you to be imprisoned in the House of Correction in the County of Suffolk for a term of not more than two years, this sentence to take effect from and after the sentences imposed upon you to the Massachusetts Correctional Institution.

"You have a right to file a request for leave to appeal to the Appellate Division of this Court within three days."

The court clerk who was reading Judge Forte's sentences took a deep breath. He had never had to read what was about to fall from his lips:

"Joseph F. McGinnis. The Court, in consideration of your offense, as set forth in Indictment No. 1292, sentences you to be imprisoned in the Massachusetts Correctional Institution at Walpole for and during the term of your natural life.

"On Indictment No. 1293, the Court sentences you to be imprisoned in the Massachusetts Correctional Institution at Walpole for and during the term of your natural life, to run concurrently with the sentence on No. 1292.

"On No. 1294, the Court sentences you to be imprisoned in the Massachusetts Correctional Institution at Walpole for and during the term of your natural life, to be served concurrently with the sentence imposed on No. 1293.

"The Court, in consideration of your offense as set forth in Indictment No. 1295, sentences you to be imprisoned in the Massachusetts Correctional Institution at Walpole for and during the term of your natural life, this sentence to take effect concurrently with the sentence on No. 1294.

"On No. 1296, the Court sentences you to be imprisoned in the Massachusetts Correctional Institution at Walpole for and during the term of your natural life, this sentence to be served concurrently with the sentence on No. 1295.

"On No. 1297, the Court sentences you to be imprisoned in the Massachusetts Correctional Institution at Walpole for and during the term of your natural life, this sentence to run concurrently with the sentence imposed on No. 1296.

"On No. 1298, the Court sentences you to be imprisoned in the Massachusetts Correctional Institution at Walpole for and during the term of your natural life, this sentence to run concurrently with the sentence imposed on No. 1297.

"On No. 1301, the Court sentences you to be imprisoned in the Massachusetts Correctional Institution at Walpole for and during the term of your natural life, this sentence to run concurrently with the sentence on No. 1298.

"On No. 1302, the Court, in consideration of your offense, sentences you to be imprisoned in the Massachusetts Correctional Institution at Walpole for and during the term of your natural life, this sentence to run concurrently with the sentence on No. 1301.

"On Indictment No. 1292, the Court sentences you to be imprisoned in the Massachusetts Correctional Institution at Walpole for a term of not more than ten years and not less than eight years, this sentence to run concurrently with the sentence imposed on No. 1302.

"On Indictment No. 1290, the Court, in consideration of your offense, sentences you to be imprisoned in the Massachusetts Correctional Institution at Walpole for a term of not more than three years and not less than two and one-half years, this sentence to run concurrently with the sentence on No. 1302.

"On No. 1260, the Court, in consideration of your offense, sentences you to be imprisoned for two years in the House of Correction in the County of Suffolk, this sentence to take effect from and after the sentences imposed upon you in the Massachusetts Correctional Institution.

"You have three days within which to file a request for leave to appeal to the Appellate Division of this Court."

There was only one audible comment from the eight defendants as they heard their fates. It came from McGinnis. He turned to a court attendant, shrugged and said, "Why doesn't he give me about nine more lives?"

18

"**W**HERE'S THE MONEY?"

Millions asked that question in the wake of the sentences.
The Boston *Record* asked it editorially, on October 10, 1956,
and added:

> The last chapter of the fantastic Brink's robbery case has
> yet to be written. It won't be written until the $1,218,211
> which the raiding gunmen whisked away on the night of
> January 17, 1950, is located and recovered. To date, only
> about $68,000 has been accounted for; and somewhere, ob-
> viously out of reach of the authorities, the rest of the huge
> sum is buried or otherwise concealed.
>
> Where is it? Who has it?
>
> Effectively functioning justice has made certain that the
> vanished loot won't do eight Brink's robbers much good—
> at least not in the foreseeable future.
>
> Joseph F. McGinnis, the alleged ringleader, is serving
> nine life sentences—concurrently or simultaneously. The
> seven other defendants are beginning single life sentences
> as well as additional prison terms of eight to ten years for
> breaking and entering with intent to commit a felony.
>
> In the impregnable fastness of the maximum security
> State's Prison at Walpole, these men, who attempted the
> perfect crime and almost succeeded, are going to have
> seemingly endless time for thought, and we don't think much
> of it will be pleasing.
>
> If they ponder upon the money they cannot spend and its

whereabouts, their walls will assume a thickness and their bars a stoutness far in excess of the builders' dimensions; and the agony of frustration, which the poet Dante called the most writhing pain of Hell, will grip and gripe them increasingly.

There is a powerful lesson here for American youth and particularly for those impressed by the utterly false notion that the Brink's robbers were big men and bold men.

There is nothing big about them now as they exchange their names for numbers; and if any trace of boldness lingers on in their attitudes, it is wasted on the Walpole guards and officers, who are used to that sort of thing and can always cope with it.

Law-abiding society is grateful to the Federal Bureau of Investigation, the district attorney's office, the jurors and judge who put these men where they belong and for so long a time.

Confronted by an extraordinary test of duty they met it courageously and admirably, and our whole way of life is the better because of them.

There were other cries of "Where's the money?" The $100,000 Reward Committee set up immediately after the robbery* received a number of claims presented by persons who asserted they had complied with the phrase "for information leading to the Arrest and Conviction of Persons involved in the Holdup of the Office of Brink's, Incorporated, 165 Prince Street, Boston, Massachusetts, on January 17, 1950."

A strong case was made by Dean Meredith, the Towanda, Pennsylvania, chief of police who recognized Specs and Gus on June 12, 1950, and brought about their arrests on charges other than the Brink's case.

One William H. McMasters of Boston, who claimed to

* Henry M. Leen, former Assistant United States Attorney; Edward O. Proctor, former Assistant Attorney General of Massachusetts; Timothy J. Murphy, former Assistant Attorney General of Massachusetts; Charles A. McCarron, attorney, and Edward Johnson, official of the Boston Chamber of Commerce.

have submitted the plan that "flushed" the Brink's robbers, also applied. So did a Boston attorney named Vernon Marr, who furnished information that on the night of the robbery he saw two men dressed in pea coats and rubbers. He gave police such details as he remembered, upon reading the next day's reports on how the robbers were dressed.

One Wendell A. Haynes of Poultney, Vermont, told the Reward Committee that on January 19, 1950, he spotted McGinnis driving in that state.

Wayne Lineberry of Galax, Virginia, who described himself to the committee as "an old man who grew up in the back hills of Virginia," applied for the $100,000 on the ground that he had sent information about the culprits to "a post office box in Mount Vernon, New York."

Hilda Hamilton, Rochester, N. H., felt she was entitled to a share, at least, for her earlier "solution" of the case: it was the work—the robbery was—of "college students, because they are intelligent, could room together as a group, and could have developed the spirit necessary to accomplish such a robbery."

A Honduran named Antonio Martinez based his claim on elaborate deductions which corresponded to a great degree to those that had been published in United States magazines. The Commercial Assurance Company, the "Lloyd's of London" Smith had spoken of, filed civil action to regain its payoff.

The committee soon ruled that it would withhold distribution of the reward "until the last avenue of appeal has been closed."

By that time, in the immediate wake of the sentencings, appeals followed appeals. The FBI report on this activity reads:

APPEALS

On October 15, 1956, counsel for Anthony Pino, Joseph McGinnis, Vincent Costa and Adolph Maffie filed motion with the clerk of the Suffolk Superior Court that they will appeal the jury verdict to the Massachusetts Supreme Judicial Court.

On October 17, 1956, attorneys Lawrence F. O'Donnell and Henry Sontag, filed similar appeals on behalf of their clients, Thomas F. Richardson, Michael V. Geagan, James I. Faherty and Henry Baker.

All counsel in their appeals declared that the defendants were aggrieved by certain opinions, rulings, directions, judgment, verdict and sentence in the trial.

On February 27, 1958, attorneys Paul T. Smith, Robert DeGiacomo and Henry Sontag filed with the clerk of the Superior Criminal Court a list of Assignment of Errors in this case on behalf of defendants Anthony Pino, Joseph McGinnis, James V. Costa, Henry Baker and Adolph Maffie. Attorney Lawrence O'Donnell, for defendants Richardson, Geagan and Faherty, has been granted an extension of thirty days in which to file his Assignment of Errors.

The following is the number of Assignment of Errors on behalf of each defendant, which will form the basis of appeal to the Massachusetts Supreme Court:

BAKER	132
PINO	132
COSTA	134
MC GINNIS	142
MAFFIE	132

A review of the Assignment of Errors shows that, for the most part, they are duplicated in the case of each defendant. Many of the Assignment of Errors deal with the Court's ruling regarding Motions to Quash and Pleas in Abatement.

A number of the Assignment of Errors have to do with failure of the Court to exclude testimony of witnesses, stating that such testimony concerned a collateral issue tended only to support the statement of an accomplice, namely O'Keefe, and that the admission of this testimony was highly prejudicial.

A number of the Assignment of Errors are also concerned with the closing argument of District Attorney Garrett Byrne,

Suffolk County, which has been characterized by the defense attorneys as inflammatory.

One of the Assignment of Errors makes reference to failure of the judge to exclude remarks of District Attorney Byrne regarding the presence in the courtroom of Special Agent in Charge E. J. Powers, and SA John P. Larkin, when neither of these people testified during the course of the trial.

The Assignment of Errors filed on 3/21/58, on behalf of Michael V. Geagan, Thomas Richardson and James I. Faherty are very similar to those filed in behalf of the other defendants except that exceptions have been taken to the introduction of evidence, such as finding of guns and bullets and hair dye in the apartment of these men when they were arrested.

The Massachusetts Supreme Court affirmed the convictions of the Brink's robbers on July 1, 1959. On November 16 of the same year the U.S. Supreme Court denied a request of the defense counsel for a writ of certiorari. The costly, tedious appeals machinery had been put back in motion.

At Walpole, the men were given an exotic first-night dinner. The prison kitchen saved them warmed-over chop suey. They were assigned individual cells in a new block for two weeks of interviews and classification. Life promised to be austere, the Boston *American* of October 10, 1956, noted:

> They'll get up at 6:30 A.M., have breakfast and then start their day's work in metal fabrication, the foundry, the print shop or the laundry. If any of them is adept at clerical work they may be given that type of job. There is some form of recreation almost every evening at Walpole, but prisoners are in their cells at nine. At 10:30 it's lights out, and at 11 P.M. the prison radio system, which the convicts hear through head sets, is turned off.

By the following month, the Boston *Traveler* was able to report that the bandits had become "model" prisoners.

"I wish we had a hundred guys like them," a veteran guard was quoted as saying. All the robbers were "working quietly and efficiently."

McGinnis was helping with the prison's plumbing and electrical work. Pino and Costa were together in the prison warehouse, loading and unloading supplies. Baker was a clerk in the foundry, checking the performance of foundry workers. Richardson was carpentering. Maffie and Faherty had drawn laundry service. Geagan was in housekeeping.

"The Brink's bandits are pleasant and polite to all guards," the *Traveler's* reporter Jim Harrington noted. "They are aloof from other inmates. When they have free time, they meet together at 'fraternity corner' at the prison. They talk constantly about a new trial.

"To all the other inmates, they are the 'big shots.'

"The young convicts, especially, regard them with almost 'reverence,' guards say. But the group keeps to themselves. They do their jobs each day and look hopefully to the future.

"One veteran guard said, 'They'll do their bit and never give anyone trouble. I only hope some of the punks here can learn a good lesson from them.'"

The case was not ended for Fat John Buccelli.
An FBI report reads:

John Buccelli, a well-known Boston and New York underworld figure, had served time with Tony Pino at the State Penitentiary in Charlestown, Massachusetts, in the early 1940's. Buccelli had been sentenced to serve five to seven years following an armed-robbery conviction in 1940; and Pino was received at the State Penitentiary in 1938 to serve two consecutive sentences of three to four years in connection with a burglary.

An extremely stocky man, Buccelli weighed nearly 300 pounds and was often referred to as "Fat John." He was born in Brookline, Massachusetts, in September, 1914, and resided with his wife and two sons in Bellerose, Long Island, New York, during the period when the Brink's robbery was being planned and carried out.

Following the Brink's robbery, Buccelli was interviewed by FBI agents on three separate occasions. He gave conflicting accounts of his activities on January 17, 1950, and was evasive in answering the questions asked him. Careful checking of his background did not disclose him to be a participant in the Brink's robbery; however, it did show that he was an associate of Pino, Geagan, Gusciora and other members of the robbery gang.

On the night of June 3, 1956, Jordan Perry, a small-time Boston hoodlum, was arrested in Baltimore with $4,635 identifiable as part of the Brink's loot. Perry stated that he had obtained this money from a man known to him only as "Fat John."

A search of the office which John Buccelli used on Tremont Street in Boston led to the recovery of an additional $51,906, which was identifiable as part of the Brink's loot. As a result of his possessing this money, "Fat John" Buccelli received a two-year prison sentence.

After serving this sentence, Buccelli resumed a life of crime. While out on appeal in connection with a narcotics conviction, he met his end.

The *Traveler* told it more graphically:

"FATS" BUCCELLI SHOT
Body Found in Auto—Bullet Wound in Head

A notorious Boston gangster, linked with the Brink's case and a narcotics gang, was shot to death in his car in the South End early today (June 19, 1958). John F. (Fats) Buccelli, 44, was found bleeding from the head and slumped behind the wheel of his 1957 Imperial sedan.

It was first believed the heavy-set underworld figure had been killed when his car rammed into the rear of a trailer truck on Chandler St., at Trement St. But Medical Examiner George W. Curtis revealed after an autopsy that Buccelli had died from a bullet wound in the head. No gun was found at the scene.

Two Boston detectives, meanwhile, were sent to Beverly to question a man captured in a wild 100-mile-an-hour chase. In the car, police said, was a gun which had been fired once. The Boston investigators will compare the bullet removed from Buccelli's head with the gun in Beverly.

Buccelli was the sixth figure in the Brink's case to meet death. Two died of natural causes. Three others are missing.

"He was murdered," said Dr. Curtis.

Police arriving at the scene at 3 A.M. found the sedan's front grill pushed in about twelve inches. The car was behind the parked truck. Buccelli was bleeding profusely from the mouth and ears when pulled from the car by police. He also had lumps on his forehead and the back of his head, police said.

Police grew suspicious that it was more than an ordinary accident when they noticed that the left window of the driver's side of the car had been smashed. They theorized that the killer might have smashed the window with a heavy instrument, possibly a baseball bat, before shooting the paunchy Buccelli to death.

There were no skid marks in the area that would indicate the car had come to a sudden halt in an effort to avoid the truck.

And what of Specs?

He was to serve longer at the East Cambridge jail—a transient trap—than any inmate in its history. About 10,000 convicts entered and left as he languished there establishing his unenvied record: the confessed burglar who waited longest for the disposition of his case.

While not in solitary, he was kept isolated from the ebb and flow of fellow-prisoners. Guards described him as a model prisoner, one given to hours of reading and study in his cell. He did his exercising in the prison corridor rather than in the yard. He became so much of a fixture around the place that guards occasionally used him as an impartial arbitrator in fracases involving inmates.

That he was regarded as a human clay pigeon by the state

was made abundantly plain on January 19, 1959, when he was spirited out of the jail under heavy guard to pay his last respects to his mother, Catherine, dead at eighty-five and resting at a Dorchester funeral parlor. Cars of well-armed police guards escorted Specs to the funeral home. More than a dozen detectives were deployed at the home itself, including some who posed as mourners in the room where the old lady, who had known so much distress in life, lay in death.

Specs' sister Mary met him as he entered. They walked to their mother's coffin, knelt and prayed. Then Specs was taken back to prison under the same heavy guard. He decided not to attend the Mass and burial service, not that he feared for his life but he wanted to add no further chaos.

The question of what to do about Specs had been the special interest of District Attorney Byrne for months before that. And it was to remain so. On the tenth anniversary of the robbery, January 17, 1960, Byrne told Jerome Sullivan of the Boston *Globe*:

> Hasn't he paid enough? He's been behind bars for nine of the last ten years, compared with only four for the Brink's convicts. After paying the maximum three and a half years in Towanda on a firearms violation charge, he came back here and has done another five and a half years, and he still owes another three-to-twelve-year term in Pennsylvania for burglary.
>
> Is it to be a life sentence for a man who gave all to his commonwealth and his country? Doesn't Pennsylvania take into consideration what he has done and the time he has paid both here and there?
>
> Where would we be—the Commonwealth of Massachusetts or the FBI—if it weren't for Specky? He cracked the Brink's case. Is this his reward—a life sentence behind bars here, or death in the Western State Penitentiary in Pennsylvania?
>
> What does a man have to do? Specky's life certainly isn't any inducement to anyone else to come forward with in-

formation in a criminal case, is it? Is he to pay with his life for doing his state and his country a service?

If he is put on the street he has a better chance of survival than if he is sent back to Pennsy to pay for the same crime for which he has already served his time.

Byrne had frequently visited Specs in jail and each time had been impressed by O'Keefe's particular concern about serving time at the notoriously tough pen at Pittsburgh. He was convinced that the treatment Gus had received there had played a role in his eventual death. He was convinced, too, that at Pittsburgh he would not be considered a defender of the commonwealth, a boon to the Federal Bureau of Investigation or a "guest of the court," but, instead, an informer.

Byrne's efforts to spring the man who had meant so much to the successful completion of the long case were, for a considerable period, frustrated by legal considerations. The recurrent appeals of the eight lifers appeared to require priority, just as the Reward Committee had ruled that there would be no division of that impressive sum until all appeal ammunition had been expended. A brief for the appellants, filed early in 1959 by Paul Smith, charged that the "overwhelming prestige" enjoyed by FBI Director J. Edgar Hoover caused the public to accept implicitly his statement, prior to the trial, that the Brink's case was solved.

"The effect of the news release, as well might have been anticipated by the Department of Justice and Suffolk County enforcement and prosecutive officials, not only was sensational but also set the stage for indictment by press and trial by press," Smith's brief said in part.

But at long last the shackles began to fall from Specs.

On June 22, 1960, Specs was taken from prison and driven under extreme precautions to Superior Court. A cheap suitcase lay at his feet in the rear of the sedan he shared with jail master David S. Robinson. Specs had eleven cents in the pocket of his characteristically neat dark-blue suit.

Once in the courthouse he was taken in tow by the district attorney and whisked to the courtroom of the same Judge Forte who had presided over the long trial of four years before. There he repeated his old plea of guilty to a charge of armed robbery, and to indictments accusing him of breaking and entering in the nighttime and "confining and putting in fear" the Brink's guards on duty at the time of the robbery.

Byrne stepped forward immediately.

"May it please the court," the DA said, "the defendant Joseph O'Keefe has already served fifty-three months in jail for his part in the Brink's armed robbery.

"There is no penitentiary either in Massachusetts or Pennsylvania wherein he could serve any future sentence for his past crimes without being prey to murder or cruel and inhuman punishment because he testified as a witness for the commonwealth against his confederates in the Brink's case.

"Without the co-operation of the defendant O'Keefe the multimillion-dollar robbery of Brink's, Incorporated, would never have been solved.

"His testimony as a witness for the commonwealth during the trial of the surviving eight Brink's bandits was a major, contributing factor in their conviction.

"To sentence Joseph O'Keefe now to any additional punishment would constitute a fatal blow to law and order and to the well-being of society in America.

"I recommend that Indictment No. 61 of 1960, to which the defendant pleaded guilty on January 16, 1956, be placed on file. There are compelling reasons for this recommendation. The alternative would be imposition of a sentence and granting credit under General Laws (Ter. Ed.) c. 279, section 334, which reads as follows:

" 'The court on imposing a sentence of commitment to a correctional institution of the commonwealth shall order that the prisoner be deemed to have served a portion of said sentence, such portion to be the number of days spent by the prisoner in confinement prior to such sentence awaiting and during trial.'

"Sentence under the alternative would not accomplish the desired result, which is immediate release of the defendant O'Keefe. He would be committed to Walpole even on a sentence upon which he is eligible to immediate discharge because of the fifty-three months he has served awaiting trial and sentence.

"There would be inevitable delay, red tape and some incarceration in a place where as before noted he would be in mortal danger.

"I therefore renew my recommendation that Indictment No. 61 of 1960 as to the defendant O'Keefe be placed on file. I further recommend that the companion indictments numbered 62, 63, 64 of 1960 be placed on file without plea.

"If the defendant was sentenced to five to seven years in Walpole he would be eligible for complete discharge at the expiration of four years and one month—forty-nine months. Defendant O'Keefe has been incarcerated for more than fifty-three months." He recommended three concurrent sentences of three to four years each.

"It is my honest belief," Byrne concluded earnestly, "that this man should not serve one more day in prison. I feel that he has paid his debt to the Commonwealth of Massachusetts in full."

Judge Forte quickly concurred. Court Clerk Edward V. Keating, acting on instructions from the bench, told O'Keefe:

"You are deemed to have served the sentences just imposed. You are ordered discharged from custody, unless held on some other process."

Pennsylvania would have taken him immediately. High Sheriff William Reece of McKean County, Pennsylvania, was waiting for Specs at his next stop that day: in Boston Municipal Court. He presented a mittimus, a writ authorizing O'Keefe's imprisonment on the sentence that had been imposed in Superior Court in Pennsylvania, March 4, 1954.

Specs' lawyer, Joseph M. McDonough, promptly blocked the mittimus by starting the machinery which would move Specs' extradition case to the office of Governor Foster Furcolo. Pending the outcome of that action, Specs was provided with $5,000 bail on a charge of being a fugitive from justice in Pennsylvania, and the case was continued to August 3, 1960.

He was free to leave a scene that had been familiar to him, off and on, since the age of eight.

"Is the defendant aware of the risk he will be taking if he goes back into the community?" the municipal court judge, Francis X. Morrissey, asked in plain concern.

"He knows all about it," McDonough, his lawyer, answered for Specs. "He is willing to take the chance."

As Specs turned away he was surrounded by reporters and cameramen.

"Have you anything to say?"

"Not a word."

"Any plans?"

"Nothing to say . . . nothing to say," said the man who had said so much.

They would not take that for an answer but crowded into an elevator with him and followed him to the side door of the courthouse. Specs ducked into a car driven by an old friend, a plainclothesman of the Boston police department, Tom Barry. The car started away from the curb of the narrow street and a press car started firing up to give chase. But a third car, manned by a young detective associate of Barry pulled in front of the newsmen and blocked them—impervious to shouts of rage and threatened retribution—until Barry had O'Keefe out of sight. The maneuver reminded Specs of a similar plan of long before, one involving Costa and a crowded truck.

"O'Keefe's destination was unknown," a Boston reporter glumly recorded.

Specs:

"Tom took me to the first good meal I had had in years, a steak place named Valle's, about fifteen miles out on Route 9. I had a piece of roast beef I'll never forget. Then he brought me downtown again, where Kehoe was waiting for me. I borrowed enough from him to buy a hat. Then I tried to get a room at a nice place named '1200 Beacon,' in Brookline.

"They told me they had no vacancies. Maybe they didn't, at that.

"I went to my sister's, and from June until October, when I appeared at the attorney general's office to fight going back to Pennsylvania, I never showed myself publicly."

Specs was public enough that day, however. The *Record*, in reporting the occasion of October 6, 1960, headed its story:

"SPECS," TERRIFIED BY "ASSASSIN," FLEES

In a flight of panic to escape an imaginary underworld assassin, Joseph J. "Specs" O'Keefe, the state's star informer in the fabulous Brink's robbery, bolted from the State House yesterday, raced through heavy traffic to Boston Common, and disappeared toward Tremont Street.

O'Keefe had left the office of Attorney General Edward J. McCormack, Jr., after appearing at an extraordinary open hearing to fight rendition to Pennsylvania, where he faces a three-to-twelve-year term imposed in 1954 for breaking and entering.

An open elevator waiting for him opposite the double doors of McCormack's office caused him to freeze in panic. Then he ran along the third-floor corridor, scuttled past the Hall of Flags, plunged down the outer stairway leading to Beacon Street and continued his headlong race.

It was a flight from terror. He believed an assassin—one of those he claims has vowed to "get him"—lurked at the bottom of the elevator shaft. What O'Keefe did not know was that the elevator had been held deliberately by State House police to escort him to the basement and let him out a side door. Nor did he know that the Capitol police had put some of their men into plainclothes and that they were waiting to guard him. All he knew was the paralyzing fear in which he has lived since he "sang" at the trial of his eight accomplices in the $1,218,000 Brink's robbery and sent them all to prison for life.

He knew the underworld code for that—that death is the penalty.

O'Keefe did not even remain to hear Assistant Attorney General William M. Sullivan, who conducted the rendition hearing, announce that it would be several days before a recommendation will be made to Governor Furcolo.

O'Keefe did not speak at the hearing, but his counsel, Joseph M. McDonough, spoke at length and declared: "To send him back to Pennsylvania is to give him cruel and inhuman punishment. The underworld would get Joe O'Keefe, and instead of his live body we would have a dead corpse."

McDonough said he was only paraphrasing the remarks of District Attorney Garrett H. Byrne of Suffolk County, when O'Keefe was freed. Byrne said O'Keefe had violated the unwritten code of the criminal and would be a "prey, a sitting duck, for murder or cruel and inhuman punishment at the hands of the underworld."

McDonough reminded Sullivan of the service O'Keefe had rendered to the state in the Brink's case, and declared: "Pennsylvania may give you all kinds of assurance of his protection, but if the headlines some day say he was found murdered or maimed in his cell there, it won't be on my conscience."

E. C. Potter, deputy district attorney of McKean County, acting as a special assistant attorney general for Pennsylvania, argued that neither "sympathy nor gratitude" for O'Keefe should have any bearing on his rendition. There was no question of his guilt or innocence in the Pennsylvania case, Potter said. "O'Keefe was convicted."

Specs now says:

"That was a laugh, that business about being 'terrified by assassin.' I bolted that day to get free of the reporters and

274

camera guys. During the whole session they had never let up on me. I didn't want to talk to any of them. I just wanted to get away, and I did."

Potter's plea was most determined. But it failed to move the attorney general's office or the governor. On November 4, 1960, Governor Furcolo announced he would refuse to deliver Specs to Pennsylvania law "because it would mean certain death at the hands of some underworld executioner."

Joseph James O'Keefe was free, wholly free, under one of the most remarkable amnesties in the annals of the commonwealth.

19

IT HAS NOT BEEN AN EASY FREEDOM.

"Rehabilitation," treasured word of modern penology, has a tendency to collapse like a bubble the moment man leaves the cell where that metamorphosis supposedly took place.

Specs tells it better:

"What's life like? I live as quietly and as inconspicuously as I can, and not in fear, really, but because I don't want to intrude on the public consciousness.

"A person like myself is never free, I guess. People 'see' me at different places and make a report. The other day John Larkin of the FBI, a real good guy, called me to ask me if I had been at Boston's North Station in a Cadillac the day before. I haven't been in a Cadillac since they had running boards. It was just another phony story somebody had called in.

"A good legit man I know, Joe Mealy, knowing how badly I need a job, called me and said he had a job for me as a chauffeur. All I had to do was renew my driver's license. It was the best news I had had in years. I rushed downtown to the Motor Vehicle Bureau, but I was turned down. I went to see the registrar himself, his name is Clement Riley, and he told me I was 'an improper person to hold a license.' It hurt me to do it, but I pleaded, begged for that one humanitarian act. I tried to explain to him that here was a chance for a legitimate job, that it would be as much a part of

276

rehabilitation as the time I had served in prison, the culmination of it. I told him what a terrible thing it is to have to depend on family and friends for subsistence, when I should be helping them.

"Finally, Riley said that if he issued me a license it might hurt Governor Furcolo politically—it was around election time. But even after the governor had had the guts to make the decision not to send me back to Pennsylvania, and the election was over, the fellow still wouldn't give me a license. I shouldn't be bitter. But I wonder how he sleeps at night?

"I spent a couple weeks in New York, at Christmastime, mostly around the New York City unemployment office. But every job, even the most menial—and any kind of work would have sufficed—specified 'No Police Record.' I could have falsified the application and taken a chance that they'd never get around to finding out. But that would be starting out all over again, doing something I've turned my back on.

"I'm tied to Boston by these and other things. I must go some place where I can work. I seek anonymity. I could brazen things through in the Boston area, and may have to. But that could lead to terrible trouble.

"Somebody could get killed . . . me or somebody else. It's incumbent upon them to kill me. Their business is to instill fear. Their ego is such that they'll have to try again. And being around Boston makes me available. It's stupid."

During his last days in the East Cambridge jail Specs was visited by a Hollywood producer who offered him $5,000 down and $5,000 upon his release if he would consent to make a trailer to be used in connection with a film purportedly about the Brink's robbery.

Specs was not interested. He didn't like the man's manner. "He kept telling me how much smarter he was than other picture people—how many guys out there he had screwed on deals," Specs recalls. "I figured that if he conned his friends, what would he do to me, a complete stranger?"

"The picture is practically in the can right now," the producer told him. "You know, we can complete it without you."

"Fine," Specs said. "Please do."

The producer tried another tack. He sought O'Keefe's permission to entitle the quickie *I Robbed Brink's*. Specs shook his head, but it didn't discourage the man from never-never land.

"Then we'll write in a part for your sister and call it, *My Brother Robbed Brink's*—how about that?"

Specs said he had a headache, and would the visitor please excuse him?

But it was a decision that later caused him to wonder about his judgment, particularly when he recalled his determination—bordering on a crusade—to provide a college education for the boy he helped haphazardly to raise.

The old days, the old ways, beckon—but not enticingly enough.

He was a few minutes late for our appointment to meet in the lobby the day I was checking him out of New York City's ancient and hallowed Plaza, where he stayed during the course of our long interview.

"I'm sorry I'm a bit late," O'Keefe said in his quiet and gentlemanly way. "I had to spend a little time . . . unpacking."

"Unpacking?" I had noticed he had his suitcase in hand.

Specs chuckled and shook his head. "I pack my clothes, shoes, toilet articles and so forth," he explained, "and then their towels, soap, light bulbs, ashtrays . . . whatever. I was closing the suitcase when a terrible and I guess wonderful thought hit me. I said to myself, 'What the hell am I doing this for? I don't *have* to do it any more. Any more ever.' It took me a little time to put the stuff back."

I paid the modest bill at the cashier's cage, to his distress.

"It's hard for you to understand, I guess," he said as we walked slowly away. "All of my life I, and most of the people I ran with, would have found it impossible to do what you

278

just did without saying, inside, 'Now, how will I get this back . . . how do I take it back from them, so I won't be a sucker?' "

We were abreast of the archaic treasury department of the stately hotel. Specs looked blandly through the grill and past a matronly cashier. And then he sighed, ever so briefly.

"It would be so easy," he said.

He shrugged and we moved on to the men's bar. There was time for a drink before his plane back to Boston.

After a few sips I asked him if he ever heard directly or indirectly from the men he had put away for life, and beyond.

Not directly, he said. Only indirectly, through anniversary feature stories and the like. There had been a story in a Boston newspaper, I told him, to the effect that Tony Pino had been elected within the prison to membership on a joint guards-convicts grievance board.

The mellow mood of Joseph James O'Keefe stiffened imperceptibly.

"Anthony must have rigged it," he said.

A B O U T   T H E   A U T H O R

BOB CONSIDINE, well-known columnist, author, and veteran war correspondent, is a top figure in contemporary journalism. His "On the Line" column appears regularly in newspapers from coast to coast. Among the books he has written are *Thirty Seconds Over Tokyo*, *MacArthur the Magnificent*, *General Wainwright's Story*, *The Babe Ruth Story*, *Innocents at Home* and *Brother Rice*. He is the author of numerous magazine pieces, and has written for motion pictures.

Mr. Considine is a past president of the Overseas Press Club. He and his wife live in New York City; they have three sons and a daughter.